Contact information:  The Why Guy Group c/o Face Book.

Write to:    P.O. Box 2222
                    Deer Park, WA 99006

D0916218

Special thanks to:

Janice Branter.
We met on Face Book. She is a retired English teacher who graciously edited this book. She didn't always agree with my findings, but she still applied her skills to help my conclusions make sense.
Thanks again Janice

My wife.
Like any best friend would do, she analyzed my writing and helped me hone my communication skills.

Kent Lindsay.
Thank you for editing the graphics for my book cover.

Paul Noble.
Thank you for turning me on to a free photo web site that supplied me with the photos for my book cover.

Thank you, all those who have encouraged me over the years and have supplied their personal testimonies and thoughts within these pages.

# TABLE of CONTENTS

Page:

# About the author

The Why Guy, obviously a pen name, is a devoted husband of a beautiful wife, and an adoptive father of two dogs and a cat, all of whom he loves with all of his heart.  He does not consider himself a Bible scholar or a theologian, but in this regard, he coined a phrase by calling himself an "Opinionist".  ☺

He is a published author, songwriter, and musician, and has been involved with a few secular bands throughout his life, but was never so satisfied as when he was encouraging people to sing praises to God.  At the age of 15 he had a dramatic life changing encounter with God that consisted of a vision of Christ.  Soon after, He received an overnight gift of playing the guitar, and shortly after that joined a praise team at the church he began to attend.

Much later in his life he became a private music teacher who had the privilege of instructing students ranging from 8 to 80 years old on the guitar, banjo, mandolin, and bass.  In his small town, he was contracted by the school district for a year to teach music.  In the same time period, he and his wife owned a music store for 11 years, which allowed him to obtain the knowledge to tutor beginner students on the piano, as well as the flute, clarinet, alto and tenor sax, trumpet, and bass clarinet.  In his spare time he still tunes pianos.

The author was heavily involved with prison ministry where he was given the opportunity to take his band J.C. & Co. to facilities such as: Walla Walla State Pen., Coyote Ridge, and Airway Heights in the State of WA.

For over 30 years, He had the honor to lead praise and worship as a member of his church, or as a special guest to congregations and youth groups in churches such as: Four Square, Vineyard, Calvary Chapel, Southern Baptist, Presbyterian, Nazarene, Catholic, Methodist, a Mormon Ward, and a variety of non-denominational fellowships.

On and off for years, with permission from staff and patients, he would take his guitar into hospital rooms and sit at the foot of the bed and play soft soothing music as a means to possibly distract the patients from their suffering. He did this in various hospitals in CO, CA, Utah, and WA.

At the age of 50 he built his own log home where he and his family currently reside.

Presently, he is a self employed leatherman by trade, and has owned and operated his part-time business for over 32 years.

Now for fun, he has over 300 YouTube videos conveying the true Good News message. Search YouTube under "The Why Guy" or type in the address:
https://www.youtube.com/channel/UCMCWBse_z8tDsMLmjUweArA/videos?
Consider looking up the author on Face Book. He has a group called The Why Guy group.
It would be great hearing from you.

# Prologue

There was once a fatherless little boy who was oftentimes left alone from the age of four. His mother became pregnant with him while she was 15, so naturally she was out and about trying to have her own life, as well as to try to make a living to support her and her little boy.

This all took place in a small town where there was no crime, and it was common and not neglect from his mother, for a little boy without a father to roam the streets of this small town. Everyone knew who he was, and the town folk nick named him Little Joe the Wrangler who always had a pack of dogs following him
wherever he went. This was the reputation this little boy had.

A couple of years later when he lived in a house where the owner had divided the upstairs from the downstairs, thus making it into two apartments. On one particular day he was home alone, and as he was heading outside to play, he approached the back door of the split entry that divided his downstairs apartment from the vacant upstairs dwelling. As he reached for the back door knob, he heard his name being called, echoing off the walls of that small staircase. He turned around and answered with a resounding "WHAT?", as any little boy would do. He could hear his voice echoing off the walls as well. There was no one in sight.

The little boy turned to proceed outside, and he heard his name a second time. The lad didn't answer, but instead he walked up the short flight of stairs, and put his little hands next to the glass of the upstairs apartment kitchen door window to look inside. He already knew it was unoccupied, so he tried the doorknob of the locked door. With no understanding of who or what called his name, he turned around to go down the stairs and out the back door.

Again, as he reached for the doorknob, he heard his name a third time. This time the little boy turned around and asked the question, "Is that you God?" By this time, he knew in his heart that it was. Not waiting for an answer, he turned and went outside. This experience remained a vivid memory for the rest of his life. I've often wondered about that little boy--why didn't he wait for an answer?

Unfortunately this little boy grew to be an angry young teen due to a lot of physical, emotional, and mental abuse. The young, bitter, angry teen would lock himself away in his room, like most teens often do. One day while watching Wild Wild West, the angry teen responded to a knock on his door. This scenario happened three weeks in a row, from a visiting four year old boy named Tony.

The angry teen rejected the little boy the first two times, but the third time he finally let him in.  Little Tony jumped up on the bed, next to the angry teenager, and held him close.  Eventually little Tony told the angry teen that Jesus loved him and asked the teen to visit him at church.  The angry teen didn't want to go to church, but he couldn't say no, because he didn't want to discourage the little boy.  There's far more to this story than what is written here, but this pretty much sums it up.

Two weeks went by and little Tony had not returned with his parents, whom his father was the pastor of the church the teen was invited.  It was driving this angry teen crazy, because he knew he had to get to that church and keep his word to this little boy.  So on one Sunday evening in a small home, where they had gutted out the upstairs, making it into a sanctuary, leaving the downstairs as an apartment for the pastor and his family, the angry teen found himself sitting on the back row, angry and bitter because little Tony wasn't there.  Apparently he was being disciplined and had to go to bed early.

The angry teen was furious that he had to sit in this crazy place waiting for it all to end.  Those attending equalled about eight people.  At the end of the service, everyone but the angry teen went forward to pray around a platform. As the angry teen sat alone judging the spectacle, he was shocked by an apparition, a vision of what he knew was Christ. This didn't surprise him as much as who was standing next to Jesus--it was an apparition of himself. The shocked teen saw the love and the peace in this incredible being he knew was Christ. Yet, what he saw in the apparition of himself was an ugly person who allowed anger, bitterness, and hate to rule his life. The obvious difference between the two apparitions caused this young man's heart too break--to break like it had never broken before. This young man crumpled to the floor in a fetal position, sobbing. Crying to himself while mumbling "God, I want to be like this Jesus. I don't want to be like that other guy!"

The teen eventually got off the floor, his arms feeling as if they weighed 50 lbs each, and wiped the tears from his eyes. What was odd about the whole incident, even more so than the vision itself, was how nobody else present knew what had happened. It was almost as if time stood still. No one recognized, witnessed, or understood what just took place, except this teenager.

Approximately a year later, this teen started going to a youth group. All he desired to do was worship God in song. On one of those quiet times he prayed to himself, "God, if you teach me to play the guitar, I'll play for you for the rest of my life." The following week, a member of that youth group came up to the teen and handed him a guitar, and told him they were supposed to give it to him.


The following morning, the mid-teen woke up and as soon as his legs swung to the side of his bed, he  picked up the guitar and began to play it.  Not just play with it, not just play at it, but actually began playing it.  He played chords, finger-picking, strumming, and thought that was normal, and wondered why he didn't do this a long time ago.  It seemed so easy, resulting in writing his first song within a week.


Approximately a year later, along with a group of young people, the same mid-teen took his guitar to a New Year's Eve gathering in someone's home.  He noticed in the room that there was a banjo on a stand, so he asked for permission to hold it, because he had never seen a five string banjo before.  With permission, the teen picked it up and began to play it in front of at least 25 witnesses.  The following Sunday, the homeowner/banjo owner came to the teenagers church and gave the teen his banjo.  He told the young man, "I've been taking lessons for 5 years, and I never sounded as good as what you did the other night.  Besides, this gives me an excuse to buy a new banjo."

A couple of years later, the older teen had a catastrophic hang gliding accident. He shattered his left arm and elbow, and the doctors talked of amputation. The damage was that severe, but they called in a specialist to assemble the bone fragments against a piece of stainless steel with the teen's understanding  that he would never have normal use of his left arm ever again.

Within a week of being released from the hospital, the teen went to visit a church where a guest speaker named Malcolm Smith was teaching. There's more to this story as well, but to keep the story short--after the service, the teen went forward to get prayer.  As he was taught to do, he had his right arm raised while worshiping in song.  During this time, he audibly heard in his left ear, "raise your left arm".  The teen turned to see who the fool was who told him to do it, because he was in so much pain as it was.  The teen was in agony, thus the reason why he went forward in the first place.  He heard the audible voice again saying "raise your left arm", and shortly thereafter a third time, "raise your left arm and you will be healed".  Each time, no one was there. There is far more to this story highlighted in this book.

A couple days later, the teen went to the doctor's office for a check-up and an X-ray.  The X-ray technician ran out of her booth and told the teen how he healed extremely fast, and that he should come and see.  The teen saw the X-rays of a piece of metal stuck to a perfect piece of bone, with no scarring on the bone. The surgeon wanted to know what happened. The teen explained the best he could, and the doctor left the cast off, after only four days. The doctor said, "obviously you don't need this anymore, but take it easy on that arm". That was the only instructions the teen received.

Approximately 6 years later the little boy in this story was now a grown man who had a young bride. The young man found himself out in his garage, walking in circles, complaining to God about his new wife. He blamed God for making the mistake of having him meet and marry this woman. In his anger, the young man was audibly shouting to God about how his wife didn't understand him, and how they argued all the time. The young man was stopped up short by a booming voice. He didn't know if the voice was in his head or outside of himself, but he knew who it was. He heard God speak again, and that conversation saved the young man's marriage.

Now let's proceed a few years later to a sister-in-law's home with this middle aged man. At the home of his sister-in-law, she had a piano. He sat down and began to play it. It just happened instantly--those kinds of things happen sometimes when God has a plan for a purpose.

Years later, much older now, this older man was given a revelation of a truly loving God. The older man thought he already knew of a loving God, but he really didn't. The older man gained the knowledge of how he had been deceived by ignorant, but well meaning, very loving people who claimed that their God was going to send countless souls to hell. When the older man discovered the deception, it made him extremely angry just to think of all those years he could have known this truly loving God, but instead he always had this pent-up anger just below the surface. He had a lack of love for the very God he was singing praises to. For most his adult life, he ignored and pushed aside his lack of love and mistrust in God. The anger was always there, yet it shouldn't have been that way, due to all those years of deception.

Shortly thereafter, the older man began producing YouTube videos and years later wrote a book called In Defence Of God's Love. His videos and book are about his newfound freedom and peace, while at the same time exposing the lies and the deceit of religious dogma, also known as doctrines of men.

The older man began having conversations with others on Face book which resulted in making a lot of great friends, but unfortunately, he made a lot of new enemies as well. There were those on Face book that had tried to convince the older man that he's the one that is actually deceived about hell rather than themselves. Then there were others who tried to convince the older man that God really doesn't exist.

The older man was amazed at some beliefs considering what he had gone through in his life. The older man couldn't help but to sadly laugh. However, there is one thing that genuinely caused him to laugh--the notion that God doesn't speak, audibly or otherwise! That's hilarious to the older man considering what he's heard, and the changes and miracles that took place in his life because of what was heard.

The little boy of this story still lives within that older man--still wanting and wondering, still excited, and at times he still gets angry with God. Wanting and waiting for God to do something, to do anything to show the world and religion how wrong they've been about Him. Sometimes the little boy in the older man gets tempted to no longer believe in God, even though what has happened in his life points to the contrary. What a spoiled little boy.

Folks, many details have been left out, but this an accurate true story, and it's the reason why I do YouTube videos and have written this book--it's all because of that spoiled little boy.

# Chapter One:

## The Question of Huh?

I feel that curiosity is a very wise thing. To ask yourself and others; why do you believe what you believe?--is wisdom. I really believe this with all my heart now, but there was a time I didn't. I was discouraged from asking questions of "why?". You know, those questions that usually began with a "huh?".

I've discovered that most clergy, whether they're pastors, teachers, or priests don't embrace curiosity. Yes, they encourage you to have enough curiosity to learn, but you've got to learn within the parameters of their understanding--of their teaching. Otherwise they may call you rebellious, and consider your curiosity a threat to their authority--more on "authority" later.

Asking too many questions in general, especially directed to the clergy, will elicit an indictment of you for having a lack of faith. Their assertion is nothing more than a cop-out, exposing the real reason behind their claim... an abundance of pride and ignorance. They will then follow up by encouraging you "to trust God", which on the surface is true and valid, but what they're really asking of you is to have blind trust.

These teachers are essentially asking people to have blind trust in them, their teaching, their education, their institutions, and the conclusions they have come to about spiritual matters. If you question their teaching they will feel threatened, whether consciously or subconsciously--their authority will feel threatened, because they have invested so much time, energy, money, and prayer into their occupation. It's more than an occupation with these people--in their minds it's a calling of God. Don't get me wrong, I'm not questioning their sincerity, and I know the vast majority of them love you with all their hearts. They also feel a responsibility for the spiritual health of people with whom they have dedicated so much emotion, time, and energy.

They have been indoctrinated into believing the "authority", spoken about earlier, is a God-given authority, and they also feel that they will have to answer to God for not following through with their commitment. I try not to use the word deception too loosely, but in this case I feel it's appropriate, because we're dealing with a false responsibility--which I'll also explain later.

Yes, these people in their "God-called" occupation will have their pet Bible verses to prove their position even though historically the long term affect, the "fruit" of their occupation, has produced what the world views as a following of lemmings. The flavor of lemming is dependant upon the ministry's capability to promote their own specific version of traditions along with their brand of doctrines of men.

It is written and said Christ is the Author (that means the beginner) and the Finisher of ones Faith. It's clear--the clergy, a pastor, a teacher, or priest is not the Author. Also, He who began a good work in you will complete it unto the glory of God. Was it flesh and blood, a person who Authored your faith and began a good work in you? I don't think so! A clergy with a false sense of authority may want to take the credit for Authoring your faith, or beginning a good work in you, but the glory belongs to God and Him alone.

Glory? I definitely have heard glory being tossed around promoting a specific denomination, or a particular belief (that usually causes division),--how about an exaggerated membership number? As of this writing, there are about 33,000 different denominations, about 400 different Bible colleges, and about 40 different versions of the Bible. A rhetorical question: Do all these things really and truly bring glory to God, i.e., point people to God, or are they designed to point people to a denomination and/or church?

Another rhetorical question: Am I the only one who has heard boastings about the size and accomplishments of congregations? Is it unheard of that evangelists, pastors, teachers, and priests boast about their "authority in the name of Jesus"? Yet, God is the One who initiates the relationship between His Spirit and mankind. God's love and grace Authors and finishes, begins and completes the necessary salvation of healing from ignorance in regard to His love--in this case, being saved from ignorance! By being saved from wrath, best defined the Greek as being saved from our own violent passions, and brought into a love relationship with God, ourselves, and humanity--this being the truest definition of salvation.

What part does the clergy play? Their only "authority" should be categorized as being an encouraging servant. To encourage people "to study and show themselves approved", and if that study happens to bring an understanding in opposition to that of the cleric--so what! Righteously judge both positions. How so? The answer will be covered a little later--read on. Unfortunately righteous judgment and dialog is usually not even considered among church leaders, because of that before mentioned deception called: "Authority"!

The perspective that matters most belongs to God, and from His perspective these men and women of faith are no better or valuable than anyone else who has the Spirit of God abiding in them.  As a servant there may arise a need for the clergy to input their thoughts into the mix, and some may be called upon to research and find out if their thoughts and input are from God or from traditions via doctrines of men, and again--just like anyone else, their input needs to be judged.

I've personally been very close with so many pastors and teachers throughout the years, and been an active part of what's considered leadership and authority.  The 30 plus years that I led praise and worship has given me an insight into the inner workings of church life, and I know what motivates these people called clergy.

I've had a number of pastors approach me, who have had a paradigm shift in thinking--they came to the realization that the vast majority of what they've learned in their Seminary was a waste of time and money.  They became aware that most of their education was based on people teaching from traditions and doctrines of men--blind leading the blind, dogmas that had been handed down from generation to generation.  It was devastating to them to realize... so much waste.  These pastors were brought to a place where they were not afraid to ask the question, "Huh? Something is not adding up."

Things that makes you think "huh?" is a great place to start, but don't stop there. Some great questions to ask yourself about teachers of any kind are: Where are they going with the answer to my question of "huh"? Why are they answering this way, and where did they get their information? With every response it's wise to wonder what the motive is behind their answer. Most of the time they're not sure about anything and are only "winging it". This is nothing short of dishonesty and exacerbates ignorance. With that said... I am not implying to abandon grace, time, and patience when it comes to someone's ignorance, but in order for it to work--the person "winging it" needs to admit their ignorance and show a little humility.

Most people are insecure to one degree or another, and only want to prove a point--to feel they're right regardless whether it's the truth or not. We all "fall short" and "see through a glass dimly" when it comes to ignorance, but I've discovered one doesn't have to be scholarly knowledgeable to have wisdom and be enlightened by the Spirit of God. The wisdom and enlightenment I speak of will be defined and repeated over and over again in this book. It can't be said enough. Everything, I mean everything has to and must be based upon the foundation of: "God is love"! If this truth is skewed and tainted, by whatever foundation, or theology, one's understanding will result in uncertainty, and it will crumble.

Remember "judge it" mentioned earlier? Based on God's love I give myself and whomever I meet this advice:  Whatever you read, whatever you're told, whatever you teach, and whatever you're taught--judge it!  I can't say it any stronger, but judge it. Judge all things in wisdom via the enlightened truth of:  "God is love".  Whatever answers you happen to get to your question of "huh?", does it endorse God's character?  Remember, we've already determined God is love.  Do the answers you get to your question of "huh?" define that love? Do the answers you get to your question of "huh?" cause you to trust God more or does it cause you to trust God less?  Judge it!  If it's less it's the wrong answer, and the one giving the answer is deceived, and maybe unknowingly they're deceiving you as well.  Last but not least, do the answers bring out in you what is so rightly called: The fruit of The Spirit.  Judge what is brought out in you!  If the fruit is rotten the answers are not of God, but of the minds and doctrines of men, based on opinions with the motivation to only "prove a point". Speaking of proving a point--try this one on for size and judge it... is fear part of the fruit of The Spirit?  If fear is involved, it is NOT of God because God's "perfect" love casts out fear.  What kind of fear?  In first John it spells it out clearly... FEAR OF PUNISHMENT FROM GOD!

In conclusion to this chapter called " The Question of Huh?"--the answer to the question of "huh?" is: "God is love", and any other answer is nothing more than "noisy gongs and clanging cymbals." In the next chapter let's examine what a noisy gong and a clanging cymbal might look like when perverting love in conjunction with trust, and what those consequences might produce.

# Chapter 2

## The Perversion of Love, Trust, & Consequences

Fear and trust are oxymoronic, as in polar opposites of each other. My wife gave another option to my claim by saying "A person can still trust God in the midst of their fears". She's absolutely right, even though not many of us are successful with that kind of trust.

This chapter is not about the kind of trust my wife was referring, but it's more about a perverted kind of trust promoted within Christianity. If I didn't just lose you with my previous statement, and you're not screaming HERETIC at the top of your lungs--I will soon explain in detail what I meant, but before I do so, allow me to share one of the corner stones in my personal foundation.

Be forewarned, I'll be using a small amount of strong language, and my tone may be perceived as anger. Please don't be put off by it, and try to understand I'm making an attempt to defend a love that has been perpetually attacked for centuries. Why else would I title my book "In Defense of God's Love"?

For me, it all came down to this simple truth: I could never trust a God I didn't love, and I could never love a God I couldn't trust. If you think about it, that's the main problem the people of the world have with the Christian message. You don't think so? Just bring up hell for an example.

Those of us who love God expect the people of the world to love and trust a god who had and will send countless billions to hell. How do they trust a god like that? Our expectation is oxymoronic in of itself, and Christianity actually expects the world to love a god who would do such a horrible thing. It doesn't add up, and that tells me there is something extremely wrong with that doctrine of men. The hell doctrine is a perversion of love, and it's obvious to me that fear is the power behind that perversion.

Fear. I've heard it said: "The fear of the Lord is the beginning of wisdom". Unlike the fear my wife mentioned, this too is not the kind of fear that I'm addressing--meaning, the English word fear is not what that scripture reference is really talking about. This is a Hebrew verse and one has to look at the Hebrew culture and customs to identify the intent of a word rather than an English translation of the word "fear". The intent is telling us to have a deep respect for the power of God, it's not telling us to fear God as in being afraid of Him.

Love.  1st John 4:18 states:  "There is no fear in love but perfect love casts out fear", so what kind of fear?  It continues by saying:  "...because fear involves punishment", punishment from whom?  The context is referring to God as the "whom".  The verse finishes by saying:  "...and the one who fears is not perfected in love."

I haven't forgotten about the perversion of trust I mentioned in the 2nd paragraph, also I've intentionally left the love issue hanging in the wind, considering the title of this chapter is: " The Perversion of Love, Trust, & Consequences".  The perversion of trust and love will soon be addressed, but first let's take a look at "consequences" from a unique perspective.

Consequences.  One of the colossal hang-ups within Christianity is what's known as "consequences".  What I've always heard people say is:  "If there are no consequences, that would mean people could go out and do whatever they want and get away with it!"  What they are really saying is those type of people deserve hell, and hell is the consequence.

Allow me to digress. The above kind of thinking proves to me beyond a shadow of a doubt, that a person who thinks like this has absolutely no understanding of God's perfect love. If their belief system is built upon a flawed ignorant foundation--it causes me to question their understanding of God, thus making the rest of their message suspect. Speaking of ignorance... I've heard it said: "God still loves all those people suffering in hell." I used to blindly believe and say the same things. Now I look back on what I used to say and what others still believe and wonder how on earth did I not see such blatant contradictions and perversions of God's love?

I realize I'm stepping on toes while addressing matters that people believe in their heart as true, yet my intent is not to offend, but simply to share a different perspective. From my newer perspective, I believe it to be a perversion to believe in such a place as hell, and at one time I was right there with those who were shouting "Turn or burn"! Proof of what I'm calling a perversion will become more evident throughout this book, yet I know when it comes to the human psyche--if something is believed strong enough--no amount of evidence will convince a person otherwise--this saddens me.

While still addressing the theme of an oxymoron,  a polar opposite--I have finally figured out what is wrong with the religion we know of as Christianity.  It seems as if  Christians think it's a good thing that God inspires fear in them, even though that fear is in direct conflict with the verse in 1st John that states:  "There is no fear in love but perfect love casts out fear", all while Christians are making the claim that "God is love".  This makes no sense!  In the next few paragraphs I'm going to begin to combine love, trust, and consequences, along with a short paragraph on justice--how they all perversely interact within Christianity, and how to avoid centuries of mistakes.

The first step one must take to rid themselves of oxymoronic thinking in regard to God's love is to make it crystal clear in one's mind--is God love or not?  Simple!  Second, one must examine if their definition of love is perverted in any way.  As a starter, go to the famous love chapter 13 in 1st Corinthians, and compare what it says to how you believe God should respond to sin, or better put-- sinners.  Do they match?

Trust. I uniquely define a perversion of trust as a byproduct of fear. As an example of what I'm trying to say is... Christians are afraid to disobey God i.e. sin, because they "fear" there will be consequences, and they "trust" God to implement those consequences. On the surface, my conclusion sounds logical and reasonable to the religious carnal mind. Yet, it's perversely in direct conflict with what Jesus openly claimed is God's character.

Examples of God's character:
John 3:17 - "For God did not send the Son into the world to judge the world, but that the world might be saved through Him.

John 5:22 - The Father judges no one but has given all judgment to the Son

Again, is His character love or is it not? Does love elicit an eternal punishment for the deeds of a short lifetime? Putting deeds (plural) aside--what about the single deed of unbelief? Does love elicit an eternal punishment for the single deed of unbelief within a short lifetime? The answer would be yes, and justifiably so in the minds of most Christians who have a perverted view of how God obtains trust within someone. The affirmative answer of yes is the kind of oxymoronic thinking that is not love, and it's a perversion.

If a gun was pointed at your head by a would-be assassin, would you feel threatened, would you "trust" in the ability of the killer to follow through with their threat?   Is love involved in this kind of scenario? No?  Yet, this is the kind of perverted trust Christianity is promoting with a... you can trust me, but first you must love me or else-- believe or else-- endorsing a turn or burn message.  My view of this kind of perversion is:  If a belief is not perfected--it's perverted in some way, otherwise it would be perfect! In other-words, knowing and understanding perfect love is what will perfect a belief, and the above examples of the Christian message is anything but love, and anything but perfect.

Justice?  A belief that God will implement a fear based, horrific consequence for disobedience is a perversion of "perfect love" as well as a slander to God's character.  Remember the question I keep asking?  Is God love or not?  The argument is... God is also "just"!  I would agree and say yes, but I would follow up with the question:  Is His justice based on His "perfect love"?  This question brings us right back to the perversion of love previously mentioned.

Love.  Even though John states there is no fear in love, Christianity's belief of God's character has been perverted as well.  If my statement is not true, then explain to me how the perfect love of God casts out fear!  Fear of what? Fear of punishment-- punishment from whom?  From God!  This oxymoronic, perverted thinking has been taught and believed for centuries.  How so?  Because a perverted love doesn't cast out any kind of fear, but actually encourages fear instead.  Fear from whom?  From God!  For what purpose?  To punish you for disobedience.  The exact opposite of what 1st John is saying.  I hope this made sense.  If not, reread it until it does--it's critical in understanding the perversion of love!

Back to consequences.  I am not saying nor implying there are no consequences for disobedience--for sin.  Let's address some of those consequences found within scripture.  I'm referring to consequences from God specifically rather than consequences in general.

Example of a consequence mentioned in 2nd Corinthians 5:19: "God was in Christ reconciling the world (cosmos in the Greek ) unto Himself NOT COUNTING MEN'S SINS AGAINST THEM"! The argument: "You mean you can just go out and do whatever you want and God's not going to count that against you?" If you're in this camp, your argument isn't with me, your argument is with Paul. There is no other way to interpret this scripture. This is one of many self-contextualizing verses, meaning it's true, appropriate, and applicable no matter who it was being written to at the time, or when it was written. Also note--nowhere within the context of this verse, nor within the chapter are there conditions of "you must first...".

Isn't judgment a consequence? John 5:22 tell us "Not even the Father (God) judges anyone"! (*WHAT?! I thought God was going to judge the world*) The verse continues by saying "but has given all judgment to the Son." (*Okay, finally somebody's going to judge--we're finally going to see some consequences.*) Jesus spoke in John 12:47: "If anyone hears my saying (*okay... judgment time...* ) and does not keep them (*all right... BAM!... here we go*) I WON'T JUDGE HIM. I did not come to judge the world but to save the world." (*POOF!*) That sure let the air out of that consequence.

Is there scriptural evidence of an agreement between the Father and Son in regard to judgment i.e, consequences?  John 3:17: "For God did not send his Son into the world to judge the world but the world would be saved through Him."  Yes! Christendom claims this will happen, but only if you first believe, believe, believe.  However, in rebuttal to that notion, and in context referencing unbelievers-- Romans 3:3 - "What then? If some did not believe, *their unbelief will not nullify the faithfulness of God,* will it? May it never be! Rather, let God be found true, though every man be found a liar".  Christianity has been advocating a lie for centuries by claiming it's all about the belief and faithfulness of the individual rather than the faithfulness of God.


Christendom demands and requires consequences, so below are a few examples of consequences, but from God's perspective, His position is based upon His faithfulness.  Yes, I consider God's faithfulness a consequence of sin, of no sin, or whatever label happens to come to mind. Also as a consequence, He is going to complete the work that He has started in you.  Another consequence of God is the power of His conviction, as in the Spirit of God that is more than able to touch the hearts of men and women--to turn them around, to change their minds, known as repentance.

There's a consequence of God that states: It is God who works in you both to will (to choose) and act (behave) according to His good purposes. These are only a few of many examples of God's consequences that endorse His loving character and nature . I hope you are catching this, because it's by His power, by His might, and in His timing, He will implement whatever consequences necessary to fulfill His will. Bottom line is this... I consider God's faithfulness to be steadfast, regardless of our behavior.

Getting away with... ! Love doesn't let anyone get away with anything. Does a loving parent use the wrongs committed by the child as a means to teach them what is right? Or does the loving parent torture their child--continually--without end? So the next time you think, speak, or hear someone say: "You mean they're going to get away with...". Sin has its own price. No one gets away with anything... not really. It may seem like it at first, but things have a way of adding up in the conscience which will later have an impact in defining one's character. Without forgiveness (of oneself-the kind of forgiveness God is really asking of people), the sin seed will continue to grow and later produce the kind of fruit within a person that will eventually stink! That's what sin does.

Ask the "getting away with" question to a person who is hooked on drugs. Are they getting away with anything? The horror of always feeling desperate most of the time, without that fix? How about the prostitute? That young man or woman who just wants to be loved, and feeling like they're not--to fill that gap of being desired, by selling their bodies. If not for that reason-- maybe it's the only way they know how to survive and make a living. Are they actually paying a consequence? Our prisons are full--is this a consequence? Turn on the news--there is so much hate in the world, especially politically--is that a consequence of sin?

My dear reader, I must ask: Why do you think God hates sin, and doesn't want us to be involved with it? It's because of those consequences that harm us. This is how love operates. If you have any kids, think of your own children doing the things they do to harm themselves, and how that would make you feel. I hope this chapter has made sense. Judge it, as in: Does it endorse the non-perverted true character of God? Let it sink in that you can trust God with a real trust, not a perverted trust. Why? Because God is love, not a perverted love, but the perfect love.

Consider this... God isn't limited to this lifetime (thank you God), and He's not limited to time as we understand it. He created it! It's only going to be a matter of time, once a body dies in the midst of those consequences--the person will be free of them. People will be free of those temporal consequences, then the eternal consequences from God will continue. He will persist in working on a person, believer and unbeliever alike. It's not just for the here and now, i.e. this lifetime. I can not say this often enough... God is more than capable to implement His consequences of starting a good work in someone long after they die.

Death. Death does NOT stop God! Limiting God to this lifetime is such a hang-up within Christianity, yet most will claim Christ conquered death. Why else can Peter claim in: 1 Peter 4:6 - "For the gospel has for this purpose been preached even to those who are dead, that though they are judged in the flesh as men, they may live in the spirit according to the will of God." In the next chapter I will be asking the question: Does Death Stop God?

# Chapter 3

## Does Death Stop God?

This chapter will be intentionally comprehensive, wide ranging, and possibly the longest chapter in the book. I didn't feel I had much choice due to so much of our understanding of God is largely based on our own limitations, and those limitations are far spread. Simply put: to a degree mankind has recreated God in its own limited image. Stick with me. There will be something written you may not have thought about before, and there will be some things written you may deem heretical. Something for everyone.

"This is it!" "This lifetime is the one and only opportunity you'll have to accept Christ or reject Him." "For a Christian, this life will be the only hell we'll have to endure, but for an unbeliever, this life will be the only heaven they will ever experience!" From time to time, I've heard all of the above statements within Christian circles. In all honesty I used to make similar statements myself for which I now humbly apologize.

I've searched scripture for some evidence of limits being placed on God, or a restriction of His capacity to work within a person to convict, promote, and encourage a God-inspired kinship with a person regardless if one is alive or dead. Frankly, I've found nothing within scripture having any substance to support the notion of limiting God in relationship to anything. Contrarily I've discovered numerous verses within scripture to support a God who is recorded as being "Almighty", "Sovereign", and unlimited in enacting His will. Pertaining to God, whenever the word "sovereign" is mentioned within some Christian circles, usually a misinformed mind will immediately fall back on a "puppet master" mentality. This is an ignorant view and not at all the true definition of sovereign within scripture. The sovereignty of God will be addressed in chapter four.

With respect to unlimited authority, John 3:35 tells us that the Father (God) has given ALL into Jesus' hands, then we read it is the desire of the Father to save ALL, and He has given Jesus all power and authority to do His will. A rhetorical question: Why don't Christians believe Him? I suppose another good question might be: Does death stop Jesus? I believe what Christ did in "conquering death" has far greater implications other than raising Himself from the dead, considering others were raised long before His own resurrection.

There are those who say they have had experiences that do not define a resurrection, nor a near death experience. It's now claimed by many, they've literally been to a torturous hell rather than having an experience through a dream or vision. My point... One must literally die to literally be in hell, so technically their return is a resurrection, yet none will make that assertion. Regardless of how it took place, they all make a declaration of warning to the rest of us. I don't question their sincerity, but I must ask why is it, regarding every testimony of those who believe they were exposed to hell--they all claim it's a place of no escape, yet they're here telling us about their escape.

As a result of their escape, occasionally some are selling books, while others are invited for speaking engagements--all the while getting attention like they've never received before. Some who call themselves Christians, who have had this experience, will claim hell is a place designed for unbelievers, as in those who have not made a commitment for Christ. Then you have testimonies of those who didn't become a true believer in Christ until they experienced hell. In both cases, they stand firm about the reality of their experience--wouldn't you? I would too if I didn't know what I know now!

I wish to address and show a disagreement to these testimonials without slander and malice towards the people who make them.  In other words... I believe that they believe their experience was true, but I also believe I might have a unique answer other than the conclusion they have all reached.  The conclusion reached by those who were already believers in Christ is:  Hell is a place designed for unbelievers to reside who...

 "pursued a course of sensuality, lusts, drunkenness, carousing, drinking parties and abominable idolatries"! (1st Peter 4:3)

This verse pretty much sums up their answer, their conclusion, and the Christian belief in why hell needs to exist.  This conclusion creates a conundrum, because those who didn't know Christ to begin with were obviously considered unbelievers BEFORE they had their hellish experience.  By the way, if this verse represents the offenses deserving of hell, then why isn't hell mentioned anywhere within context to the 1st Peter verse?

How is this a conundrum?  If hell is a place for unbelievers, then why were these visiting unbelievers allowed to return?  God apparently let them come back and no one else? Convenient.  Were there not countless billions of unbelievers already residing in hell that were not allowed to return and share with their loved ones about the experience, similar to the ones writing books?  To add to the conundrum... by allowing only a select few to return--wouldn't this imply God is a respecter of persons, and/or gave room for the notion that God simply loves those who returned more than those who didn't return?  This is in direct violation to the character of God, and it is not how love works.  But wait!  There is an answer.

Before I provide an that answer, I must address a hypocrisy, or the very least another violation of what all believers in Christ claim is true.  Christians claim the Bible, above all else is their book of authority.  Most have given it the title of:  The Authoritative Word of God.  Others go a step further and call the Bible:  The Inerrant Word of God.  The hypocrisy I speak of refers to the very people who make the above claims about the Bible, and then they will ignore countless Bible verses that may oppose the aforementioned testimonies.  Simply put, people will actually believe these testimonies and the books written about them, over what they themselves consider The Word of God.  These actions have to be described as either hypocrisy or deception.

With that said, let's now refocus on the "hell sojourners" who claim were in hell and why.  If unbelievers in Christ are those that populate hell, (ignoring the previously mentioned conundrum), and these hell visiting testimonies confirm the notion it's a place for unbelievers who (1st Peter) "pursued a course of sensuality, lusts, drunkenness,... " and so forth--then on the surface the Apostle Paul is in disagreement with Peter, because in Romans 3:3 Paul is saying:

"What then? If some did not believe, their unbelief will not nullify the faithfulness of God, will it? May  it never be! Rather, let God be found true, though every man be found a liar".

This verse in Romans that Paul has written is telling me God is faithful to the unbeliever, and the above books and testimonies are a lie!  Their very testimonies go directly against Paul proclaiming God is faithful to unbelievers, because according to the testimonies all unbelievers have been abandon by God from which there is no escape!  By no means am I calling those who give these kinds of testimonies blatant liars, even though this verse in Romans implies that, but what I am saying is those giving their testimonies have misinterpreted their experiences, and they themselves are believing a lie.

Interesting side note and question: Why are there no examples of people within scripture, both Old and New Testament, that had hell experiences like the ones portrayed in this chapter? Some will say... what about the Lazarus & the rich man parable? It doesn't apply for three reasons:

1. It was a parable using symbolic language. Those that testify of being in hell say it's a real place, meaning there is nothing symbolic about it.

2. The rich man wasn't allowed to return. The common denominator regarding the testimonies are: They were allowed to return.

3. Later on in this book I will prove the rich man wasn't in hell in the first place. I bet number three got your attention!

Along this same line of thinking--isn't it odd, over the span of about 4000 years, the Old Testament never mentioned hell? Then all of a sudden the topic of both hell and demons show up when Jesus does? Without having all the answers of why there are these two oddities that cause a division between the Old Testament and the New--these oddities alone should be enough reason to question the validity of hell and demons, as well as questioning one's understanding of both.

Back on topic in regard to the question of: Does Death Stop God? Sarcastically asking, apparently hell does? Without sounding overly simplistic--those who are in hell are dead, right? And Christians who claim they've been there all say the dead are unbelievers, also correct? For a moment let's ignore those who were unbelievers before they had their hellish encounter, and focus in on unbelievers in general. Contextually describing unbelievers in 1st Peter 4:3, this verse states:

"...having pursued a course of sensuality, lusts, drunkenness, carousing, drinking parties and abominable idolatries."

Then three verses later within the same context it answers the question: Does death stop God?

1 Peter 4:6 - "For the gospel has for this purpose (What purpose? Regarding the unbeliever in verse 3) been preached even to those who are DEAD, that though they are judged in the flesh as men, they may live in the spirit according to the will of God."

This verse in 1st Peter 4:6 is undeniably talking about dead unbelievers! Wait a damn minute! (pun intended) I thought hell was eternal death for unbelievers who "pursued a course of sensuality, lusts, drunkenness, carousing, drinking parties and abominable idolatries"?

Christians hate verses like the one in 1 Peter 4:6, along with hating the dozens of the verses that claim God is going to reconcile all of His creation-- losing none. (I have supplied an extensive list of those verses in the back of this book) Christianity dances around, make excuses for, ignores, or just refuses to believe verses like these. Why? Do you think maybe there's a degree of indoctrination taking place within Christian circles? Generally speaking, even without indoctrination it's in the nature of man to fight back against a wounded pride and ego. Simply put, it takes far too much humility that most are unwilling to apply to admit themselves wrong. I believe it all comes down to one problem... because of deception and ignorance, these verses go against their perverted sense of love, consequences, and justice I spoke about in chapter two.

If hell is real, one must ask: Does hell stop God from saving people? It sure didn't for those whom He supposedly let return so they can attend speaking engagements--sarcasm intended. It has been said; without a hell, there will be no judgment, i.e. consequences for the wrongs committed by evil doers. My answer to that understandable, yet shortsighted conclusion is as I previously stated... sin has its own price. Sin produces it's own judgment clearly mentioned in:

1st Peter 4:6 - "For the gospel has for this purpose been preached even to those who are dead, that though they are JUDGED IN THE FLESH AS MEN, they may live in the spirit according to the will of God."

Did you get that?  This verse proves beyond a shadow of doubt, death does not stop God.  For those who are dead have already been judged... in the flesh... while still alive... as men, yet in the spirit they will live.  Does this sound at all like spiritual death that Christianity has promoted for centuries?  Not only will they live in the spirit, but will live according to the will of God!  Some will be screaming heretic about what I just wrote and totally disregard what this verse is saying.  All I've done was quote the verse in 1st Peter, so your argument isn't with me.  People need to investigate this for themselves.

In order to prove my argument that death does NOT stop God, I must digress and continue with the topic of judgment.  The reason:  Christianity has been deceived into believing evil doers "will get away with it" without God's judgment of hell!  Using sensuality and lust mentioned in 1st Peter as an example--what I hear in response is this:  "You mean to say I can just go out in the world and pursue a course of sensuality and lust and get away with it?"  Sure... go for it if that's what you want to do.  Go for it and do you know what will happen?  You will be judged in the flesh.

I am going to prove there is no need for eternal punishment. However, there absolutely is a need for cleansing and purification after death, and who better suited to do this than a loving God, who death cannot stop? All of us will be punished, better put disciplined, because it is claimed "God punishes/disciplines those He loves", and "God so loves the world...". Are you getting it? And according to 1st Peter that punishment/discipline is for sinful acts done "in the flesh". Discipline is not a judgment! Just because you've already been judged in the flesh, doesn't mean you won't encounter further discipline and purification later, because love continually disciplines.

Even without God's direct involvement, best described as reaping and sowing, to one degree or another a person is going to pay a price in the here and now, i.e. the flesh. Understand this... sin has its own price, it's own judgment. Using the same example previously used in 1st Peter, any man or woman who want to go out and pursue a lifestyle of sensuality and lust will pay some kind of price. That's simply how life works.

You don't agree?  Am I sounding too religious for you?  I'm simply being practical in exposing a price, a judgment one must endure.  Sensuality and lust can never be satisfied--it always desires more and more.  Sure it's fun for awhile, but it's never satisfying in the long run.  If this were not true, then why do most who engage in this kind of lifestyle eventually choose to be with only one person--the way God intended in the first place?

Unfortunately in most cases, even after a commitment to one person, the price and judgment for the preceding lifestyle usually causes broken marriages and relationships.  How might this work?  Simple... carrying around memories produces desire, and desire can lead to dissatisfaction for the one you're with.  This explains why the divorce rate is so high.

I've just described and have given an example of a price one pays along with  judgment people can put on themselves.  God doesn't have to judge anyone for anything.  To an unknown degree, an automatic reaping and sowing seems to be doing the job, for the general purpose of learning right from wrong.  This is why in says in John 5:22 that God judges no one.  Then in John 3:17 God tells us He didn't send Jesus to judge us.  Jesus confirmations this in John 12:47 where it says Jesus judges no one either.

The choices we make do all the judgments necessary for the purpose of bringing us face to face with our mistakes, and to pay a price. Most are too dishonest to admit those mistakes, so as a people, we go on and on making the same mistakes, centuries after centuries until we die. Then we can be rid of those judgments of the flesh and live in the spirit according to the will of God. Living in the spirit according to the will of God just might mean starting from scratch for the unbeliever. So, does death stop God? Does God love the unbeliever? Does death stop love?

At this time I want to give what I believe is the real answer to those hellish experiences from sincere people who claim they've been to hell and have returned to warn us. Jesus spoke about the faith of a mustard seed--something as small and tiny as a mustard seed--tells me three things: One, it tells me it only takes something small and tiny: Two, has the power to take something as big as a mountain and move it into the sea: Three, it tells me that faith is unbiased. What I mean by "unbiased" is this... is moving a mountain into the sea a good or bad thing? Is it a right or wrong way to use such a power? In this mustard seed story, there's a contextual sense of irrelevancy from Jesus by not addressing the motive for casting a mountain into the sea. I can't help but to conclude faith is unbiased. Because it's unbiased it also tells me it's a power in of itself.

Remember my warning in the first paragraph that this chapter would be wide spread? With that reminder I must say before I can wrap up this chapter, I need to briefly go a little further in addressing "faith". In doing so, I will give evidence to why I believe faith is the key factor in producing the experiences the witnesses of hell claim they had.

It's not my place to judge ones heart, but let's assume George Lucas is an unbeliever, and just maybe within the realm of God's faithfulness towards unbelievers spoken about in Romans 3:3, He gave George some insight with that famous line of: "May the force be with you" or "use the Power of the Force". I can easily substitute "force" with the word faith considering how Jesus described faith using the mustard seed analogy. Because of that analogy, I believe faith is a power... a force... it's a gift that God gives to every man, woman, and child that has ever existed. For what purpose? To cast mountains into the sea? Hardly! We all know it's an analogy. An analogy about what? The mountain represents whatever it is in our lives that would hinder our survival. Not solely for the physical, i.e. healing as such, but the survival of the inanimate such as peace and joy, etc..

Since faith is unbiased, and a power in of itself--that power--that force can be used to produce and have both a negative or positive result.  Example:  A gun is unbiased, yet very powerful in the hands of someone using it.  That same power can be use to protect or to murder, as in opposite extremes.  Also, the power of the gun is measured by the size, its strength as in its caliber.  I've heard similar questions asked of Christians pertaining to the strength and size of their faith, and I might add--the caliber of their faith.

My point to all of this:  The faith (the force) is strong in people, including those who have had various dreams and visions of hell.  My unique answer is this:  Due to one having such a strong faith in the existence of a hell--I believe their faith has produced their experiences.  This unbiased, powerful faith created those experiences, and they are as real as any other experience.  As a possibility, this is how I see it happening.

By glaringly paraphrasing Jesus using His "faith of a mustard seed" story, I can easily say: Consciously or subconsciously, the unbiased, powerful faith, the size of a mustard seed gave you the ability to say to your belief in hell, cast me to that place I believe exists, because I've been taught as if it where truth. Because of your faith, that place will be created in your mind, or in whatever dimension those things happen. Once you leave that place and return, it will dissolve into the realm of the false, like all things not of God eventually do. (end paraphrase) We all have a choice to fuel faith via the will of God, or to fuel faith by fear. It can't be both, as in the perfect love of God casts one out, while the other remains. God's will remains! His love never fails!

But what of those who claim they didn't believe in hell until their experience? I would ask this question of those are making this claim... are you also wanting us to believe you never were or have never been consciously or subconsciously influenced by culture, stories, Hollywood, or Halloween?

Lastly I need to address those who say you were actually there. My conscience wont allow me to supply a title of your books, nor the You Tube links where these claims were mentioned. To those of you who say you were actually there--you're asking the rest of us to ignore the absent evidence of bodily damage. No bruises, burnt flesh and no scars of any kind. Not even a hint of odor resulting from singed flesh or clothing. What? No clothing? For those who were naked during their horrendous trial, miraculously you find yourself dressed upon returning. Later you claim God healed you of all the abuse and trauma, and with some... apparently dressed you. How nice of God for doing that just for you, while countless billions are suffering far worse than your brief painful encounter... as God idly stands by and does nothing for them. This is your testimony of a God you claim is love?

Let God be found true and every experience be found a lie. In other words, don't trust your experience, but trust in the love of God. Otherwise, it slanders the very character of God. You can't have it both ways--you cannot believe in the character of a loving God and His faithfulness to unbelievers, and also believe unbelievers are going to hell. It's oxymoronic and it makes no sense considering God created all things, including time and death. Maybe the word "sovereign" comes to mind--next chapter.

Book Chapter 4


Sovereignty of God versus Free Will of Man


What about the free will of God? The term "Sovereign God" has been one of the most misconceived expressions within Christianity. It's presumed a person who believes in a sovereign God would no longer have the ability to choose. That notion couldn't be further from the truth! In this chapter I'm going to prove how a sovereign God works abundantly well in union with the will of man.


The main reason for this misunderstanding within Christendom is due to how Christianity has shifted away from the true definition of sovereign, by redefining what is known as the "free will". Don't get me wrong--God has indeed created a will within mankind, but "will of man" and "free will" are not one and the same. Free will is in direct opposition to that of a sovereign God whereas biblically the will of man can actually compliment and endorse a sovereign God. In this chapter I'm going to prove how a sovereign God works abundantly well in union with the will of man.

Within this chapter I will be bouncing back and forth in describing the sovereignty of God and how I view free will. There are far too many paradigms of how both are understood and applied, so keeping them separate is impossible. With that said, I am going to properly define "a sovereign God", but first I need to comment on free will and how it differs from the will of man.

Within Christianity the term "free will" has grossly been misrepresented to mean something it does not mean. To one degree or another, free will is taught and defined as:

Free will means:

- To make a choice by having the ability to choose, or...

- God created us in His image, so this must mean He gave us a free will, or...

- Free will is proven in the garden story--Adam and Eve had a choice to be disobedient or not, or...

- To be in charge of one's own destiny, or...

- To be responsible for one's own decisions.

The next erroneous step taken by Christendom is to then apply the misaligned definition of free will to the role of obtaining, or keeping a relationship with God. Is it, or is it not in the mind of a Christian, that it is solely on one's own willingness to make the right choice? That choice being--choose Christ in order to begin a relationship with God. Before going any further, I must point out how I intend to liberally use the phrase "free will" for communication reasons only, by no means am I endorsing such a belief.

Technically free will would include how one would have the ability to choose when, where, and why one was born, along with the choice of a family tree. Let's not forget eye and skin color, etc. The argument I hear is: "Just because you were born, by no choice of your own doesn't mean you're not in control of your own destiny." That argument actually makes sense... to a carnal mind. Let's look at that argument a little deeper.... In other words it's being proposed that an individual is in complete control, as in sovereign over their own destiny, by the choices they make. Did I get that right?

In order to get to the bottom of all this, I must ask ten thought provoking questions to clarify Christianity's definition or belief in free will:

One: Where did Christianity get the above definitions mentioned in paragraph 1?

Two:  Are there verses in the Bible clearly defining a free will?

Three:  Are there examples in the Bible of how free will is manifested?

Four:  Are there examples in the Bible of how free will had influenced someone's destiny and what that outcome was?

Five:  Is the phrase free will found anywhere within scripture?

Six:  Does free will have its limits?

Seven:  If there is a free will, who created it?

Eight:  If free will was created, is it more powerful than the One who created it?

Nine:  Does God have a free will?

Ten:  If number nine is true, which will has more power?


The answer to these 10 questions will be answered throughout this chapter, but not necessarily in the order displayed here.  See if you can identify them.

My heart beats--not by choice, nor by free will!   Similarly, a person breathes, and can't help it because it's an automatic function.  Sure you can hold your breath, but see how long your free will lasts while giving it your best shot.  There are far more examples other than these two obvious ones I've just mentioned, and these simple examples also prove free will has no influence on something that was created to have an automatic function.  Let me emphasize--**"Something that was created to have an automatic function"** is something important to be remembered, for it is the foundation to understanding how a sovereign God operates.  Please keep in mind the phrase:  "Something that was created to have an automatic function" in an upcoming chapter covering the question of:  Does "all" mean all?

I just proved in the previous paragraph how free will has its limits. Not only that, but some can hold their breath and temper better than others, so this tells me free will is inconsistent. Free will is irrelevant when it comes to your race, eye color, etc., even though technically this is the truest definition of free will. Putting that fact aside... thus far I've given indisputable examples of how free will has its limits, is inconsistent, and is irrelevant in many cases, yet Christianity teaches this limited, inconsistent, sometimes irrelevant free will is the all encompassing powerful key to determine ones eternal destiny. (huh?) Since there are obvious limits, can we at least agree God is the one who created those limits--for a purpose? Yet, again... Christianity is basically claiming that the very creator of that free will, who has put limits on it, has no jurisdiction over it! (again...huh?) That makes absolutely no sense if you think about it.

I've also discovered something interesting while doing the research for this chapter--ego and free will fit together like a hand in a glove. I see the ego as a continual power supply that feeds and fuels the free will. If not, then why is it, if someone gets offended in some way--the hurt ego will fuel the free will to react. If it wasn't for the ego no one would care about insults, and without ego--free will could be construed as irrelevant, or the very least objective.

My point for this strange detour in thinking... if it wasn't for the ego, one wouldn't care if God was in charge and sovereign over one's destiny. The Christian free will doctrine is driven by pride and the ego, the opposite of the humility pronounced as a virtue within Christendom. It takes true humility to admit our choices, i.e. our free will is not in charge of our eternal destiny, but instead--it is the love of God, through the gift of grace, and the accomplishments of Christ--requiring no prideful, ego driven free will of an individual to put the finishing touches on one's own eternity.

I want to be clear... WE HAVE A WILL, and yes, the ability to choose. If we didn't have a will then how would God have the ability to work in it? As in:

"For it is God who is at work in you both to WILL and to act according to His good purposes." Phil. 2:13

God really is sovereign, yet I believe not in control over everything. WHAT? Remember that "automatic function" mentioned in the fifth paragraph? Just because you have a sovereign God who created your will, it doesn't mean He is in control over every thought, every action, and every automatic bodily function.

Yes, God can work within any and all aspects of our lives, and will influence our wills. But control? I don't think so--no person is a puppet or a robot (puppets & robots will be addressed later in this chapter). However, what God is in total control of is the final outcome of the choices we make, i.e. the consequences caused by our actions. It is a sovereign God's authority and responsibility to righteously judge any and all eternal outcomes. Christianity indeed will claim that God is great! God is good! God is love! God is all powerful--all the time! They'll even quote Jesus in saying: "Not my will, but let thy will be done", yet get this... (it would be funny if it wasn't so sad) according to traditional Christian beliefs in reference to the doctrine of free will... God is NOT great enough, nor powerful enough, nor sovereign enough--His will is not powerful enough to be able to save you without your "free will"! Are you catching this--without your free will--which is a creation of God—at which He obviously set limits to, and He's in control of the outcome, yet it's claimed that one cannot have salvation without the sanction of one's own free will!


Whatever you want to call it: Free will, will power, choice, and/or the ability to choose--it has limits as well as abilities. By design God created both, and those limits or abilities cannot, nor will not go beyond the non-limited will of God--unless of course you believe in an itty-bitty little god. Maybe your free will is more powerful than that god. Is there scriptural evidence promoting God's will over man's? You bet there is as seen in these examples:

- Proverbs 16:9 – Man devises, God directs his steps (what about free will?)

- Proverbs 19:21 – Man devises, but God's counsel stands (so much for free will)

- Job 42:2 - "I know that You can do all things, and that no purpose of Yours can be thwarted.

I have an interesting question:  Sweating drops of blood proves to me Jesus was fully human at the time, so when Jesus prayed... "Not my will but Yours"--was Jesus only submitting His will to God's, or was He acknowledging God's sovereign will and authority over His own?  I find it interesting how Webster's dictionary seems to be in agreement with what appears to be the same definition of God's sovereignty characterized by Christ, as in: "Sovereign - unlimited original authority superior to all others."

Through the ages, man has obviously perverted what they would deem "authority superior to all others", by the examples and actions portrayed by kings and dictators. The cruelty displayed throughout history by these individuals has, understandably so, grossly tainted how most view the word sovereign. However, we cannot and must not attach this horrific world view to a loving sovereign God. I know for a fact none of our kings and dictators loved their people with the kind of love God "is"!

Christianity has an oxymoronic understanding of sovereign, as in:  A sovereign God can coexist with man's free will.  By the very definition of sovereign, one cannot have it both ways--it's either one or the other.  Properly defined sovereign is like pregnancy, as in there is no such thing as part sovereign, or somewhat sovereign.  The word sovereign implies something exclusive and complete in and of itself.  God is exclusive and complete in and of Himself, and God is sovereign--God is also love, thus we can fully trust a sovereign God because of His love.  I hope that made sense.  For those who believe being created in His image is a sign of our own sovereignty--the problem with that kind of thinking is one cannot take a fragment of God away from God, and still view God as exclusive and complete.  Meaning, one cannot take a portion of God's sovereignty away for a free will believer to use and abuse it as one wish's, and still claim God is "Almighty".  In other words, one cannot take an allotment of sovereign away, and have it remain sovereign.  That would be like taking a portion of God away and have Him remain God--that wouldn't make sense to very definition of God.

I as well used to believe, and I used to share how God did not create robots so I had to conclude it meant God created us with a free will. I now have concluded an either/or scenario, either God is sovereign or man is, rather than adopting the Christian idea of claiming you're either a robot or you have free will. Another similar way I've heard it said is: "Either God is a puppet master and you're a puppet, or you have a free will." Is there even the smallest chance God is bigger than that--than just the two options of robots or puppets? Before the end of this chapter I would like to share a third option that is not only biblical, but also endorses the character of God's love.

But first I have to address The Garden of Eden story that implies without a free will, Adam and Eve would have been nothing but "puppets on a string". This is the ideology that is used as a defense of free will. I must ask those that believe this way... where did you get that from and who taught you that? Those of you who have children--are your children puppets? Up to a certain age, are you not sovereign over your children, yet they still have wills of their own? Are you in complete control of their lives? It's obvious to everyone that children have their own STRONG wills, and in this context, a loving parent is there to properly influence those wills. Why is so hard to believe God is any different, if anything He's much better at it!

When teaching your children or correcting them, do you not manipulate the situation for the best outcome for both you and your child?  Nothing could be easier to understand—God manipulating circumstances to teach and correct His children.  Yet, I know of parents who treat their children in the loving manner I've mentioned above, who go to church and learn of a doctrine of men called a "free will".  These same parents consider God their loving Father (heavenly parent),yet they choose to ignore a biblical principle that teaches of that same loving Father as being sovereign.  Then they go back home after church and behave with their own children as a loving sovereign God would with them, and then deny God's sovereignty by exalting their free will.  It's almost as if these parents are saying, "Oh no You don't God… don't You dare use the same parenting tools we use in teaching and correcting our children!"

What I've personally witnessed in most cases, if I bring up the above scenario to their attention, they will passionately defend their free will, and some to the point of anger--with the same breath they demand their right to choose.  This proves my point of how Christians have erroneously redefined free will I previously mentioned in paragraph one.  I find it interesting how the average Christian will defend their free will and never consider defending God's sovereignty—His free will, even though one is blatantly biblical, and the other is only presumed to be so.

I was taught in reference to The Garden of Eden story--the infamous tree along with the infamous fruit--it was at that point in time God gave that couple the opportunity to choose to obey God or not. The problem I see with this theory, is that a person must jump to a conclusion that the well known couple were not given any other opportunities to make a choice of obedience before that time. Choice! Choice? We're continually told it's all about choice, and the act of choice started at the Tree. Preachers also continually use "The Garden" story to prove how, at that time, we were given the opportunity to choose to love God or not. I want to ask them... are you telling me that Adam and Eve did not love God until that point in time, or never had a choice about anything before that moment?

It doesn't make sense to put the burden of "choosing your eternity" on people, and then base the reason on The Garden of Eden story. If The Garden story is true, here's why it doesn't make sense to compare what happened to Adam and Eve with respect to us. They walked and talked with God, we didn't and we don't--not like they did. They knew first hand of the God of creation--we didn't. They knew God from the beginning of their very existence--we have to learn of Him and hope that knowledge has not been perverted in some way. Apparently they were not born with the sinful nature as the Bible claims we have. If this nature were not true then why would Paul state in Romans 7:18-20:

"For I know that nothing good dwells in me, that is, in my flesh; for the willing is present in me, but the doing of the good is not. [19] For the good that I want, I do not do, but I practice the very evil that I do not want. [20] But if I am doing the very thing I do not want, I am no longer the one doing it, but sin which dwells in me."?

Adam and Eve didn't go through any of what Paul mentioned above... at least not in the beginning of their journey. So to compare how they made choices to how we make choices is pure lunacy.

Adam made his choice out of a full knowledge and understanding of what that choice was all about, and why he was making it. I believe he knew exactly what he was doing. Some will claim deception! Reread the account--only Eve was called deceived. My point: From the beginning Adam and Eve had a full knowledge and understanding what was going on in their lives. They knew what God expected of them from the get-go. They knew who God was better than we do, and they still made bad choices, yet we're supposed to make the right choices while not knowing a fraction of what they understood? They already had a cultivated relationship with God--a friendship with God before partaking of that fruit-- before making that choice. We have never had an opportunity or a relationship like that before making our choices!

The Christian community seems to demand of the people of the world--that have never known God--that they should make the right choice to follow God--that they never knew, or experienced, or cultivated a relationship with--to instinctively jump on board the God train. Know this, I have no choice (pun intended), but to come to a conclusion that any significant choices we make, has to be done with knowledge and understanding of what we're choosing and why we're choosing it. Please keep in mind of a difference between a head knowledge and a Spirit knowledge. How that needed Spirit knowledge is obtained--will be fully covered in the chapter I'm going to write about referencing the Faith Of Christ.

Allow me to offer this analogy: If I've never drank coffee in my lifetime--meaning I've never tasted it, and if someone were to put two cups of coffee in front of me and say one is vanilla flavored and one is not--choose your favorite without tasting them. To whom would that make sense? Every Christian would agree my coffee analogy wouldn't be a fair way of making a choice, yet that's exactly what's expected of people when they're instructed to choose God.

Speaking of tasting... it's written in Psalms 34:8:

"O taste and see that the LORD is good;"

Ah ha, but you must come to Him first so you can make the "choice" to taste.  This statement is nothing more than a doctrine of men instigated by the religious carnal mind.  A sovereign God would respond with:

John 6:44 – "No one can come to Him UNLESS HE DRAWS THEM" (it's obvious you don't choose Him first via any kind of will, free will or otherwise).


I've been giving example after example of why God is sovereign, how His sovereignty works, and why free will is irrelevant in the long run.  All along I have not denied the existence of our wills, nor the ability to make choices.  So, the question comes to mind:  What is our responsibility, and how do we initially gain the knowledge that we need, so we can make the right choices?  Some people will say by the word of God.  I'm not claiming the Bible in it's entirety is solely the word of God, but God does use the Bible as a wonderful tool to lead, draw, and teach people-- no doubt.  I'm sure most will agree--simply reading the Bible and knowing scriptural references is nothing more than a head knowledge without the Spirit of God's interpretation.  But, by making the claim it's the only means by which God gives the necessary knowledge is shortsighted, ignorant, and is on the verge of slandering the Spirit of God, and His competence.

By alleging every relationship with God has to start with the Bible is lunacy--biblical principles maybe, considering within those pages it speaks of the ability of the Spirit of God to draw all mankind to His love.  If the Bible never existed, the Spirit of God is more than sufficient enough to instigate and perfect a relationship.  Philippians 1:6 -

"For I am confident of this very thing, that He who began a good work in you will perfect it until the day of Christ Jesus."


Since John 6:44 is telling us God instigates a relationship via a "drawing".  The very act of drawing by God is obviously a way of gaining knowledge, but is best described as a conviction.  In the Greek, "conviction" implies a bridging of God's thoughts to our own.  A rhetorical question:  Is it possible a degree of knowledge accompanies the bridging of thoughts?  Another way God might draw people could be defined as a "still small voice" whispering into the inner hearts and minds of a person.  Perhaps God will manipulate circumstances to get one's attention.  In most cases it's because of someone sharing God's love with their fellow man, along with a combination of all of the above.

I have a few questions for those who think their experience initially was due to an invitation, or an insight from someone else. Who manipulated circumstances to bring the two of you together--the appointment--that divine appointment? Who encouraged them, via that still small voice to share the hope that is within them? Who was it who convicted their thoughts to share with you in the first place? Personally, as it does in most cases, an appointment is how it happened to me. I think we all know the answer to these above questions of who was in charge.

As an angry teen, I refused to listen to anyone, including God, and I wasn't about to read a Bible. God knew exactly what it would take--He sent an innocent four year old little boy named Tony. I'll be sharing that story in an upcoming chapter.

Sovereign God? It's all about God. He will use whatever circumstance, and at times manipulate a circumstance to initiate a "first contact" with our minds, that most of us incorrectly define as our hearts. Someone has got to get the credit, and if it goes to us, it's called "boasting", but with God it's called love--love doesn't boast. Love gets the credit, the glory, i.e. God gets the glory. A sovereign God operating in love will use whatever it takes regardless of whether it's using the Bible, a dream, a vision, another person, a song, and I'm sure the list could go on and on.

"For it is (a sovereign) God who works in you both to will and to act according His good purposes." Phil. 2:13

Do you remember me asking earlier:  What is our responsibility, and how do we initially gain the knowledge that we need so we can make the right choices?  I've already supplied numerous examples of how God gives us knowledge, but what part do we play once we've obtained that knowledge?  Answer: Our responsibility is to eventually yield.  "Eventually" is the key word, as in "due time" best described in 1st Timothy 2:6 that reads:

 "Who gave himself a ransom for all, to be testified in due time."

Since a sovereign God is competent, as well as outside of time, He takes one heart/mind at a time, at the perfect time, in the perfect place, using a perfect circumstance for that person to make the right choice to choose Him.  But what if a person doesn't yield, as in using their free will to choose to refuse that knowledge?

The conclusion Christians jump to is: Then they're lost, and if they die there is a price to pay for their refusal, and that price is eternal hell. This is simply a doctrine of man, and nowhere in the Bible does it say anything like that! In other words... there are no examples in the Bible of anyone who had been exposed to God's love, as in Him instigating a relationship, who were convicted in their minds (heart) of His love for them, and then they refused, died, and ended up in an eternal torturous hell. It never happened, yet Christianity teaches it as if it had, does, and will continue to happen.

A sovereign God who is outside of time is a mystery to me. The exact methodology of how He continues after death is an unknown to all of us. But if one were to speculate on that unknown, it must be based upon love--His love, and what His love has done in the past. It seems obvious to me His love will continue to do as before--after death regardless of a "free will", as He did with the living. Consider rereading chapter 3: "Does Death Stop God?"

As a reminder to what I've written in a previous chapter, I will supply a page if not pages of scriptural verses that clearly point out it's a sovereign God's will that all men will be saved, and how that is accomplished. All mankind including the worst scumbag you could ever have known to exist, down to the nicest little old lady who never missed going to church a day in her life. In spite of a free will, God knows exactly what it's going to take to touch each and every heart. Since death doesn't stop a sovereign God, it may not happen in this lifetime, but God is competent and knows what He is doing.

Now for that third option I spoke of earlier. I encourage some of my readers to use that "God given free will" you claim you have, to choose the option of believing in a sovereign loving God who works within your will to teach you how to behave in accordance with love. The alternative would be to choose the option of--it's entirely up to you and your free will, and believing you'd be nothing but a robot or a puppet on a string in the hands of an egomaniacal control freak, or the very least a puppet master. If you believe the latter, consider the possibility--you have created a god in your very image. Speaking of the ability to "choose"... by adopting the free doctrine--realize you're "choosing" to ignore scripture verses that plainly state God is sovereign, His will cannot be thwarted, and He will accomplish His plan to reconcile all of creation. Not only that, you're "choosing" to ignore the zero times "free will" is mentioned within scripture.

Choices!  Can our choices change a sovereign God's will?  Emphatically NO!  From what you've read so far it's obvious I have differing views on what sovereign means than what most Christians have been taught to believe.  My simple approach to most things is I try never to put God in a box.  I'll address the box issue with this question:  Why can't the All Mighty, All Powerful, Creator of the universe, be sovereign while at the same time create us with wills, along with the ability to make choices on our own?  I believe that's exactly who He is and what He did because, "Ultimate Authority" i.e. Sovereign  DOES NOT MEAN "control".

Christians, on the other hand, are notorious box builders.  By believing sovereign and control are one in the same, which results in, or appears to put God in a box.  I'll explain it this way… If God is sovereign it must (box) mean He is in control of all the bad, the pain, and the shit people do.  Or, if God is sovereign it must (box) mean we have no wills and we're puppets and robots.  These are perfect examples of how some will put God in a box.

Again I will clarify… God's sovereignty means: In His "Ultimate Authority" (not control), He uses every good and bad choice we make. He gives us the ability to choose, allowing us to use our own wills to bring about pain or joy, or nothing of consequence. Unlike some in the "God is sovereign" camp, I believe we are in temporal control in most instances, but we have absolutely no "Authority" to dictate any eternal ramification caused by our choices and wills.

"God reaps where He has not sown"--spoken of in Luke 19:21. As in principle only this verse is also telling me--with God nothing goes to waste. I believe this "nothing goes to waste" would include both our good and bad deeds. Because He is Sovereign as defined in Hebrew as: " The supreme Father, Caretaker, Ruler, Judge, and has the Ultimate Authority". The Hebrew definition is describing a sovereign God who has the ability to use the good and bad choices we make as a learning tool, to eventually bring all of us--all of creation to Himself, regardless of the actions His creation chooses to make!

The above paragraph makes more sense to me rather than God giving up who He is, as in "sovereign", just so we can make our own choices. To reiterate:  We have wills, God is still sovereign-- we can make choices, God is still sovereign--most of the time we are in control of our own actions, God is still sovereign.  One does not negate the other.

Due to my research, I have some closing thoughts of how I define "free will".  Free Will stands alone, considering the word "free" can be interpreted as meaning:  Without Gods influence, that is… free of God's influence unless I allow it!  True free will is freedom from God, as in who needs Him--unless I call on Him.  Free will implies and is taught--God will not force Himself on anyone—God is a gentleman (tell that to the Apostle Paul).  I have my own free will to accomplish what is necessary for making decisions in life, as well as what is required of me to procure eternal life--considering it's my choice that determines that.  My free will is sovereign and is powerful enough to override the will of God, thus making the creation sovereign instead of the Creator.  Free will means the ability to make your own destiny apart from God's choices, thus proclaiming you are a sovereign person apart from God.

None of the aforementioned definitions are scriptural, yet I've heard the same if not similar claims from within the Christian community. All of it is based on assumption and conjecture, better known as doctrines of men. The "will of man is not capable of doing any of what was mentioned in the above paragraph. The "will of man" is a gift God has given mankind, whereas "free will" is nothing more than a counterfeit gift that man gives to itself. Search the heart, search the mind, search whatever you have to, and most importantly… be honest! You'll discover free will is a pride issue, whereas a humble person would never consider their wills would be superior to God's. Christians will sing songs about "God is the potter and we are the clay", and proclaim to one another "in Him we live and move and have our being", then hypocritically insist on having a free will.

To conclude this chapter let's briefly recap what has been covered thus far. Chapter 1 encourages everyone to question just about everything. Chapter 2 exposes perversions within Christianity, thus the reason to question most everything. Chapter 3 explains scripturally how death cannot stop God from completing His will, and in this chapter we've discovered how a sovereign God has the power and authority to expedite His will over the will of man. In the next chapter I'm going to touch on how, in most cases within scripture, "all" actually means everyone when we read verses like:

1 Tim 2:4 – God will have ALL to be saved

# Chapter 5

## When Did "All" Become A "Select Few"?

All?  What does "all" mean in scripture?  That little  three letter word could possibly be the most important word in the entire Bible to understand.  If someone's understanding or belief about something is erroneous, wouldn't it make sense to sow a few seeds of doubt about it to make a person think?  That's precisely what this chapter is about.  Frankly, that's what this whole book is about.

We all need to remain humble and teachable so we (myself included) don't end up being stuck in a rut, and getting nowhere with our understanding--not only in reference to the word "all", but about most things in general.  With that said, what it takes is a simple Greek word study of the word "all".  By doing so it would eliminate any doubts and misunderstanding in our approach to the good news... well... that's how it worked for me.

Let me be clear... I am not claiming to be a Greek scholar. However, with the internet at our fingertips, any of us can obtain a better knowledge of what words mean like never before. This was my approach: First I researched the languages the Apostle Paul spoke. He called himself a Pharisee of Pharisees, which would mean he was well versed in the Torah, thus telling me he spoke Hebrew. Also, as a Jewish scholar he would be required to read and understand the Talmud. The Talmud was written in Aramaic so he most likely spoke Aramaic as well. He was born in Tarsus, considered by historians as a Hellenistic city. Hellenistic, as in the dialect of Greek Paul was raised with, better understood as Koine Greek versus Ancient Greek. Yet, all dialects had some things in common, which were: Passive, Neutral, and Active word usages as well as Feminine or Masculine. I didn't research the pertinence of Feminine or Masculine, but I zeroed in on how the Passive, Neutral, and Active word usages were relevant to my research, and boy did I find a treasure trove!

---

Since this book is written in English, I'll first give a Webster's definition of the word "all", and then later explain how more complex it is in the Greek.

Definition of ALL in English:
The whole amount, quantity, or extent of every member or individual component of:
*all* men will go
*all* five children were present

Synonyms: everyone, everybody, each person, every person

It appears as though *all* means *all* in context to a person or thing, yet when Christians read the same English word *all* in their English translated bibles-- suddenly or miraculously it changes its meaning to only mean a select few! The reason? Christians have been duped for centuries into believing the word *all* within context to people is conditional. Conditional on "what" will be addressed shortly.

To build a foundation of understanding of what I mean by "duped", I would like to bring up what I call: Ignorance promoted by blind-faith.

A few examples of blind faith are:

- Believing whatever the pastor or priest says.
- Thinking the early church leaders had a better grasp on things than we do.
- Defending the position of Bibles being error free, even though none agree about everything.
- God somehow protecting the Bible from errors created by man within its pages.
- Believing every biblical story to be literally true, while ignoring man's perpetual habit to exaggerate, and to use metaphoric language.

Christian ignorance in the form of blind-faith is a terrible witness, giving the world cause to ignore the Good News message. We're viewed as just religious kooks that scientifically and historically have been proven wrong, over and over again. This shouldn't be. We need to be on top of things, well-educated and honest, rather than doling out multiple forms of deception. One example of deception is this: Deceiving the church and trying to convince the world into believing that the word *all* doesn't mean *all*. It only takes the tiniest amount of research to disprove such an erroneous belief.

Just because a Christian is taught to believe someone is not part of the *all* doesn't mean it's true. As an analogy, let's say you were deceived and misled into believing the notion of having a lot of money was somehow evil, and with blind faith you chose to believe it. With that said, let's also continue by saying you had a wealthy relative pass away who left you millions--simply put, you'd be considered by every definition available--a millionaire. Even if you didn't believe it--you'd still be a millionaire. If you had no concept or understanding of what it would be like to be a millionaire--you'd still be a millionaire. If people around you told you, you were not a millionaire--you'd still be a millionaire. Then there would be people like myself who were trying to convince you, you were a millionaire, and you chose to ignore us--you'd still be a millionaire. And, if you died without using a penny of it—you would have died being a millionaire.

Think of Jesus as your wealthy relative: Because of the actions of Jesus, faith was given to you as a gift through grace--you were reconciled to God. If you had no concept or understanding of what it would be like to be reconciled--you would still be reconciled. Even if you don't believe it or confess it--you're still reconciled. If people told you, you were not reconciled--you'd still be reconciled. And if there were people like myself who were trying to convince you, you were reconciled, and you chose to ignore us--you'd still be reconciled. And, if you died without acknowledging or experiencing the riches of a vivified, reconciled life—you would die still being reconciled. And, not just you only, but *the world,* for *everyone,* and as this chapter contends... the "all".

I will now begin to prove to anyone who has eyes to read, and a heart/mind to comprehend how wonderfully gracious God really is. Now, because of The Christ--from God's perspective--your beliefs, your actions, and what others say, has absolutely nothing to do with who and what you are. You are *the world* that God so loved, you are the *every* knee that will bow, and the *all* that will know God! As the title of this book states: "In Defence of God's Love", this chapter is trying to make another attempt to convince you of who you are, because of God's love.

Do you the reader remember the "automatic function" I mentioned in chapter four referencing how it takes no will of our own for the heart to beat, or to take a breath--it being an automatic function? That function was pre-programmed in creation. I submit the exact same pre-programming of salvation became an automatic function, because from God's perspective Christ was slain BEFORE the foundation of the world--for "all".

This pre-programming I speak of has grossly been interpreted as Arminianism or Calvinism, depending on who you speak to. I will prove it's neither. First Arminianism: To interpret pre-programming as Arminianism wouldn't make sense, considering Armenians believe in the "election" of a few believers, and yet I'm promoting an election of *all* people that will eventually become believers, since death doesn't stop God!

On the other hand, my "pre-programming" view will be understood as Calvinism by some, considering pre-programming can be skewed as meaning predestination. Calvinism proclaims a predestination of "a few", even though I'll be sharing dozens upon dozens of scriptures that are SHOUTING a Good News message for *ALL* people! The exact opposite of Calvinism. Yes indeed the scriptures speak of predestination, but the implication and context is only referring to God's will, His plans, and His ability, rather than the eternal destiny of mankind.

For the next four paragraphs I intend to scripturally support my position of pre-programming. Romans 8:29-30 is telling us God has predestined everyone He knows. (Is there anyone God doesn't know?) Predestination for what purpose? To be conformed--all those He knew--to the image of His Son. Later in the same verse it tells us "these whom He predestined, He also called; and these whom He called, He also justified; and these whom He justified, He also glorified." This sure sounds like pre-programming to me.

Here's another example of what I consider pre-programming: In 1 Corinthians 2:7 it plainly states "God predestined before the ages to our glory". To whose glory? To those spoken about in Romans 8. "Before the ages"? God's plan to reconcile all of creation was predestined or pre-programmed before any of us were born.

Ephesians 1:5 is telling me "God has predestined us to adoption as sons through Jesus Christ to Himself, according to the kind intention of His will". Who are the "us"? All those He knew in Romans 8. Predestination or pre-programming promotes an election of *all* people that will eventually become believers through adoption.

Last example: In Ephesians 1:11 it says "we have been predestined (pre-programmed) to obtained an inheritance". Who is the "we"? You guessed it--the ones He knew spoken about in

Romans 8. Later in the same verse it says "according to His purpose who works all things after the counsel of His will". Am I misreading this, or does it say God is the One doing it according to His will? I see nothing in context about anything being dependant upon the will of man.

The common denominator between Armenians and Calvinists is they both believed in an "election" of a selected "few", only differing in the method of how God would do the selection. There is logical reason for this division that I call madness--they both believed in the doctrine of hell. Common sense tells me, without the belief in hell, both Armenians and Calvinists would have had no need to select only "a few" to be acceptable to God. Described as a "few" faithful believers by the Armenians, or described as the predestined "few" God chose to be with Him by the Calvinists. The doctrine of Armenianism, of Calvinism, or of hell--the word *all* is in direct opposition to all three doctrines.

In English, "Universal" is the best word to describe *all* and *everyone*--defined as:

*an adjective*
"-of, affecting, or done by ALL people or ALL THINGS in the WORLD applicable to ALL cases."

Universal sure sounds like the word "all" to me, best described in Acts 3:20-21:

" - and that He may send Jesus, the Christ appointed for you, [21] whom heaven must receive until the period of "restoration of all things"(universal) about which God spoke by the mouth of His holy prophets from ancient time."

Before you quickly label what I'm saying is Universalism--let me be abundantly clear... it is not! Universalism pronounces all paths, all religions, all beliefs lead to the same point. I am saying the opposite by stating Christ is the ONLY WAY, the ONLY TRUTH, the ONLY LIFE, and no one can come to the Father except through Him. It's obvious there's a huge difference between Universalism and what I believe and what I'm promoting in this book. Also, something else to consider--when you label someone it makes it easier to dismiss them, so listen up before being tempted to add another label of heresy to the list.

Historically, the early Christians practiced and believed in Christian Universalism, easily proven historically and scripturally as in:

- Four of the six schools that taught theology during the first 5 centuries after Christ all taught "ultimate reconciliation," or another way of putting it: Universal Reconciliation. Those schools were: Caesarea, Nisbis, Alexandra, and Antioch.

- 1st Timothy 2:6 is only but one of many verses that declare a salvation of ALL. This verse plainly endorses a universal declaration by using the word "all", with nothing in context referring to it being conditional upon any acts or requirements from the person who is part of that "all". This verse also endorses a "coming age" inference by stating: "Who gave himself a ransom for all, to be testified in DUE TIME."

- Sarcastically asking, is the word Cosmos describing a select few in: "God was in Christ, reconciling the Cosmos to Himself, not counting men's sins against them." 2 Cor. 5:19 (?) Once again, there is nothing in context separating one man from another, nor is it conditional.

- Christianity will agree with half a verse that says in Adam "all" die, meaning everyone is going to eventually die. You can't get more universal than that! However, the second half of the verse state that in Christ the SAME ALL are going to live, meaning the same (everyone) is going to eventually live in Him.

- Universally, death cannot stop God. (Read chapter 3)

- Repent means to change your mind. Conviction is a bridging of God's mind to your own. Are there only a few that God wants to convict, thus causing repentance, or is it everyone, as in universal?

- "For God so loved the world" makes God's love universal. Since His love never fails, and His mercy endures forever, how can anyone think this only applies to a select few?

- "Every" is another word for universal, so is it true or not that "Every knee shall bow, and every tongue confess, that Jesus Christ is Lord to the glory of God the Father."

Most of what is considered heresy today was indeed taught as truth long ago. So what happened? The infestation of pagan beliefs has so thoroughly become traditional, and has been taught as Orthodoxy within Christianity. Then when someone like myself tries to expose the real "heresy"--instead of honest research and debate, I am the one labeled as a heretic.

This chapter boils down to understanding and properly defining one little word: "ALL"! Sarcastically speaking, and from my personal experience, it seems everyone but Christians know what "all" means in English. So, lets delve into what it means in the Greek, both in the New Testament as well as in the Old known as the Septuagint. In doing so, we'll bring to light why there's such a huge misunderstanding in Christendom, and expose the ignorance of why they don't believe all means all. I'm not trying to sound condescending, but when people read words--it's perfectly natural and obvious they are going to read those words with the understanding of their own language and culture, without considering the original language for whom it was originally written.

As I've said before, I am not a Greek scholar by any mean. However, we have Greek dictionaries available to us right at our fingertips. So, with that said it's time to get a little technical (sorry about that). In the Greek within scripture, the word "all" incorporates eight different adjectives, one noun, and one adverb. I am only going to address the adjectives, because the samples of scriptures I'll be using--only uses adjectives for the word "all". To start, allow me to articulate what I wrote earlier in this chapter--the word "all" in the Greek can be a passive usage, a neutered (neutral) usage, or an active usage. In the Greek dictionaries these words are usually displayed as: "pas", "neu", or "act". Here are a couple of examples of how the neutral "all" is used in scripture.

Neutral/Neutered: Matthew 5:34 - "But I say to you, make no oath at "all", either by heaven...".
Matthew 9:26 - "This news spread throughout "all" that land."

There's many more example of this within scripture, but there's really no need to further explain the "neutered/neutral all", due to its irrelevance to this chapter.

Lets see what an "active all" looks like, and how it would be applied in this modern day example of: We "all" played a good game, we "all" participated, and we "all" had an <u>active</u> part in the outcome of the game.  It's plain to see it takes an action on the part of the "all" in order to be included as part of the "all". Now lets look at a couple of biblical examples of how the Greek translates an "active all" within scripture.

Active:  Matthew 10:22 - "You will be hated by "all" because of My name..."  What makes this an "active all" is defined by participating in hate, as in the very ACT of hating.  In other words, there would be no hate unless "the all" engaged in, or cooperated in the act.
Matthew 14:20 - "...and they "all" ate and were satisfied."  Again, they ate--a required action on the part of "the all" in order for "the all" to be satisfied. Now for The Good News for us "all" (Passive).


Now for The Good News for us "all" (Passive). The rest of this chapter is going to be dedicated exclusively to the "passive all", how it's applied in scripture, and why it's such Good News to all mankind.  "Passive", in application to the word "all" simply means no one has a choice of being part of the "all", as in no action is required to be included. Below is a list of three modern day examples we would all understand:

1.  Something happened that has a direct impact on your life, but you didn't even know about it--you are a passive participant--meaning no action on your part would make a difference.

2.  If you were in a building and an earthquake hit hard, killing "all" who occupied it--you would be a passive participant--meaning no action on your part would make a difference.

3.  In a hunting accident, a stray bullet seemingly out of nowhere struck you--you would be a passive participant--meaning no action on your part would make a difference.


   Did I happen to mention--"meaning no action on your part would make a difference"?  This statement is most critical to understand when examining the "passive all" in the Greek and later transcribed into the Bible.  All the above modern examples are reasonably easy to understand, have actually happened to people throughout history, and some are called "acts of God".  Ironic how Christianity will give God the credit for what's known as natural disasters, all along acknowledging people had no choice of what was done to them, yet refuse to give God the credit for the salvation of the "passive all", as in no choice of their own, orchestrated through the power of His grace.

Christians don't understand, and have never been taught there is such a thing as a passive, neutral, and an active "all". In context to salvation, whenever they read the word "all", they interject in their minds a belief it's conditional on obeying, confessing, repenting, and believing. I'll be repeating these conditions later on in this chapter, but by believing in these conditions--it would require from the Greek an "active all", rather than a "passive all". Whenever a "passive all" is involved, one will never see contextually within scripture any conditions such as obeying, confessing, repenting, or believing. I know this goes against traditional teaching, but this is simply how the word "all" is defined in the Greek.

If one is in disagreement with my assessment of the "passive all"--your argument is not with me, it is with every ancient and Koine Greek dictionary at our disposal. It is clear--the "passive all" means a person who is part of the "all" has no active role to play. There is nothing a person can do about being included, considering the word "all", in of itself, means there are no exclusions. Any participation or by not participating--a person can't add to it, nor take away from it. This sure sounds a lot like GRACE! Why? Because the "passive all" in the Greek confirms how grace works!

For the next few paragraphs, I will give example after example of how the "passive all", through the power of grace, is recorded within scripture. Note--whenever the word "all" is used in a passive application, the Greek root word is "PAN". I don't claim to understand this fully, but depending on other words within the same scripture in relation to the word "all", PAN might end with a "ton", "tes", "tas", or "ta". Examples of these are: Pan (purest form), Panton, Pantes, Pantas, or Panta. These Greek words are used within scripture to define "all" as follows:

Pantes:

- 1 Cor 15:22 – "In Adam ALL die, in Christ ALL live". In this verse the word "all" is a passive word, meaning we had no part to play in the outcome. In Adam we're "all" going to die--this is a fact, people are going to die! We may have an active role to play in the method, but in context--that's not the point. It's stating there is no active role we can play in ultimately stopping the process--we simply have no choice in the matter. The same passive "all" is being used IN CHRIST "ALL" WILL LIVE--no choice--"all" are going to live. I know what I'm about to say will tweak many of religious minds, but with a "passive all", it's irrelevant if you believe, repent, or whatever condition the religious folks throw at you. Because it's not up to them or you. If it required an action on your part, then you would have something to boast about. Yet, we're specifically told that life with God is totally dependant on a free gift of grace so we

96

wouldn't have anything to boast about.  See why the passive word "ALL" is so important in this verse?

- Rm 5:15 – In Adam "ALL" (pantes) condemned, in Christ "ALL" (pantes) live  (Condemned simply means death and the word "all" is identical in every way to 1 Cor. 15:22)

- Jn 12:32 - Jesus will draw "all" (pantes) mankind unto Himself (Mankind has no choice in this drawing process--free will means nothing.  Yes, we have a will to run around and do whatever it takes to live this life, but in the end--Jesus will draw everyone unto Himself regardless of the human will.)

Pantas:
- Rm 5:18 – Therefore just as one man's trespass led to condemnation for "ALL" (pantas), so one man's act of righteousness leads to justification and life for "ALL" (pantas) (In the same fashion three verses earlier, the word condemnation means death, and this verse is almost identical to that of 1 Cor. 15:22)

- 1 Tim 2:4 – God will have "ALL" (pantas) to be saved (God's will gives no choice to the "all" He is going to save)

Panton:
- 1 Tim 2:6 – Salvation of "ALL" (panton) is testified in due time (Not only is this verse telling us that "all" will be saved, but that it's

only a matter of time, by telling us it's not limited to this lifetime or age.)

- 2 Cor 5:15 – Jesus died for "ALL" (panton)

- 1 Tim. 4:10 - We rely on the living God, Who is the Savior of "ALL" (panton) humans, especially of those who believe.  (This verse is clearly not separating humans from one another regardless if they're believers or not.  Unbelievers are still part of the "passive all", not because they are believers (obviously), but because they are humans.  The point--you as a human, as mankind--you have no choice with the fact that we "all" rely on this living God who is the savior of the "passive all".)

Panta:
- Col 1:20 – "ALL" (panta) reconciled unto God (The "all" being reconciled unto God means "the all" has no choice, no active role to play in being reconciled unto God. Another verse Christians hate because some claim they've said the sinner's prayer, so that's their part to play, and that's why they're part of the "all".  If this prayer was required to be part of the "all"-- in the Greek it would have been an "active all" to be reconciled rather than a "passive all".

Pan:
- Hebrews 10:10 - By the which will we are *(present tense-done deal)* sanctified *(past tense)* through the offering of the body of Jesus Christ once for "ALL" (root - pan).

Reader--please take special note of the following three verses:

- Jn 3:35 – The Father has given "ALL" (root - pan) into His hands (meaning God gave Jesus "ALL" things)

- Jn 17:2 – He (Jesus) has authority over "ALL" (PAN) flesh to give eternal life. (Jesus gives eternal life to "ALL" that His Father gave Him in Jn 3:35, and this "ALL" in Jn 17 is an example of the purest form of pan. Since this is a "passive all"--Jesus gave eternal life to the "all" who had no choice in the matter. Once again this "passive all" is telling us no amount of obeying, confessing, repenting, or believing had any active part to play in becoming a member of "the all". If there were requirements such as the aforementioned obeying, confessing, repenting, or believing--then the Greek language would have made it an "active all", and then we could boast about it. I know most Christians won't agree with this, because of centuries of indoctrination. I encourage anyone to look it up in an Ancient or Koine Greek dictionary and try to prove me wrong.)

- 1 Tim 2:4 – God will have "ALL" (pantas) to be saved. (God's will gives no choice to the "passive all" He is going to save)

Note: Jn 3:35 is plainly telling us that the Father has given "ALL" into Jesus' hands--then we read in 1st Timothy it is God's will to save "ALL", and He has given Jesus "ALL" power and authority to do His will (which is to save "ALL"). Why don't Christians believe the Father or the Son in this?

I believe the reason the "passive all" is not taught or is ignored by Christendom is because of ego and pride within all men. In this case-- Christians who hate the thought of not having a choice when it come to salvation, which is what a "passive all" declares. Christians are the ones who want to declare it was by their choice, their free will to accept or reject salvation. In reality--as a member of the "passive all", it is accomplished by the Faith of Christ--given as a gift to "all" (passive) mankind, so no one can boast about it being their free will or choice. Once again... If salvation had anything to do with free will or choice then it would be an "active all", rather than a "passive all" in the Greek.

Hopefully some lights have gone off inside the heads of those who happened upon this book. To one degree or another we in Western Christianity have been taught through a lens of prejudice and self-righteousness. We are prejudiced against the unbeliever because of their refusal to believe as we have done. This kind of prejudice defines us as self-righteous.

Please, don't get me wrong--it's super important to obey, confess, repent, and believe--for the purpose of this lifetime. It's called a vivified life, not a vivified after death. What Christ accomplished for "all" was accomplished with no help from any of us. God is going to reconcile all of creation and our petty little choices are not going to stop Him. I'm sure somewhere in the mix is our will, and our God created abilities to choose, but it's only within the parameters of: "For it is God who works in you both to will and to act according to His good purposes."

Below is an extremely important list with a theme of: ALL, EVERY, and WORLD. Intelligent religious folk have a tendency to throw the baby out with the dirty bathwater. Two examples of how this is done: Proof texting and context. Proof texting is only applicable and warranted if a scripture is taken out of context. However, every scripture verse previously shared and in the list below--is self contextualizing, meaning they are true in and out of context--they are applicable to any and all situations, to all people, regardless of who wrote it, to whom it was written, and why. The baby and the dirty bathwater? The baby is the theme and the dirty bathwater is substituting the truth in the below verses with a label of proof texting. This is done for the purpose to self justify ignorance, indoctrination, and doctrines of men that keep a person from seeing the theme.

Okay, but before we get started... first a little FYI: None of the below scriptures are conditional on obeying, believing, confessing or repenting. If that were true, it would say so and written somewhere within context, and not only that--they wouldn't contain the Greek root word "pan". In this list, EVERY verse with the word "all" in them is the root word PAN, thus making every verse a "passive all" in the Greek. After reading this list with the understanding of a "passive all", I challenge any of you to even try to keep the excitement down to a minimum. (Note: There will be a repeat of a few verses already covered in this chapter, but I thought you would want a complete list available here.)

Theme: ALL, EVERY, WORLD

Genesis 12:3 --- ALL peoples on earth will be blessed through Abraham.

Genesis 22:18 --- ALL nations on earth will be blessed through Abraham's offspring.

Psalms 22:27 --- ALL the ends of the earth and ALL the families of the nations will acknowledge God.

Psalms 33:15 – God fashions ALL hearts

Psalms 65:2 – To You (God) ALL flesh shall come

Psalms 86:9 – ALL nations will worship Him

Psalms 145:9-10 --- The Lord has compassion on ALL His creation and ALL He has made will praise Him.

Psalms 145:13 --- The Lord loves ALL His creation.

Psalms 145:14 – He raises ALL WHO FALL (even backsliders?)

Samuel 14:14 – We must ALL die; we are like water spilled on the ground, which cannot be gathered up. But God will NOT take away a life; He will devise plans so as NOT TO KEEP AN OUTCAST BANISHED FOREVER FROM HIS PRESENCE. (do you honestly still believe in eternally being separated from God in hell?)

Isaiah 25:6-8 --- God will prepare a feast for ALL PEOPLE, He will destroy the shroud that enfolds ALL peoples, the sheet that covers up ALL nations. He will eliminate death, wipe away the tears from ALL FACES and remove the disgrace of his people from all the earth.

Isaiah 45:22-23 --- God has sworn an oath that (ALL) every knee will bow before Him and every tongue will swear by Him.

Isaiah 49:6 --- God's salvation will be brought to the ends of the earth.

Jeremiah 31:33-34 --- ALL men will know God, from the greatest to the least.

Matthew 18:13 --- Like the man who owes a hundred sheep and is not willing to lose even one, God is not willing that any one be lost.

Luke 2:10 --- The birth of Jesus is good news for ALL the people. (nowhere in context is this conditional)

Luke 3:6 - ALL flesh shall see God's salvation

Luke 15:4 - If ANY (all) stray He goes after that which is lost until He finds it

John 1:29 --- Jesus is the Lamb of God who takes away the sin of the world. (not conditional)

John 3:35 – The Father has given ALL into His hands (meaning God gave Him ALL things)

John 4:42 – Jesus is Savior of the WORLD

John 5:25 --- Even the dead will hear the sound of Christ and ALL who hear will live.

John 5:28 – ALL in the grave will hear & come forth

John 6:37 --- Everything (ALL) that God has given to Christ will come to him.

John 6:39 – This is the will of the Father Who sent Me, that of ALL He has given Me, I should I SHOULD LOSE NOTHING, but raise them up at the last day.

John 12:32 – Jesus will draw ALL mankind unto Himself

John 12:47 – I do not judge ANYONE who hears my words and does not keep them, for I CAME NOT to judge the world, but to save the WORLD. (Jesus came to save ALL)

John 17:2 – He (Jesus) has authority over ALL flesh to give eternal life.  (Jesus gives eternal life to ALL that His Father gave Him)

Acts 3:20 – (Restitution of ALL) And that He may send [to you] the Christ (the Messiah), Who before was designated and appointed for you--even Jesus, Whom heaven must receive [and retain] until the time for the complete (universal) RESTORATION OF ALL that God spoke by the mouth of all His holy prophets for ages past [from the most ancient time in the memory of man].

Romans 3:3-4 --- The unbelief of some will not nullify God's faithfulness.

Romans 5:15 – In Adam ALL condemned, in Christ ALL live

Romans 5:18 – Therefore just as one man's trespass led to condemnation for ALL, so one man's act of righteousness leads to justification and life for ALL

Romans 8:38-39 --- Nothing can separate us from the love of God that is in Christ.

Romans 11:15 – Reconciliation of the WORLD

Romans 11:32 He has shut ALL up in unbelief to show mercy to ALL

1 Corinthians 3:15 – ALL saved, so as by fire

1 Corinthians 15:22 – In Adam ALL die, in Christ ALL live

2 Corinthians 5:15 – Jesus died for ALL

2 Corinthians 5:19 --- Through Christ, God was reconciling the world (ALL) to Himself.

Ephesians 1:10 – ALL come into Him at the fullness of times

Ephesians 1:11 --- God will bring ALL things under heaven and on earth under Christ.

Ephesians 1:22 - Therefore He has put ALL things in subjection to Christ

Ephesians 4:10 --- Christ ascended higher then all the heavens to fill the whole (ALL) universe.

Philippians. 2:9-11 --- Every (ALL) tongue will confess that Jesus is Lord (In 1 Corinthians 12:3, Paul writes that no one can say "Jesus is Lord" except by the Holy Spirit)

Colossians 1:20 – ALL reconciled unto God

1 Timothy 2:4 – God will have ALL to be saved

1 Timothy 2:4 – God desires ALL to come to the knowledge of truth

1 Timothy 2:6 – Salvation of ALL is testified in due time

1 Timothy 4:10 --- God is the Savior of ALL men, especially (not exclusively) those who believe.

Titus 2:11-12 --- God's grace, which brings salvation has appeared to ALL men.

Hebrews 2:9 --- Jesus tasted death for everyone (ALL).

Hebrews 7:25 – Jesus is able to save to the UTTERMOST

Hebrews 8:11 – ALL will know God

II Peter 3:9 - ALL come to repentance

1 John 2:2 – And He is the atoning sacrifice for our (believers) sins, and not OURS ONLY, but ALSO for the sins of the WHOLE WORLD. (you still think you're "special" because you're a believer?)

1 John 4:14 --- Christ is the Savior of the world (ALL).

Revelation 5:13 --- Every (ALL) creature in heaven, on earth, under the earth, and on the sea will sing praises to him who sits on the throne and to the Lamb (Christ).

Revelation 21:4-5 --- God will dwell with men and he will wipe every (ALL) tear from their eyes, death, mourning, crying, pain and the old order of things will pass and everything will be made new.

Were you able to keep from getting excited? If none of the above verses gave you hope for all humanity, then you need to reexamine what you believe, and why you believe it. These verses should have encouraged you to trust in God's abilities--if not, get as far away as you can from whoever is teaching you otherwise. They are wolves in sheep's clothing and have no idea what love is--not just love, but "perfect love", and with God's help, I will illustrate what this means in my next chapter.

WOO HOO!! Preach it!!

# Chapter 6

## Perfect Love

Scripturally speaking I've discovered a huge difference between "perfect love" and love. Every Christian I've met is very familiar with "the love chapter" in 1st Corinthians chapter 13, yet the word "perfect" is nowhere to be found within the chapter. Every wonder why? As I said before, because there is a huge difference between "perfect love" and love at which a foundation first needs to be laid before the difference can be exposed. Wouldn't it be wise to understand how love is described and how love operates within scripture before pointing out how different it is from perfect love?

Notice how "perfect" is nowhere to be found in: "Love is patient, love is kind. It does not envy, it does not boast, it is not proud. It does not dishonor others, it is not self-seeking, it is not easily angered, it keeps no record of wrongs. Love does not delight in evil but rejoices with the truth. It always protects, always trusts, always hopes, always perseveres. Love never fails" (1 Corinthians 13:4-8). To add to this theme, I've heard songs sung about the Romans 8:39 verse of how "nothing can separate us from the love of God". Weird question: Is this love, that nothing can separate us from, referring to perfect love or the love described in 1st Corinthians? We shall see once we've properly defined perfect love.

Before I get too far into this chapter, I want to point out how the verses both in Romans and 1st Corinthians are self-contextualizing. Meaning, they are true and applicable to every situation, every circumstance no matter who wrote it or who is reading it.

I have a cousin who insists the verse in Romans that states "nothing can separate us" was written to and is for believers only! I'm sure he's not alone in this belief, so does this mean God's love is separated from some people and not from others? Does the famous verse of John 3:16 say for God so loved "some" that He gave His Son? The key word I want to emphasize is the word "nothing", as in "nothing can separates us from the love of God". Just previous to proclaiming nothing can separate us--it's written "nor any created thing". Is the unbeliever a created thing? Is the will, as in the ability to choose within an unbeliever and believer alike--a "created thing"? My point: Nothing means nothing, and just because it was written to believers it doesn't mean it was only about the believer.

Is there any place God is not?  If God is love, is there any place love is not?   Christianity almost portrays how God is only love if one is a believer, making God's love conditional, and not just conditional but contingent upon a belief in Him.  I will ask again, is there any place God is not?  Some will claim God is not in hell since hell is an eternal separation from God.  Others will go a step further and allege a person will suffer endless pain while in eternal separation from God.  Which one is true, they both can't be!

Allow me to address another belief within Christianity and work my way backwards.  God is love, and since it's believed God is not in hell--that would mean love cannot be in hell--right?  According to Christian beliefs, hell represents an eternal separation from God regardless of the involvement of pain or otherwise--true?  It is also believed the Latin word hell (infernum) is a derivate from the Greek word Hades--technically this is not true, and I'll cover this misnomer in detail later on in future chapters.  But, just for the sake of argument let's say the word hell is a derivative of Hades.

Lastly, Christianity teaches how the word Sheol is the Hebrew equivalent of both Hades and hell. If that is true, that would mean Sheol would be a place where God is not--where love is not, due to the fact of His love being eternally separated from people who reside there--correct? For those who believe this way, please explain what the hell/Sheol was King David talking about when it's recorded of him saying:

"If I make my bed in Sheol, behold, You are there". (Psalms 139:8)

Also interesting how it says in Isaiah 14:11:

"Your pomp and the music of your harps have been brought down to Sheol".

Is Christianity actually trying to get us to believe God's "splendid display" of love, along with His music is allowed in hell, but He Himself is NOT?

The scripture verses above should prove beyond a shadow of doubt that the Christian hell cannot be found anywhere within the Old Testament. Furthermore, the notion of being separated turns out to be bogus, and the thought of it being forever (eternal) is disputed in Samuel 14:14:

"We must all die, we are like water spilled on the ground which cannot be gathered up, but God will not take away life.  He will devise plans so NOT to keep an outcast banished FOREVER from His presence."

This verse sure describes a God of love to me.  Now you can understand why this scripture below can state:

"For I am convinced that neither death, nor life, nor angels, nor principalities, nor things present, nor things to come, nor powers, nor height, nor depth, nor any other created thing, will be able to separate us from the love of God, which is in Christ Jesus our Lord."  Romans 8:38-39

I have a very good friend named Phil who helped me build my home--you don't get better friends than that. Phil is one of those who adheres to traditional Christian thinking, so naturally he doesn't agree with very much of the content in my videos on You Tube, but we love each other just the same. I use him a lot as a sounding board, especially because he doesn't agree with me theologically most of the time. He is a wise man and a man full of love, so I had nothing to lose by asking him about his view in reference to God's love and the existence of hell. Because of his view of God's love, Phil couldn't wrap his mind around a God who would torture people with endless fire for an eternity. So instead, he believes that hell is only an eternal separation from God, requiring no pain, because being separated from God's love would be torturous enough. Sound familiar?

What I find ironic about Phil's belief in hell is there is nothing in scripture that says or even implies such a belief, yet he considers the Bible a book of authority for his Christian beliefs. Rather than debating scriptures that state the opposite of Phil's belief in hell--I instead chose to give him a figurative slap in the face to get his attention. Sometimes it's necessary to use these tactics in order to get people to think about what they believe and why.

So, I asked Phil:  What about all those people throughout the ages and down the centuries who have never heard the name of Jesus, and have never had the opportunity to accept or reject Him?  If you believe they're eternally separated from God, how does that add up in regards to God's justice and love?  Phil responded with:  "God will make a way for them, because God is just".

That was his answer, and I doubt he realized it was a doctrine of men designed to make an excuse for his theology and the existence of hell.   Even though rhetorical, my next question was:  "If what you say is true... wouldn't it be wise of us who have heard and accepted the truth of Christ... to keep our big mouths shut--never mention the name of Jesus, or Christ, or ever share the good news message?  By doing so, are we not opening the door of opportunity for them to reject Christ, thus closing the door for God to make a way for them later?  Think about it Phil, according to your belief it's because of us and our big mouths-- someone may be condemned to spend an eternity separated from God."   Phil accused me of "twisting it" rather than taking a hard look at what he believed.  If the man wasn't twice my size I would have grabbed him around his neck and said:  Phil... don't you see... that doctrine you fall back on--YOUR DOCTRINE IS TWISTED!  (Even if he were of small stature I wouldn't have done that.)

I'll be the first to admit I may not know what love is in its entirety, no one does, but let's just say I'm on a learning curve just like everyone else. It may seem oxymoronic but, I will boldly say I do know with precision what love is not! Along with countless billions, I grew up with a perverted sense of love, and that perversion has made its way into Christianity. It's not surprising, considering the fact that people are people, and we all carry our baggage everywhere we go.

By bringing to light what I have personally witnessed as a perversion of love, it's subliminally taught (sometimes openly) within Christendom. My "perversion of love" statement is not meant as an insult, and by no means is it the general rule of how Christians actually behave on a regular basis. What I mean by that--Christians as a whole are some of the most loving people on the planet. When I talk about perverted love within Christendom, I'm referring to the system--not necessarily the individual, but I'm referencing the doctrines of men that slander God's character of love.

Example of what doctrines of men produce:  As an on-again off-again youth leader, as well as a praise and worship leader, I discovered most children, especially teens feel as if they can do nothing right in the eyes of their peers, their parents, and God.  The vast majority of these kids never grow out of it when entering adulthood.  If they're still going to a Christian church, doctrines of men insist on pushing an agenda of "never being good enough"!  Depending on the church one goes to, there are a number of hoops one has to jump through in order to be accepted by others, and most importantly approved by God.  Consider rereading chapter two titled:  " The Perversion of Love, Trust, & Consequences".


Permit me to give a personal testimony of what love is not.  I grew up thinking that physical, emotional, verbal, and mental abuse was normal.  What I experienced was not love, but I thought it was.  Being the only child, who could I compare myself to?  I could write a book alone on how God healed me of most of the trauma, and is continuing to heal some of the residue.  As it's been said:  "A lifetime of abuse takes a lifetime of healing".  (author unknown)  Most memories of my childhood were those of condemnation--not in the biblical sense, but in a modern English sense.  Earthly condemnation of any kind is not love.

I was like most angry teens thinking I could do nothing right, and once I grew too big to be physically abused--both parents would confirm their rejection of my worth by calling me vulgar names. This was not love, but I thought it was, and all along as part of the mix--from time to time my mother would keep telling me she loved me. This was not love, but I thought it was. This was how I grew up thinking--this must be how love is expressed. Abuse someone, then tell them you love them. Then as a mid-teen, I started going to church and was told how important it was to honor my parents in order to be acceptable to God. This was not God's love, but I thought it was. I went for years secretly hating my parents, and feeling condemned by God for doing so.

Later in life as a married adult, part of the healing process required me to intentionally live hundreds of miles away from my widowed mother. At one time, over the phone, my new bride had to reprimand my mother by telling her if she didn't have anything good to say about her son, not to call again. Kudos to my wonderful wife, and at that time I unfortunately didn't know how to properly return my wife's love. Because of her love for me, I started getting a glimpse of what real love was. My biggest regret is how it took over twenty-five years of our marriage before I learned to return her love. As of this writing, we've been together 39 years.

Much later, when I spoke at my mother's funeral I could see the scorn directed towards me from people I had never met.  At the time I couldn't understand why this was happening until I started putting all the pieces together.  I began to realize, even after death, the previous slanderous seeds planted by my mother over the many years were still reaping a harvest.  At the end of her life, my mother asked me for forgiveness for all she had done, but the seeds had already been planted in those people who never knew of my mother's repentance.

Since I believe forgiveness is a choice and not an emotion--naturally I chose to forgive my mother.  However, there was no trust, no friendship, and no relationship to build onto that forgiveness.  Later in the parking lot of the funeral home a distant relative told me my mother loved me very much.  Maybe so... in her "own way", but what my mother showed me was a PERVERTED love.  Perverted love is NOT love, and most certainly it's not perfect love.  Considering it's within the context of this chapter, I feel it is important to pontificate again in order to share of my first encounter with "perfect love".

One night, I heard a light knock on my bedroom door, and because I was an angry teenager I shouted "what do you want?" A voice from a small child asked if he or she could come in. I abruptly said NO! Exactly one week later, I knew it was the same time, because I was watching the same weekly TV show--I heard the same light knock on my bedroom door. Of course this piqued my curiosity, so I cracked open the door, but only enough for my eyes to see a cute little boy who I later found out was four years old, and his name was Tony.

Little Tony asked, again for the second time, if he could come in? I wasn't quite as abrupt as the first time, but I said no and I told him to return to his parents in the living room. He said okay, hung his little head and walked off. The following week, same time, same channel watching the same show. Knock, knock. I knew who it was. I felt sorry for the kid, because I found out from my parents that some preacher invited himself over to out house to talk religion, and each time he brought his wife and his little boy Tony.

This time when I opened the door, little Tony looked up at me and again asked if he could come in, but with a caveat--he promised to be real quiet, so I let him in. As an angry, physically abused teen, I couldn't remember the last time I allowed anyone to touch me, but as I climbed back on my bed to watch my show--little Tony jumped up right beside me and threw one arm around me, making himself comfortable while watching TV with me. I, on the other hand, was NOT at all comfortable. I wanted to throw that kid off my bed and brush his cooties off me... but I just couldn't.

Sure enough, he was quiet and still until a commercial. During that commercial, he told me Jesus loved me and he loved me too, and thanked me for letting him in. I didn't reply. A few commercials later he asked me if I would come visit him at church sometime? THAT'S when the alarms started going off in my head! Within an instance, the thoughts crossed my mind of... NO!!!..., but if I tell him no, he's going to ask why. The best way I can put this is--I instinctively knew not to discourage this little boy about God, so my only response was to say yes. Nothing much was said after that--the show was over, he left my room, and he went home.

Next week, same time, same TV show, but no Tony. I heard his dad in the living room, but still no Tony. I was shocked at how disappointed I was. I later found out he was being disciplined and had to stay home. Another week went by and still no Tony. I never found out why, I didn't care. All I knew was I had to keep my word to that little boy, and get my butt to that stupid church. I went to the following Sunday night service.

With the friendship brewing between my parents and the preacher, I grudgingly tagged along, while inwardly I was excited about keeping my word to little Tony. The church was nothing but a small house with the upstairs gutted out to make a large meeting room, and the basement was a parsonage for the preacher and his family. No more than ten people were there, yet no Tony--he had to go to bed early for some reason. I was pissed! I sat in the back row, on a chair as close to the exit door as I could find. I just waited with my arms folded tight over my chest, angry at the world for making me come to such a stupid place as this.

I have no idea what the sermon was about--I wasn't listening, and I didn't care. In his closing statements, the preacher invited everyone to come forward to kneel around a carpeted platform, and pray together. Of course nine out of the ten people complied, with one exception--you guessed it--ME! As they all were praying, I sat there judging them for the fools I knew they were, and out of the corner of my left eye, at the 10 o'clock angle, no more than 8ft away--don't ask me how I knew who it was but..., I saw Jesus standing there looking right at me.

Seeing Jesus didn't surprise me as much as who I saw standing next to him on his left--it was me! So much more happened than what I can put into words on a page, but within an instant I was given an awareness or a knowledge of something I didn't know existed--Jesus was an image of perfect love. However, when I looked at my image, I saw the exact opposite. I saw anger, bitterness, and hatred. It broke my heart.

The next thing I realized--I was on the floor in a fetal position weeping my brains out, inwardly crying... praying... God I don't want to be like him anymore, I want to be like this Jesus. I don't know how much time passed--I got up, sat back in my chair, wiped the tears from my face, and waited for the people up front to stop praying. Those people were no more than twenty feet away and they saw and heard NOTHING! I'm not exaggerating--it's almost as if time stood still. I never shared what happened with any of them--they were adults, and I didn't trust them, but my life sure took a change for the better. I got a taste of perfect love and I wanted more.

I've been growing in that love I met that night for about 50 years. Learning about love is pretty rocky and frustrating most of the time, its been anything but "perfect". Like most people, I'm still left wanting, wondering, and confused at times about what love is. Due to ignorance, at times I feel numb and emotionless towards God and others. This is why I say... I know what love is not, more than what I know what love is. I know it's a strange thing to say, and an unusual approach to understanding love, but I've discovered the opposite of love isn't hate--it's "perverted love" or "not love". How is this perversion of love accomplished within Christianity? I will begin to answer that question when I provide a list of "what love is not", in three more paragraphs.

Far too many things practiced, believed, and taught in Christendom are not truth, because what most people think as truth and biblical is not based on love. Love is the standard by which every belief needs to be measured. Whatever I read, whatever I believe, whatever I'm taught, whatever I teach--it MUST endorse God's character, i.e. love. It MUST cause me to trust God more, not less. It MUST bring out in me the fruit of the Spirit.

If I read something in the Bible or elsewhere that doesn't do these things, I view it as words from men and NOT words from God. When I "rightly divide" the two I find TREASURE! Simple? You betcha, it's never proven me wrong. If you find my approach erroneous, then I can't help but to go to the extreme by saying your approach portrays that God is NOT love--He can't be, if love is not the standard. If what we believe is not based upon, found in, adheres to, and compliments the character of God, then we fall short, we miss the mark, i.e. we sin. "For all have sinned and fall short of the Glory of God."

Remember me stating how I know more of what "love is not", than I do of what love is? Below is a list of a few examples of "perverted love", and what love is NOT:

- Sanctioning an eternity of torment for a short lifetime of unbelief--this is NOT love. Let's say I was a Governor, and I wanted to pass a law requiring the death penalty for the crime of jaywalking. The Christians in my city would be outraged about it, telling me how unjust I was, yet... . The word hypocrite comes to mind.

- Promoting hell causes people to not trust God-- this is NOT love. Some will admonish how they personally trust God, because they know they're not going to hell. If you ask any of them why they feel that way--the first words out of their mouth will be: "Because I"! If not those two words, then it will go along with sounding like: Jesus died for my sins, paid the price on the cross so I wouldn't have to, and I CHOSE TO BELIEVE, or I ASKED JESUS INTO MY HEART/LIFE. If a person is honest, it really comes down to Jesus providing an opportunity for you to save yourself, so your trust is--in what you have done, that's what really saves you. If you don't think this is true, then ask yourself if you'd still be saved without believing. This is an example of a perversion of trust I spoke about in chapter two, rather than a trust in the accomplishments of Christ, and the "perfect love" of God.

- Telling people to "love God or else" is fear based, horribly manipulative, and is NOT love. Sure, those exact words may not be used, but the intent of many sermons are exactly that!

- Even though God possessed a pre-knowledge of a horribly eternal outcome for someone--God still would create an individual with a "free will" to determine their own eternal destiny--this is NOT love--this is NOT God--it is a doctrine of men, it's incompetent, and it's a LIE! Honestly, as a loving parent, if you knew **long before conception** that your child would suffer an eternity of pain and torment--would you still opt to have that baby? No one in their right mind would, yet this is how Christianity portrays God. Some will claim: That's not the same--people choose to live in unbelief--the child in your example wasn't given the chance to make a choice to believe or not to believe. My answer: So the countless billions throughout time who never had an opportunity to accept your Western Jesus, were they given the same choice as you?

- Creating the majority of people to be born seemingly for the purpose of eternal destruction. Meaning, it's taught in Christendom that most people are going to hell, because the gate is narrow to enter heaven, and wide that leads to destruction. To make matters worse, apparently what Jesus did on behalf of mankind was inefficient and incomplete, because it's believed the solution is all up to the person to correct the problem themselves, by believing, repenting, and by confessing Jesus as Lord. This is another doctrine of men, it is a lie, and it's NOT love.

- Christianity ignoring dozens of scriptures in context proclaiming how God is going to save all of mankind--this is NOT love, and ignoring all the scriptures is nothing more than deception!  Consider rereading chapter five titled "ALL".

- Telling people they're going to hell--this is NOT love... it's worse, it's deception, and it's a lie! "But it plainly states in my Bible that people are going to hell!"  No, it does not, and I will prove it in upcoming chapters.

- The turn or burn threat is NOT love... it's worse, it's a lie!  A coined phrase invented by a people who claim God is love, and sing songs with words like:  "They will know we are Christians by our love".

- Teaching people to have a reason to fear a loving God is NOT love!  "Well, my Bible states to fear God is the beginning of wisdom."  The smallest amount of research will tell you the word "fear" in this verse means to have a reverence and respect for God.  By slandering God as the creator of hell (nowhere recorded in scripture) is anything but having a respect for His character or His nature of love.

- Telling people God asked us to love our enemies while believing God is going to torture His enemies for an eternity--this is NOT love.... it's worse, it's hypocritical, and it's a lie!

- Creating a place to keep a record of wrong for an eternity--this is NOT love.... it's worse, it's deception, and it's a lie considering it says in 1st Corinthians chapter 13 "love does not keep record of wrong"! Isn't hell a continual eternal reminder to all creation of the wrongs people committed in their lifetimes?

- Doctrines of men and religion have been lying for centuries, and lying is NOT love. (ya think?) In subsequent chapters I will give example after example of how scribes have lied within scripture. I'll also expose how the Ancient Latin Church had a political agenda, and had a need to perpetrate lies within scripture in order to promote that agenda.

- Beliefs and doctrines that cause you to question and not trust God's character of love-- is NOT love. Hmmm..., let's see... what possible doctrine could exist to cause someone to slander and later question God's character? An eternal torture chamber maybe?

- Beliefs and doctrines that do not bring out in you the fruit of love--is NOT love. There are numerous doctrines that produce fear within a persons heart. Fear cannot be found anywhere within scripture in defining the fruit of God's Spirit.

- Calling me names and judging my character for writing a book like this--is NOT love. (LOL)

- Telling me where I might be wrong, and doing so out of the motive of love rather than with threats of eternal damnation--THAT'S LOVE! I'm listening, but I insist you listen as well.

Everyone understands what love is, to one degree or another. "But what about a mass murderer or a rapist, there's no way they could understand love!" It's my opinion they loved somebody at one point in their life--if nothing else, their selfish acts prove they love themselves, as perverted as that love may be. I believe all creatures have been given the gift of love by God, including animals. All animals nurture and care for their young--I've seen it from the smallest animal to the largest, and of course in humankind.

I believe every creature has been created with love, and by a creator who is called love. If love is the character and very nature of God, then everything He creates simply has to have some of that nature in it. Considering who God is, I can't see any other way other than all creation was intended to experience love in some way or another. When it comes to animals, some will say they treat their young out of instinct alone, but I say it's in their nature, their divine nature. No, I don't adhere to the New Age Movement, but they do have some things right, and I believe this is one of them.

In my opinion, the best definition of love ever to be recorded is in 1st Corinthians chapter 13:

Love is patient
Love is kind
Love is not envious
Love doesn't boast
Love is not proud
Love doesn't dishonor others
Love is not self-seeking
Love doesn't easily anger
Love doesn't keep record of wrong (that's a big one)
Love does not delight in evil
Love rejoices in the truth
Love trusts
Love hopes
Love always perseveres and protects
Why? Because LOVE NEVER FAILS!
Is this not the best definition ever?

In 1st John 4:8 is says God is love, and without God you can't love. The point I'm trying to make, according to this verse, the word love and the name "God" is one in the same and are interchangeable. I don't think my algebra is flawed when I say God is love, so love that is perfected... is God. I now need to repeat how 1st Corinthians 13 defines love, but instead I'll show how God and love are interchangeable.

God is patient
God is kind
God is not envious
God doesn't boast

God is not proud
God doesn't dishonor others
God is not self-seeking
God doesn't easily anger
God doesn't keep record of wrong (that's a big one)
God does not delight in evil
God rejoices in the truth (God rejoices in Jesus)
God trusts
God hopes
God always perseveres and protects
Why?  Because GOD NEVER FAILS!


What?  No fear mentioned anywhere in the 13th chapter of Corinthians?  Now it's time to address "perfect love".  If I've heard it once, I've heard it a thousand times how perfect love casts out all fear.  No it doesn't, and the verse does not say that.  The word "all" is not in this verse. Everyone fears something, from getting sick to what happens after death, and everything in between.  Putting the misquote aside, let's examine 1st John 4:18 that states:

"There is no fear in love, but perfect love drives out fear...".

Perfect love drives out fear?  Fear of what? The verse continues by saying:

"...because fear involves punishment."

The million dollar question is what kind of fear does perfect love cast out? The previous verse 17 tells us it's referring to fear of punishment from God. Why don't these verses say love on its own casts out fear of punishment from God? Why the extra adjective of "perfect"? I believe we are witnessing an intentional contrast within scripture. It seems to me these verses are telling us that love and fear shouldn't mix, and don't work well together. But when it comes to "perfect love"--this kind of love actually casts out fear so there never can be a mix of fear and love in the first place.

The words reprove, punish, chastise, discipline, and scourge pretty much mean the same thing biblically, and are often interchanged depending on which Bible version you are reading. However, individually each word conjures up a different mental picture in the mind of someone depending on personal experience. Referring to one's own experience as a way of defining a word is carnal thinking.

The mistake people make is applying their personal experiential definition of a word like punishment, to how God would apply that word, and in how He would reprove, punish, chastise, discipline, or scourge. Below are a few biblical examples of how God uses these words:

**Hebrews 12:6** - "FOR THOSE WHOM THE LORD LOVES HE DISCIPLINES, (reproves, punishes, chastises) AND HE SCOURGES EVERY SON WHOM HE RECEIVES."

**Revelation 3:19** - "Those whom I love, I reprove and discipline"

The two above verses are actions of God done in love, and I might interject and assume--it's done with a "perfect love", because He is a perfect God, so there is no need to fear words like punish or discipline, nor should we fear any actions from God whatsoever. When the carnal mind reads Bible verses and stories giving them reasons to fear God-- one must realize those men who wrote those stories had a perverted understanding of who God was. If this were not true, Jesus would not have had to come to the peoples of Israel to correct their perverted views! Have you ever noticed how all those horrific stories ended once Jesus arrived on the scene?

With any belief, I feel it wise to ask the question of: What is the first fruit mentioned in the list known as "the fruit of the Spirit"? As an example: When reading the Bible and whenever you come across the word hell, does that word or the belief in it bring out in you love? And not just love, but also: Joy, peace, patience, kindness, goodness, faithfulness, gentleness, and self control? (Gal. 5:22) Or, does what you believe elicit a degree of fear? There is some logic to what I'm saying when I say a belief in hell induces the very fear perfect love casts out! I'll get into this topic in detail, in the next chapter.

Another way I judge my understanding of words like hell, punish, or discipline--do they, or does whatever I'm reading in scripture, compliment the character of God? The character of God is love and He manifests that love PERFECTLY... every time! A valid question--does a belief in an eternal hell endorse and compliment the aforementioned character of God? The operation of love is defined as keeping no record of wrong. Isn't eternal hell keeping an eternal record of wrongs??? Are not my last two questions simple to understand, and reasonable to ask?

The point--our love, the way we manifest love hasn't been perfected yet, so we can't apply our limited understanding--our personal experience to words like discipline or punish. But since God is both love and perfect, He is the only one who is manifesting perfect love 100% of the time. I'm not saying perfect love is unavailable to us, but according to 1st John 4:18, in order for it to be evident in our lives there can be no fear of punishment from God whatsoever. Even if the tiniest amount of fear is involved, it's NOT PERFECT LOVE. On the surface, I know this sounds ludicrous, but God's love is perfected, and because God loves us with a perfect love, we should have no fear of punishment from Him, because we should know that anything from

God is good and for our benefit--including punishment and discipline.


      Most members within Christianity will claim they're walking in perfect love, but according to the biblical definition of "perfect love" they are not!  Why?  Because as long as they adhere to a man-made pagan doctrine of eternal punishment, fear is going to be part of the equation.  It's simple math--if you believe in the existence of a hell, there's always going to be some form of fear of punishment in the back of your mind.  Isn't the very purpose and definition of hell a punishment?  So, if you believe in hell, I guarantee you are NOT walking in perfect love--it's impossible, because it doesn't add up.  In the next chapter I will attempt to answer the question of: Would a God of perfect love create such a place as hell, and after all you've just read, would He want us to fear it?

Chapter 7

Why Are People Taught To Fear Hell?

It seems as if my previous chapter titled "Perfect Love" has now transitioned into the topic of fear. It can't be helped. To a degree this chapter will continue to address love and perfect love, because I must expose fear as the greatest tool being used for deception, and how the "perfect love" of God casts fear out. Deception only works well in the dark--the perfect love of God shines the light into that darkness, so addressing both topics of love and fear is critical.

Speaking of fear--does the thought of hell induce fear in some people? Sure, I've heard some say, "I'm not fearful of going to hell!" But, are you not fearful about the unbeliever going there--how about a friend or family member? Don't you see--it's a double-edged sword as in, you're not walking in perfect love as long as you believe in an imperfect man-made pagan doctrine that was invented by men. I will prove this statement in upcoming chapters, so I encourage anyone to research the origin of the doctrine of hell, and how that doctrine goes directly against how the Bible defines perfect love. Also, if you do try to disprove how I've interpreted the definition of "perfect love"--your eyes might be opened to some things you haven't seen before.  GO FOR IT!

Would a God of perfect love create such a place as hell?  I will be repeating these types of questions more than once throughout this book, but consider this:  The creation of hell has not been recorded anywhere in the creation story nor anywhere else within the Bible.  Someone else created it, because according to the Bible--God never did!  Because of it being an invention from the minds of men, there are now a vast variety of hells, which results with no one agreeing on the severity of such a place, nor what it takes to get there?  This inconsistency should bring up a red flag within anyone.

I used to personally believe in and promote the hell doctrine for over 30 years, until I asked myself if hell wasn't true then why is it in my Bible?  That's possibly one of the best questions a Christian can ask.  The answer to that question will be addressed in upcoming chapters, but I'm not asking anyone to take my word for it.  I challenge anyone to research it, and find out who put it in there, and what was their reason for inserting the word hell into our bibles in the first place.

On the surface, words in scripture don't always mean what they originally were intended to mean.  Is there any doubt in the mind of you, the reader, what death means?  How about grave?  Yet these words were changed to the word hell within scripture, but only when in context to an unbeliever.  So, when you read words like hell, you can substitute it with death or grave, and the verse will still make sense.  Try it, and you'll see what I mean.  Also, take notice of what the word hell conjures up in your mind, then JUDGE IT?  Does the word hell make you think of death or the grave?  Hardly!  I always say, and will continue to say, judge everything you believe by the fruit of the Spirit of God.  Isn't love the first fruit mentioned as defining the fruit of God's Spirit?  I'll readdress my question this way--when you read the word hell in the Bible--does love come to mind at all, much less "perfect love"?  I'll bet the first thing that comes to mind is fear.

God never fails?  I've heard it said by various evangelists and preachers:  "Yes that's true--God is love, but...".  Why do they have to add that but?  They continue to claim God is also JUST!  We all know exactly what they mean--they're really referring to punishment, as in ramifications for sin--that's really what they're saying!  So what does God have to say about punishment?  Hebrews 12:6:

"For those whom the Lord loves He disciplines", (Translated in some bibles as "punishes" instead of discipline.)
Since God so loves the world--God loves everyone, He's going to punish and/or discipline everyone

BECAUSE He loves everyone. Everything God does is based on perfect love, so when you hear someone spout off that God is just--justice is in correlation to who God is, and He is love perfected! So, any justice or punishment God sanctions is perfect as well.

In my opinion, real justice is seeing into the heart that has committed atrocities, then to break that hardened heart in an individual so they can see and understand what they've done wrong. A truly broken heart will turn from those wrongs that caused the heart to break in the first place--that's how God's love does things. Isn't repentance the next step after a broken heart? Doesn't repentance best describe the will of God within an individual, and is God capable of causing repentance within a person? What is God capable of doing? Paul explains it beautifully in Romans 2:4:

"Don't think lightly of the riches of His kindness and tolerance and patience, not knowing that the kindness of God leads you to repentance."

An unbelieving skeptical Christian will usually respond with the usual question of: What if they don't turn, and what if they die in that unrepentant state?
As I pointed out in chapter 3, God is not limited to this lifetime, so death doesn't stop God in any way. None of us know the exact process of how the kindness of God leads one to repentance in this lifetime, so how can Christianity claim to know God can't continue His will in a life that follows this one?

It's understandable considering how doctrines of men limit God to this lifetime already, so why not the next? The point: God is going to accomplish His will to reconcile ALL, no matter if in this lifetime or the next! Reconciling all is what love accomplishes, because love never fails--God never fails. Fear doesn't accomplish anything. Fear always fails! If a person is continually fearful, thinking that this lifetime is their only chance, they will end up carrying a baggage of uncertainty about God's love, as well as a distrust in the power of His love.

When I also believed that way, I was forced to STOP and ask myself--where did I get that teaching from, or in other words, where did I get my understanding of the fear based belief in thinking there's a chance God will fail? Sure, most Christians will claim they don't believe God will fail, but unfortunately they will put the burden upon themselves in fearfully believing they as an individual might fail. Rather than blaming God for being incompetent, they accuse themselves, taking a personal responsibility for failing. This sounds right and true to the carnal mind, but in reality it's bathed in uncertainty, and uncertainty is rooted in fear. It all comes down to trusting in God--resulting in no fear. The alternative is putting your trust in yourself which produces uncertainty and fear.

A carnal mind is a mind that is lead by the five senses, and is dependant upon life experiences to determine truth. This is why scripture instructs people to not lean to the carnal mind for understanding, but to have the mind of Christ. Did Jesus walk in fear, or did He completely trust in God's love without reservation or conditions? Need I say more? When it comes to love--again most are leaning to a carnal mind--most are not giving God any credit for being amazing, because the mind of man (a carnal mind) is fearful, and cannot comprehend the vastness of God's amazing love!

Everyone is familiar with fear and how it works, so the carnal mind prefers to take the easy to understand route, rather than trying to comprehend God's love. Simply put... it's easy to fear, and it comes naturally if not instinctive to the carnal mind. If it's not fear controlling the mind, then what else could it possibly be that would keep a person from comprehending the unfailing confidence of God's love? Let's take an honest look of another example of how the carnal mind works.

I think the real reason most Christians refuse to acknowledge God's perfect love, unconditionally for ALL mankind--to reconcile ALL mankind--to save ALL mankind, is because of jealousy! What? Think about it for a moment... it just isn't fair! You're jealous that as a Christian you worked and strived to serve God.

You've done everything you possibly can do to please God. Then this other person, an unbeliever has completely ignored God during their whole life, and you're fearful they're going to get the same reward as you!(?) Let's be honest--that's exactly how you feel!

Jesus answered your jealousy in the parable of the vineyard workers in Matthew 20. Paraphrased: A landowner hired some workers to work in his vineyard. For there pay, the landowner and his hirelings agreed to how much they would get paid. Then late in the morning the landowner hired a few more, and then around noon he hired even more. It didn't stop there--three more times in the 6th, 9th, and 11th hour he hired more workers. Come pay time, THEY ALL GOT PAID THE SAME AMOUNT AS IF EVERYONE WORKED ALL DAY. THEY ALL GOT THE SAME REWARD, even though some worked all day, and others didn't have time to work at all! This parable is telling us that those who worked from sunrise to sunset were pissed--they were jealous, and they didn't think it was fair-- understandably so, to a "carnal mind".

Remember what I wrote earlier, how the carnal mind in its nature instinctively is a fearful mind? The above parable isn't designed for a carnal mind to understand, but instead it speaks of the mind of Christ--the mind of God, and it gives us another example of how "perfect love" works. Think about how the parable ends... Jesus is basically saying to us--who are you to tell Me how to operate My business--My grace?

For those who call yourself a Christian, I have a couple of questions: Is your commitment to God based on a reward, or on gratitude? Is your love for God manifested because of gratitude, or is your love dependant upon your reward? Your answers are between you and God, and I guarantee God already knows the real answers. If there is even the slightest hint of begrudging those who God deems worthy of His grace, no matter if they respond to that grace the way you think they should, by becoming a believer-- you're not operating in love. And the love you think you have is a perverted love, and you haven't a clue what God's "perfect love" is all about! I know these seem like hard words, but hopefully they will be remembered and considered later on.

Fear is not love! Predominant religions of the world all make a claim that they're either a religion of peace or love based, but actions speak louder than words. And whenever you use fear to manipulate-- that is the opposite of love. Fear or manipulation is not love--I don't care who says their religion is based on love--whenever manipulation is used it's not love! I would like to go over a list of fears that I'm extremely familiar with, and let's see how many of these sound familiar to you as well:

Fear of going to hell.
Fear of a loved one going to hell.
Fear of not being good enough.
Fear of punishment.
Fear of God.
Fear of being deceived.
Fear of the devil.
Fear of demons.
Fear of disappointing God.
Fear of rejection.
Fear of questioning authority.
Fear of questioning Bible accuracy.
Fear of being proven wrong.
Fear of not going to church.
Fear of not tithing.
Fear of not loving your enemy as God instructs.
Fear of not looking like a good Christian.
Fear of being judged by God.
Fear of being judged by others.
Fear of sinning.
Fear of failure.
Fear of not reading the Bible on a regular basis.
Fear that your prayers won't be answered.
Fear of not being positive enough.
Fear that your sins will be exposed to others.
Fear of losing friendships if you're in disagreement with them.
Fear of not being respected by members of your church.
Fear of death.
Fear of death for someone you love.
Fear of where you go after you die.

The above list is saying a lot! It speaks volumes of what is being practiced within Christendom. Christianity claims that theirs is not a fear-based religion, yet every single one of these fears listed above are endorsed and popularized within Christian congregations all over the world. I'm not saying this is being done maliciously in all cases, because some are done out of ignorance. Intentionally or not, every one of these fears are promoted to congregations and groups of people to manipulate them. Most church leaders are using fear to motivate people to do what's right. In this case the end does not justify the means. Regardless of good intentions, it's still manipulation, it's still fear, and it is not love! I have to conclude Christianity is not a love based religion, not with all these fears attached to it-- it's impossible! Honesty is a virtue held in high esteem within Christendom, so why can't its members look at my list of fears and acknowledge something is deeply wrong, deceptive and perverse because of those fears?

I used to fear much like I've described in my list, but no longer--so what happened to me? These dark (some hidden) fears in me were brought out into the light, exposing them as lies, and the fear was literally ripped out of me by God's perfect love. Even though God had a plan to remove those fears all along--from my perspective it all started by me being honest, and abandoning the self-righteous feeling of superiority over those whom I considered the "unbelievers". Later on it broke my heart to realize how I, for years believed and endorsed the kind of trash my fear list produced.


I'm hoping the reader can now see why I've titled this book "In Defense of God's Love". It should have never been necessary for a person like me to feel a need to write such a dissertation. The three best known religions of the world--Christianity, Islam, and Judaism, all are fear based and manipulative religions. However, Christianity and Islam are the only two out of the three, that promote a horrific, vengeful, wrath filled god, who's going to torture both His and their enemies forever in hell. Get this--they both claim theirs is a religion of peace. Ironic and perverse as this may sound--at least <u>some</u> Muslims are openly honest about their hypocrisy in their barbaric behavior and practices, but Christians have no excuse. They are being dishonest with themselves by choosing to ignore or deny all of the fears I previously listed.


For those who claim that Christianity is a love based religion, and then promote a fear of going to hell--they are delusional or ignorant in defining love. If the average Christian would do even the smallest amount of research, they would find out historically and technically there's no creation of hell within the Bible--the book of authority, according to Christendom. Only a deranged, deceived mind can claim God is love, while at the same time claim that the same loving God created a hell, to send those whom He didn't approve of.


Why is it preachers will declare how the perfect love of God casts out fear, and then turn right around and say things like--believe!, or else you're destined for hell?  Also, why is it whenever you hear a sermon on the perfect love of God casting out fear, they stop reading and don't finish the verse?  The verse continues by saying fear of punishment.  Can't you see the perversion?  They can't continue with the verse, because punishment from God is the exact punishment this verse is telling people NOT to fear, yet Christians claim that punishment is an eternity in hell that people should fear!  This oxymoronic belief would be hilarious if it wasn't so sad.


People rarely hear or are taught the truth about how God's perfect love casts out fear.  It's right there in context to God's punishments, in black and white, and I believe the main reason Christians choose to ignore it is because of a (you guessed it) FEAR of being deceived.  Ironic, while neglecting the meaning of this verse--the whole time they're walking in the very deception they're afraid of.

Let's specifically address some of those fears from my above list, and expose a few of the lies on which these fears have been built upon.

Fear of going to hell...
- The first question I asked myself was: Why fear hell?
- My answer at the time: It's a horrible place of eternal torment or torture, that will separate me from God and my loved ones.
- Who taught me that?
- Answer: The very people who told me God is love, and I can put my full trust in Him.
- Would a God of love create such a place?
- Answer: He must have, or else it wouldn't be in my Bible.
- When does it say in the Bible that God created hell?
- Answer: (the sound of crickets)
- Is hell part of the creation story mentioned in the book of Genesis?
- Answer: (the sound of crickets)

Isn't it obvious, once the hell doctrine is exposed for the lie it really is, all the following 15 fears will be eliminated?

- Fear of a loved one going to hell...
- Fear of death...
- Fear of death for someone you love...
- Fear of where you go after you die...
- Fear of not being good enough....

- Fear of punishment...
- Fear of God...
- Fear of being deceived...
- Fear of the devil...
- Fear of demons...
- Fear of disappointing God...
- Fear of rejection by God...
- Fear of being judged by God...
- Fear of sinning...
- Fear of failure...

I intend to greatly broaden and expound on why there is no need to fear hell in upcoming chapters--also exposing who invented the hell doctrine, and why it is in our bibles.

Fear of being judged by others...
The only reason you would have this kind of fear is because you don't believe or behave the exact same way as someone else.  Isn't that ridiculous?  Who cares what others think since you only have to answer to God.  But wait... if you're afraid of God rejecting you too, then we're right back to square one of not trusting in God's love.

Fear of questioning authority...
People look to people far too often for affirmation. This wouldn't be necessary if you knew how much God really loves and accepts you.  But wait... if you're afraid of God rejecting you, then we're right back to square one of not trusting in God's love.

Fear of questioning Bible accuracy...
A person with this kind of fear has been brain washed, and bamboozled into believing the Bible is the inerrant word of God. So, naturally if you question the Bible accuracy, you're actually questioning God Himself! Deception has to be built upon deception in order to support this doctrine of men. There was a time in recent history when the Bible was not called "The Word of God", and the scripture itself doesn't call the Bible the word of God, so what happened? The phrase simply became popular as a means to give a sense of owning God. Manipulation and brainwashing looks something like this: It's claimed God will not go against or contradict His word, i.e. the Bible. Next, because it's God's word, it's inerrant. Then comes the worst kind of perversion, bathed in ignorance, and slandering God's character by promoting fear. How is this done? By convincing people to believe the word hell was not a mistake, nor a mistranslation--bringing us right back to the fear of hell! It's so insidious!

Fear of being proven wrong...
Pride is possibly the main reason Christians refuse to even consider their beliefs are based on folklore, on doctrines of men, and are simply not true.

Fear of not going to church...
To be socially acceptable is extremely important to most of us. Church has become a social club, and by not attending church--the other members often threaten you of being a disappointment to God. The Merry-Go-Round continues... you're afraid of God

rejecting you, then we're right back again to square one of not trusting in God's love.

Fear of not tithing...
This fear is usually promoted in the Faith-based churches, also known as the name-it claim-it, blab-it grab-it churches. This fear is based on a cause and effect way of thinking. One must give to get, and most of the time it is in reference to finances, so naturally if money is involved--most wont call it "a fear" of losing out on a blessing, because fear would be construed as a "negative confession", and a negative confession can somehow stop God from blessing your finances. It's still fear based to those who are willing to be honest. With all that said, I still promote a positive mindset that's encourage in Phil 4:8: "Finally, brethren, whatever is true, whatever is honorable, whatever is right, whatever is pure, whatever is lovely, whatever is of good repute, if there is any excellence and if anything worthy of praise, dwell on these things."

Fear of not being positive enough...
This goes along with the fear of the not tithing group above.

Fear of not loving your enemy as God instructs...
I'll admit I'm on the fence with this one, yet I have no fear about not loving my enemies. I have a feeling this is an area where we'll all be learning this command for eons to come.

Fear of not looking like a good Christian...

What does a good Christian look like anyway? Who cares? The very ones who claim we shouldn't give God a bad rep are the very ones who promote hell! Let me get this straight... a person who slips with a vulgar tongue, seen drinking a beer, or smoking a cigarette--are they slandering God more than the "good Christian" who tries, judges, and condemns people to a horrific torture chamber for an eternity, in the name of a loving God?

Fear of not reading the Bible on a regular basis... I've personally been taught and told--in order to have the mind of Christ, I would have to be washed in the word. Read the word, digest the word, and daily meditate on the word. This is nothing more than a propagandized, brainwashing kind of technique that has been used in every cult and the occult for centuries. However in defense of the Bible--it is a treasure book full of words from God's heart to meditate on, mixed in with a lot of words of men to be spit on! "Rightly dividing" the two is critical when reading, digesting, and meditating on scripture.

Fear that your prayers won't be answered... I'm on the fence with this one as well. Like a lot of people, I choose on a daily basis to replace a temptation to fear with a decision to trust.

Fear that your sins will be exposed to others... We all have secrets. The problem I have is people. People judge, abuse, and mistreat other people in general, so what some might call fear--I call wisdom. I don't believe God requires anyone to be someone else's door mat to wipe their feet on. However when it comes to secrets and God--nothing can be hidden from God so I don't try, because I've finally reached a point where I trust God with my failures. Here's another oxymoronic statement, yet it's true: I trust God with my lack of trust in Him.

Fear of losing friendships if you're in disagreement with them...
This was one of my hardest to overcome. Being a praise leader and given the greatest respect from others was something I gave up. In all honesty, I never once sought those acclamations, but I will admit to it being a social perk. With a clear conscience, my only goal was to seek a unity from the congregation in bringing a smile to God's face. I've lost all of the respect I once had, and sometimes I miss it, but in retrospect I've gained so much more.

Fear of not being respected by members of your church...
See my explanation above.

I've heard at times from preachers who'd say-- when God looks at you He sees you through glasses coated with the blood of Jesus, and Jesus only looks at you through the lens of love. How dishonest can you get? If they really believed what they were saying, they wouldn't be promoting the hell doctrine the following week. They will defend their position about their lens coated sermon by making it conditional. The burden of a "you must first..." scenario is placed into the minds of people as a condition for God to see you through His lens of love. In most cases, rather than through a lens of love--it's obvious to me now, those lenses the preachers were using were in reality coated with self-righteousness, works, and doctrines of men that resulted in bondage and fear for their parishioners. I'm not passing judgment on the worth of the preachers who do these kind of things, but rather I'm judging the fruit that their teaching produce in people, and that fruit is the disgusting fruit of fear.

For far too many years my eyes were covered while wearing hell glasses with a fear coated lens. Everything I read in scripture, was while wearing those glasses, and later interpreted through the lens of the hell doctrine. I'm not implying every Bible verse I read had to be in context of hell. But in the back of the mind while reading every story, or every teaching that was about good versus evil, people making good or bad decisions, examples of the righteous versus the unrighteous, to repent or not to repent, those who obeyed God compared to those who didn't, believers versus unbelievers--there is a need for justice.

Regardless of the story or teaching referencing hell--what would be the ramification for those who were evil, guilty of making bad decisions, the unrighteous, the unrepentant, and those who disobeyed God--where's the justice? Where do they go when they die? These questions are through the hell lens I previously mentioned. Some churches are more honest about their lens than others. Some churches and church leaders simply choose to ignore the elephant in the room.

The fear based hell doctrine is that elephant in the room that consciously or subconsciously is part of the mix while trying to determine the truth about the relation between God and mankind. I'll say it in a different way--consciously or not, intentional or not, Christianity as a whole generally views scripture and beliefs through a hell lens--capitalizing on the power of fear. But once people repent (the Greek--once you change your mind) about the doctrine of hell, and fearlessly open yourself up to do some research-- you'll be amazed if not angered of what you'll find about how Christianity for centuries has been deceived.

It's so important to be willing to research the history of why the word, and more important, of why the concept of hell was inserted into the English bibles when it was not in the original Greek manuscripts, nor the Jewish scriptures, nor the Septuagint, as in the Greek Old Testament. Some will claim the word Hades was a substitute for hell and meant the same. I will later prove otherwise. My point, somebody had to put hell into scripture for a reason, which I'll address in future chapters. I do want to encourage everyone--please, if you want to be set free from all of those fears in my list, one must address the foundation of most fears perpetrated within Christendom, and most fears are in direct correlation to that disgusting hell doctrine.

Here's an example of why I call the hell doctrine disgusting: For a small town, we had an abundance of churches, and like most small towns, everybody knew just about everyone else. Owning a music store made it possible for us to know members representing every church in the community, due to the common denominator of music. We intentionally allowed floor space for a couple of chairs for friends and customers to sit and chat, and one day a young man by the name of Mike came into our music store. The two of us struck up a conversation about heaven and hell. I don't remember much of the casual conversation with the exception of one statement Mike made before leaving. He said: "...you know... if I didn't believe in hell, I would just go off and live for the devil." It stunned me into silence, and after he left I was left thinking... how sad. How sad the love of God isn't enough to cause Mike to walk in a manner that is pleasing to God, but instead fear and the threat of hell is what it takes. The words pitiful and pathetic come to my mind when I think of this story.

This should be made into a bumper sticker: "No love, no truth--know love, know truth". Or, how about "Know fear, no love--no fear, know love"? If anyone makes these into bumper stickers, please think of this book from time to time.

In reference to the gospel, I don't believe one can see the gospel as truth without having an understanding of love. Have you ever wondered why the vast majority of Christians just don't feel comfortable with sharing the gospel with friends, family, and co-workers? Ever wondered why? Have I been the only one who's felt that way? There's a Godly, yet practical reason why a person doesn't feel comfortable with sharing their gospel message.

The reason is subconscious, and is not obvious to most people. What I'm implying as being subconscious is in reference to the mind, some consider the soul--it's that place where God sometimes whispers. The Bible calls it "a still small voice". In my opinion, the word "conviction" is also another way of defining "a still small voice". In my interpretation, the Greek implies a conviction from God is a divine thought that bridges the mind of God to an individual.

From the pulpit, you'll hear all kinds of accusations directed towards you for not "taking up your cross", and filling the pews like you're suppose to. Some of these church leaders will give a mixture of reasons like: You're insecure, you're lazy, you don't care enough, you don't love people enough, you don't love God enough, and if people end up in hell...

you're partially responsible! What a load of manipulative crap!

I will agree to a point with the notion of not loving God enough, but not in the way they mean in their condescending, condemning context that is often used. Of course you don't have the kind of love necessary to share the gospel to everyone you meet, because the necessary love to begin with is based on a perversion, a lie, at which the scriptures would call a leaven in the mix. In my understanding, if I see a lack of love--that tells me there's a lack of truth. Remember my bumper sticker idea--no love, no truth--know love, know truth? I hope I've piqued your curiosity, and I hope I can share a of couple of practical, logical reasons why you don't feel comfortable with sharing your version of the gospel.

"Your version of the gospel" will be addressed shortly, but first... is there even the slightest possibility that you believe in a different gospel than the one Jesus said was the Good News, and the one the Apostle Paul said was the gospel? I'm paraphrasing when I speak of Paul's warning--if anyone comes to you--angels or whomever, who tries to share a different gospel than the one I'm sharing--let him be accursed! "Accursed" is a strong figure of speech emphasizing the importance to not pervert the gospel. Unfortunately the good news message of modern Christendom are polar opposites to the Evangel Jesus and Paul shared. I know this seems like a harsh statement to make, but I can easily prove it.

Do Christians in general believe what Jesus said is the Good News, or what man says is the good news? Are they going to share the Gospel Paul spoke of, or are they going to share the leaven induced gospel of man? People are so blind, they think it's all one and the same as if they truly are sharing the same Gospel as Jesus and Paul. The gospel message that modern Christianity is sharing is NOT one and the same with the one Jesus or Paul shared, and I'm going to point out the differences. If you have included fear, backed by the hell doctrine in your gospel message, then understand something-- Paul never mentioned Hades or hell EVER in his gospel message. This is profound considering he wrote the majority of the New Testament. Since Paul never once mentioned Hades or hell in his gospel message, yet Christianity has added it to theirs--their message is "accursed".

So, if you're adding hell to the gospel by saying Jesus came to die on the cross to save people from hell--you are accursed according to what Paul said, because it is a different gospel. Jesus never mentioned hell even once in His description of The Good News:

**Luke 4:18** - "THE SPIRIT OF THE LORD IS UPON ME, BECAUSE HE ANOINTED ME TO PREACH THE GOSPEL TO THE POOR. HE HAS SENT ME TO PROCLAIM RELEASE TO THE CAPTIVES, AND RECOVERY OF SIGHT TO THE BLIND, TO SET FREE THOSE WHO ARE OPPRESSED"

Yes indeed this is a quote from the Old Testament, but why is this important to my topic? The word hell cannot be found in the O.T., and was not believed in nor practiced within Judaism.

As a Christian, if you honestly believed that hell is part of the gospel message, then every waking moment you would be out there sharing with someone how to be spared from such a horrible place and outcome. NOooo..., but why not? Why aren't you comfortable with sharing your gospel message that includes fear, and the warning of hell? Is it because of what the preachers say about being lazy, unloving, and blah, blah, blah? Again, why are Christians not taking every opportunity? There are four practical reasons why.

The first reason: FEAR! Let's be honest with ourselves--you're fearful of what people will think. Will you be called a religious kook? Maybe you'll be looked at as a smug and self-righteous person. What? Are you saying you're more worried about what people think of you more than their eternal welfare?

Second reason: I just don't have the will. I think I know why most people don't have the will, because the power is missing! What is that power? That power is love, and who is love? God is love, right? Doesn't this tell you something--it isn't rocket science. God is the needed power to work within your will to love people, and the reason the power is missing is because your false gospel message is not of God!

Sure, people have the ability to push their own theologies, beliefs and agendas on others, but it all becomes noisy gongs and clanging symbols without the power of love. So go ahead and let the minority of self-righteous kooks keep sharing their false gospel message if they want to, but the vast majority of Christians will not, and the reason why is because God is not in it--He's not involved.

Think of it this way... If you are fearful about sharing your version of the gospel--it's obviously a fearful message, because hell is a fearful place--it then brings fear into the hearts and minds of people you're sharing it with--count them--the message is fear-fear-fear! Fear for everyone involved, then someone please explain to me how the perfect love of God casts out the exact kind of fear your false gospel message is promoting, and you claim God sanctions it!(?) It doesn't add up, and yet people have the gall to tell me that modern Christianity is a love based religion. Its been said two wrongs don't make a right, so how can two fears make it love, as in fear of sharing (for most people), and the hell doctrine produces fear in the hearts of people hearing it. Christians then declared the hell doctrine as truth, and the message is supposedly shared with love. It makes no sense!

Third reason:  With a message of hell and fear like the one I've just described above, how can anyone be certain God loves anyone?  I've heard a lot of Christians say:  "I know God loves me", then if you're honest, tell me why is it there's a nagging little voice in the back of your mind questioning how can a loving God abandon countless people to an eternal torture chamber?  That question has got to be part of the equation if fear is part of your gospel message.  I can't blame Christians for not loving people enough-- how can they when their teaching slanders and puts to question God's love to begin with?  Simply put, how can anyone be convinced of God's love when a god sanctioned eternity of suffering is involved?

Fourth reason:  God hasn't laid it on your heart.  But why?  Doesn't God want everyone to be saved?  Along these lines I've heard it said:  I'm waiting for God to open those doors to share--those Divine appointments!  I used to use that one a lot.  So I have to ask--why hasn't God opened those doors?  I believe the answer is simple--it's because the leaven of fear in your message is not the truth, it's not the gospel, and it's not from God.  In my new paradigm way of thinking, I now believe God only opens doors for an opportunity to love people.  Simple enough for a child to understand.


In conclusion to this chapter-- I'm going to shine a little light on how I view certain words in literature.  This paragraph is as good a place as any to tell the reader why I'll never capitalize the word hell in my book. I'm refusing to capitalize the word hell purely for the sake of rebellion against how one little word has terrorized people for so long, and to be frank--it pisses me off. Let's just call my little literary oddity an author's prerogative. Some might be thinking... why doesn't he feel the same about the word Hades? Hades, even though fictitious, it's the actual name of an almost cartoonish character in Greek mythology. The difference? Very few "Articles of Faith" from churches who promote the hell doctrine, rarely if ever do they use the word Hades. So, when you read the story of Lazarus and the rich man, one must ask: Where was the rich man located--Hades or hell? In the next chapter I'll prove it was neither. Last question to think about... if hell and Hades are supposed to be a place of punishment, and love keeps no record of wrong, what was the rich man being punished for?

Chapter 8

Lazarus and The Rich Dude

I feel Christendom has used the parable (Luke 16:19-31) of Lazarus and the rich man in the most abusive, manipulative, fear based, unloving, God slandering way--more so than all other stories in the entire Bible! Wow! What a thing to say. This parable is the Big Daddy over all others that Christians use to PROVE the existence of hell. In this chapter I will PROVE otherwise that:

1: Hell isn't even mentioned in this parable even though you think your Bible says otherwise.
2: No fire exists in this story, even though the word flame is mentioned.
3: No one actually died, even though it states two people died!
4: This parable is oozing with Good News, yet it has been perverted and interpreted as bad news.

I know... if you've heard it once you've heard it a thousand times--context is critical to understanding this parable. Context is much deeper than simply reading a few verses before and after the story. One important point of context is this parable is only one of many in a series of parables. So what is so significant about that? Each and every parable is about stewardship and the responsibility concerning the house of Israel. This shouldn't surprise anyone considering the physical sandal wearing Jesus said in Matthew 15:24 :

"But He answered and said, "I was sent ONLY to the lost sheep of the house of Israel."

And when speaking to the house of Israel it's stated earlier in Matthew 13:34:

" All these things Jesus spoke to the crowds in parables, and He did not speak to them without a parable."

Who were the "crowds" Jesus spoke to, and who were "them" that Jesus didn't speak to without using a parable?  Answer:  The house of Israel that Jesus said He ONLY came for.  Also, something else to consider--it's called a double emphasis, kind of like a "truly truly", or a "verily verily", meaning one needs to pay even more than the usual attention to what is being said.  Notice:  The word "parable" is doubly emphasized, as in repeated twice within the same verse.  So, what's the point I'm trying to make with these two verses?  It seems obvious to me all parables were meant exclusively for the house of Israel.  I'm not implying that other people in the future can't learn from them, but they were not spoken to, or written to, nor about Christians.  Christians were not part of the house of Israel considering Christians didn't exist at the time.

In addition to the double emphasis, we should take it seriously when Jesus said He would not teach a crowd of Jews without using a parable.  So, a Christian would have to ask themselves--since this isn't speaking to or about me as a Christian, then what and who is the parable of Lazarus and the rich man referring to?  By contextually using the Hebrew culture and their history--this will tell us everything we need to know.  I will demonstrate how their culture and history is used throughout this chapter.

To get started, and to get to the meat of any parable, I ask four basic questions:

First:  Who was Jesus speaking to?  Scripture has already told us--the Jews, as in the house of Israel.

Second:  Jesus only used parables.

Third:  Why did Jesus only use parables?  The answer is in Matthew 13:13:

"Therefore I speak to them in parables; because while seeing they do not see, and while hearing they do not hear, nor do they understand.

Fourth:  Why doesn't Jesus want people to not see, hear, or understand?  The answer is so huge and in plain site--most of Christianity can't see the forest because of the trees.  Even His disciples were wondering the same thing in Mark 4:12 when Jesus answer them:

"So that WHILE SEEING, THEY MAY SEE AND NOT PERCEIVE, AND WHILE HEARING, THEY MAY HEAR AND NOT UNDERSTAND, OTHERWISE THEY MIGHT RETURN AND BE FORGIVEN."

"Otherwise they might return and be forgiven"??? What? On the surface this sounds ridiculous to me. Is Jesus sabotaging people to keep them from understanding, and being forgiven? Not at all when you think about the timing of God's plan to reconcile the Gentiles, because it's not yet time for the house of Israel to see, understand and be forgiven. Think about this--if they did see and understand, they would not have crucified Christ! The timing and God's plan to reconcile the Gentiles is exactly what the parable of Lazarus and the rich man is all about.

I want to explain in detail how I see the parable playing out, but first we need to go way, way back in history to about 332 BC. Alexander the Great captured Jerusalem, and in keeping with the norm of Greek society, they would have ushered a few boat loads of Jews off to Greece. After awhile, Jews could no longer read Hebrew so the Greeks decided to print in their native language a Greek Old Testament, which would later be known as The Greek Septuagint. This was no easy task considering they had no printing presses, so after a couple of hundred years it was completed around 132 BC.

What on earth does the Septuagint have to do with the parable of Lazarus and the rich man? The Greek people seemed to understand something that Christians of today don't. Even though a percentage of the Greek people believed in an afterlife, and those that believed in a place known as the underworld, they never put the word hell into the Septuagint. Some will say Hades means the same, but I will prove otherwise later on in this book. Something important and logical to consider--just because there were generations of Jews raised in Greece, as a whole, were those people any less Hebrew in their beliefs? Is there even the slightest chance that Hades simply meant the grave to the Jews, yet it meant a pagan underworld, led by a pagan god in the mind of a Greek? Jews were not taught in Judaism to believe in an actual place called hell or Hades, and they most certainly were not taught to believe in other gods.

Now let's fast forward about 280 years later when Jesus is sharing the parable of Lazarus and the rich man. Jesus was born a Jew and was a Hebrew child through and through. As a child He was raised Orthodox Hebrew, taught Hebrew, and He was even considered a Rabbi when He grew up. He was raised in Nazareth, and not in Greece, and most of His followers were raised somewhere within Israel, so why is this information important? He would have never used something from Greek pagan mythology like Hades, nor something from Latin pagan mythology, as in their hell as a teaching method to instruct the house of Israel. Some may call this an assumption on my part for saying this. At this point in time, all I ask from the reader is to remember that word "assumption", because I intend to prove I'm not the one doing the assuming. This chapter will expose how Christianity has erroneously "assumed" the word hell or Hades is an accurate translation in the parable of Lazarus and the rich man.

I'm making an absolute claim that Jesus never used the word hell in this parable, yet the majority of our bibles have stated that Jesus said the rich man was in a place called hell. To the carnal and uneducated religious mind it's a simple question of who is lying--me or Jesus? How about neither? When you look back into the original Koine Greek language, you'll discover Jesus used a biblically unique word of "unseen" (αόρατο) when describing where the rich man was located. Let's compare the word hell and Hades to the word unseen in the exact same Koine Greek dictionary. The word hell is " κόλαση", and the word Hades is " Άδη". As a rhetorical question, am I the only one who sees a problem here? Even a well known children's TV show would sing something similar to: Three of these things don't belong together, three of these things are not the same.

In the ancient Hebrew culture, the word Sheol meant death or grave as a place for the dead who awaited a resurrection. In the ancient Greek culture the word Hades meant an underworld for the dead, where people were sometimes allowed to come and go. In the ancient Latin culture the word hell (infernum), when translated into English, meant an eternal torturous underworld for the dead, from which there was no escape. Reader, do all these definitions sound the same to you? Yet, Christians have been led to believe that Sheol, Hades, and hell are equivalent to one another, but only using different words representing the exact same place.

For the most part, it seems as though without a conscious thought, Christianity also expects their congregations to not only believe hell, Hades, and Sheol are indistinguishable from one another, but over time its members have been bamboozled into believing the words death, grave, and "UNSEEN", in some instances, are also carbon-copies of hell, Hades, and Sheol as well. This erroneous translation technique has resulted in replacing the word "unseen" with the word hell in the parable of Lazarus and the rich man.

By researching the ancient Latin culture, and understanding their pagan roots, I came to the following conclusion of what might have happened: The ancient Latin church came across this story and read how Lazarus and the rich man were both dead, then they viewed the word flame, and assumed flame meant fire. By combining death and fire, and being uncertain where the rich man actually was after he died, they fell back on their pagan belief in an underworld. In their ignorance, they removed the word "unseen", and replaced it with the word infernum (hell)! I could be wrong about how they went about it, but my scenario makes sense.

Now let's take an educated look at the original word "unseen", properly define it, and see what it really meant in the parable of Lazarus and the rich man. In the Koine Greek the word unseen means: Hidden, Secret, Concealed, and Clandestine. So why did Jesus specifically use the word "unseen"? More than likely it was the Aramaic or Hebrew version of a word meaning secret. This is critical to understand considering who Jesus was addressing-- He was speaking to His fellow countrymen who considered themselves "the chosen" people.

Let's not forget the purpose for a parable in the first place, as Jesus points out in Matthew 13:13:

"Therefore I speak to them in parables; because while seeing they do not see, and while hearing they do not hear, nor do they understand."

Doesn't the explanation Jesus gave for the reason for parables correlate perfectly with something He wants to keep " hidden, secret, concealed, clandestine, and unseen"? What was in this story of Lazarus and the rich man that was hidden and concealed from those listening? Was God keeping a secret from a nation He partnered with? (I believe the reason for that partnership was for the purpose of expressing His love to the rest of humanity through the Hebrew nation.) The Jews were clueless, because it was hidden, unseen to them that God wanted to incorporate the Gentiles into a "portion" of the Abrahamic Covenant, i.e. the promises of God.

I'm sure the word "portion" didn't go unnoticed. Don't get me wrong--from God's perspective we got the whole shebang in Christ Jesus by being "grafted into the vine." However, from our perspective--as long as we see through a glass dimly (1 Cor. 13:12), we're only experiencing a small taste, and only understanding a "portion" of what is to come.

Okay, we've established where the rich man was, or it would be better to say where the rich man was NOT! He was not in the Greek pagan underworld known as Hades. He was not in the Latin pagan underworld known as hell. Interestingly, even though he had supposedly died, he wasn't even in the abode of the dead--the grave, known as Sheol. Now it's time to know who the rich man was, and who he represented in this parable.

What initially caused me to take a long hard look at this parable was--out of three characters in the story, only two were named. The rich man was nameless--why is that? What was his name--did he have a name? What do we have as clues? First: He was wealthy, and second: His robes were the color of royalty. Where else in scripture do we find words representing royalty in context to Israel? A "holy nation", a "royal priesthood" comes to mind. Obviously the reason the rich man wasn't named as an individual was because in this parable he represented the entire nation of Israel.

What does being rich mean?  From God's perspective, being rich simply means to know Him, as in:

Romans 2:4 - Riches of God's kindness.

Romans 9:26 - Riches of His Glory.

Romans 11:33 - Riches of wisdom and knowledge of God.

Ephesians 2:4 - God being rich with mercy.

Ephesians 3:16 - Riches of His glory.

Philippians 4:19 - God will supply all your needs according to His riches in glory.

James 2:5 - Rich in faith and heirs to His kingdom.

The nation of Israel was sanctioned by God to be His ambassador, representing the One and only true God.  The Jewish people were suppose to be the ones rich in the knowledge of God and his character.  Israel as a whole, the "chosen people" were instructed to show the rest of the world what being rich was all about.  The rich man in this parable failed to do that--he showed little concern to the beggar Lazarus.  At the time, Israel showed little concern for the rest of the world, basically hording God's riches to themselves.

What about Abraham?  Abraham in the parable represented the same Abraham written about in the book of Genesis.  Most know and understand Abraham was the father of all Jews, and he was revered as the one with whom God established a covenant with, as in the promises of God for all of Abrahams decedents.  The Jews (the rich man) considered themselves alone as the true decedent's.  To understand Abraham's role in the parable, we'll have to go way back in time to what happened to Abraham in the book of Genesis.

The actual covenant starts in chapter 12 and goes into chapter 17, but the one verse I'm going to focus on is Genesis 15:2:

" O Lord God, what will You give me, since I am childless, and the heir of my house is Eliezer of Damascus?"

This one verse is the key to understanding the parable of Lazarus and the rich man. I'll now be transitioning back and forth describing Abraham and Lazarus's role. The name Lazarus is the Greek name for the Hebrew name Eliezer. If you read about the interaction between Eliezer and Abraham, you'll quickly realize how close these two men were. Eliezer was like a son to Abraham--a best friend--a confidant. You'll read how Eliezer was close to Abrahams "heart". Where is Abraham's heart located? IN HIS BOSOM!

So where are we so far? Eliezer and Lazarus are one and the same. In Genesis, Eliezer was close to Abraham's heart, and Lazarus was noted by Jesus as being in Abraham's bosom. Who was Jesus talking to when sharing this parable? His fellow Jews, and they knew their Abrahamic history. They also knew Eliezer was not a Jew, but was a Gentile from Damascus. Abraham wanted to give his entire inheritance, including all the promises of God, as in the very covenant, over to a Gentile since he had no children of his own. "...and the heir of my house is Eliezer of Damascus."

I've concluded the three characters in the parable of Lazarus and the rich man are as follows:

Abraham represents the promises of God.

Lazarus represents the Gentile people.

The rich man represents the "chosen people" of Israel.

The parable makes complete sense if you understand the Abrahamic covenant, and who Jesus was speaking to at the time. Now I want to address some terminology and symbolism used in the parable. Later in this chapter, I want to point out how Jesus is represented in each and every term used, and not simply because He's the one telling the story.

In this passage, when I looked up the word "flame" in the Greek--it was spelled p-h-l-a-x. Note: This verse uses the word flame singular rather than flames plural, so in this case flame does not mean fire. Phlax (flame) simply means "flash", as in a flash of awareness--to bring light to an understanding. The word flame is also where we get the word "flashlight" from. Think about it this way--if you look into the darkness, everything you don't see is obviously secretive to you--it's hidden, concealed in the darkness, and clandestine--until you shine a "light" on the area, thus giving you a "flash" of "awareness" of what was "unseen" before. This is exciting stuff folks and it fits beautifully with the true meaning of the parable. Countries like Great Britain uses the word torch rather than a flashlight, and "torch" also has its origins from the word "flame".

A strange question: Have you ever experienced having an awareness about something that really caused you anguish or misery? The medical community claims your heart beats faster, your pupils dilate, and it seems as if things are moving in slow motion. So much so it "tests" your resolve, the very core of who you thought you were! Even though I know beyond any doubt that God is going to reconcile all of humanity, I'm "tested" and brought to my knees in anguish over the death of a loved one. My point--the word "torment" in this parable means a "testing" that describes the kind of anguish I just referred to.

So, when you read how the rich man was "tormented"--it means he was "tested"--Israel will be tested, which caused anguish to the very core of who they/he thought they/he were as descendants of Abraham. What was so tormenting to the rich man that caused him so much grief? Read on, you shall see, but first... when you read the word "flame", it simply means he became "aware" of what was about to take place while witnessing the interaction between Abraham and Lazarus, and what he witnessed is what was causing his anguish.

Don't forget a "parable" uses words and terms that don't always literally mean what they seem to describe on the surface. The word "thirst" in our day means a need for a satisfying liquid in one's mouth. However, "thirst" (δίψα) in the Greek means to have an earnest desire for something, and I will add, it may or may not have anything to do with what goes in the mouth.  What did the rich man "thirst" for?  I know tongue and taste are not exclusively synonymous to one another, but in this parable you can't have one without the other.

It's obvious the rich man wanted to taste something, and "taste" (γεύση) in the Greek means to partake, or experience.  This same word "taste" was used many times within scripture while using the phrase--"...will not taste death".  My point:  The tongue may or may not have anything to do with tasting something, thus we'll see (even though the word tongue was used) how "taste" had nothing to do with the tongue in this parable.

The rich man had a "thirst" (δίψα), as in an earnest desire for water to cool his tongue.  "Cool his tongue" is a figure of speech to imply how extremely thirsty he was.  Extremely thirsty for what?  Water?  Hardly!  As a parable this is significant, because in Jeremiah 2:13 & 17:13, God is described as being a fountain of Living Water.  Living Water is another example of what the nation of Israel "earnestly desired", and I feel this is more evidence of who the rich man represented.

By using the information we found in the book of Genesis referencing Eliezer and the Covenant, along with the understanding of words translated from the Koine Greek, and knowing it was a parable and not all words should be taken literally--now let's put all this information together and see if it makes sense.

It was hidden ("unseen") from the "chosen people" of Israel, that God was going to remove the responsibility from them, and hand it over to the Gentile nations--the responsibility of showing the world the goodness of God. The goodness of God encompasses the blessings of God along with the promises made to Abraham. The rich man was witnessing Abraham chumming it up with Lazarus, a Gentile, who was considered something lower than a dog in the eyes of a Jew. This low life, known as a "beggar" at the feet of the Jews (the rich man), was now close to Abrahams heart (bosom). Witnessing a Gentile receiving the promised inheritance "tormented" the rich man (Israel) to its very core of who they thought they were.

The four things I mentioned in paragraph one I said I would prove were:

1: Hell isn't even mentioned in this verse.
2: No fire exists in this story.
3: No one actually died!
4: It's good news, not hell news!

1.  No one was in hell, because the word unseen was perversely translated into hell, so in reality hell was never mentioned in this verse.

2.  We've learned there was no fire involved, because flame doesn't mean fire.  Rather, flame means an awareness.

3.  No one actually died, because it was a parable. However, death was mentioned, but for an entirely different reason than what people might think, and I'll explain what I mean by that shortly.

4.  It's great news that Jesus has included the entire world to participate in all of God's promises made to Israel.  All of mankind is His chosen people.  Note: He is not done with the physical nation of Israel yet!

        I don't know if it is my imagination or a revelation from God, but it's as if so many things in the parable of Lazarus and the rich man seem to metaphorically point to Christ.  Let's take a look at a few words used in the story:

-Unseen:  Jesus, the truth of who He was and is, is "unseen"--hidden to the nation of Israel.  Why is that, considering the story of Jesus has been around for centuries?  Jesus answered that question Himself by saying:  "So that while seeing, they may see and not perceive, and while hearing, they may hear and not understand, otherwise they might return and be forgiven."

"Forgiven" is a figure of speech and does not mean Israel is not already forgiven--from God's perspective, but from their perspective they are not walking in His forgiveness.  How can they?  They are "unseen" to the truth that Christ took away their sins.  Why do they remain in their ignorance with all the evidence available to them?  With all of the scriptural evidence they had at their fingertips at the time, they didn't recognize Christ the first time--FOR A REASON, and for that same reason they don't recognize Him as their Messiah now.

What is that reason?  I'll be repeating this shortly, but Paul answered that question in Romans 11:25: "For I do not want you, brethren, to be uninformed of this mystery--so that you will not be wise in your own estimation--that a partial hardening has happened to Israel until the fullness of the Gentiles (Lazarus) has come in;"

Notice the word "mystery" in this verse? A mystery is something secret, hidden, clandestine, and unseen. Also notice the word "hardening". This describes a people who are in denial, and the reason they are in denial is because they are not perceiving, and the reason they are not perceiving is because it's not their time to perceive--not until Lazarus's commission is completed.

-Death: Even though nobody actually died due to it being a parable, the theme of death is critically important in this story. The rich man asked Abraham to send Lazarus back from the dead to warn his brothers, meaning his fellow countrymen. He received a true answer of how prophets have been sent to his brethren for centuries prophesying about Jesus, and it did no good--so sending Lazarus back would make no difference.

In this story, how does death point to Jesus? Jesus was raised from the dead and it didn't persuade the nation of Israel (the rich man). Symbolically, Lazarus died, the rich man died, and in reality--most importantly, Jesus died. It's written a seed cannot bring forth fruit unless it dies and is buried. We, the Gentiles are that fruit. Think about this... when Jesus shared this parable--the good news was dead--the gospel was dead. However, not long after Christ was raised from the dead--the gospel, the good news became alive in the Christ believing Gentiles.

I know I'm getting ahead of myself for the next segment with saying this, but now the Gentiles are the ones who are carrying the torch, the flame, the awareness of the accomplishments of Christ. Metaphorically speaking, the house of Israel is dead. The rich man is dead in his understanding, he is dead to the gospel, and it is still "unseen" to him (Israel).

-Flame:  Jesus is the "flame".  How so?  Since flame means a flash, as in an awareness--to me this sure sounds like a way of illustrating faith.  When I mention faith, I'm not defining our faith IN Christ which only gives a peace of mind, but I'm referring to The Faith OF Christ that gives a vivified life.  Flash, the awareness of His accomplishments as One bringing light, a "flame", a torch to what was once dark.  Our understanding of God's love for us was hidden, and "unseen" until Jesus, the "light of life", through His gift of faith, makes us "aware" of our need for His and the Father's love.

-Water:  Jesus said in John 4:10 & 4:11 He was the Living Water.  Jesus is the living water, and to this day Jesus would say if you drink of me you will thirst no more.  So far, and at this time in history, the rich man--Israel as a nation has never tasted Him--they're still thirsty.

-Taste:  Luke 14:24 - "For I tell you, none of those men (Israel) who were invited shall taste of my dinner."  The nation of Israel (the rich man) has still not tasted of His dinner, but they will according to: Romans 11:26 - "...and so all Israel will be saved;"  But when?  After Lazarus is finished with his part to play in the Abrahamic covenant, as explained in: Romans 11:25 - "For I do not want you, brethren, to be uninformed of this mystery--so that you will not be wise in your own estimation--that a partial hardening has happened to Israel until the fullness of the Gentiles (Lazarus) has come in;"  This verse reveals what happened in the parable of Lazarus and the rich man more than any other verse in the Bible.

-The Divide:  What divides the Christians of the world from Israel?  Jesus is the divide.  All Christians of the world know that Jesus is Israel's Messiah, but the Jews don't.  Some translations call it "a great chasm fixed".  I want to focus on the word "fixed".  The plan to reconcile the world has been fixed, has been rigged for a victory, and it's a done deal.  Great Divide is all pointing to Jesus--He is The Great Divide--He is what divides the house of Israel from the Gentile Nations of the world.  A partial hardening has happened to Israel "until the fullness of the Gentiles (Lazarus) has come in" (Romans 11:25), then God will change their heart of stone about who Jesus is, and give them a heart of flesh.

"Moreover, I will give you (the rich man) a new heart and put a new spirit within you; and I will remove the heart of stone from your flesh and give you a heart of flesh."

It's amazing how all of this plays out, and it has nothing to do with heaven or hell, yet this parable is the main scripture that Christians use to confirm that there's a place called hell. There is a discrepancy of how many parables Jesus actually used, but there is a common theme within every one of them-- "stewardship". The Greek word stewardship (διαχείριση) has several meanings, but in context to the parables I define stewardship as: Utilizing and managing all of God's resources, by openly displaying His love nature, and His character for the betterment of creation. Israel did not do this, but instead they slandered God's character using the law.

Their lack of stewardship took away from the true meaning of having a relationship with God, and replaced it with the law. In some instances, Christendom is doing the exact same thing while also slandering the character of God. How so? By adding a mixture of paganism, law, traditions, and doctrines of men--Christendom has replaced a real relationship with God, with a relationship with their church. I'm telling you... what Christendom has done to this wonderful parable of Lazarus and the rich man is atrocious.

As I implied in the first paragraph, ignorance, along with doctrines of men have changed the good news message of this parable into a hell doctrine that steals, kills, and destroys the trust that people might have in a loving God. The hell doctrine is by far the foremost and worst deception that slanders the character of God, and it needs to be exposed for the lie that it is.

In conclusion to this chapter, I will now tell a story using modern vernacular and terminology. Everyone, in our day should understand my short story which will explain the parable of Lazarus and the rich man. Think of my story as a parable about a parable--I call it "A Parable of a Wealthy Woman".

There once was a very wealthy woman who was the heiress of a vast fortune. As spelled out clearly in the will, her part of the inheritance required an estate fiduciary to be in control of all of her finances. This person also happened to be a distant relative--her Uncle Abram. He was the one chosen by the woman's parents to be responsible to oversee how her money was spent. There were strict guidelines established in the will that the woman must follow, or else the ramifications would be severe.

The wealthy woman was raised with a complete understanding of the specifications written in the estate bylaws, but chose to ignore each and every guideline. The will allowed her to take a healthy sum for herself and for her living expenses, but the rest was to be strategically placed to have a generational benefit to others. Instead she flaunted her wealth, and was verbally abusive to anyone she didn't deem worthy of her stature.

Her lifestyle was in direct opposition to those established guidelines written in the will. Her fiduciary, Uncle Abram, was also given specific instructions to be enacted if the heiress didn't behave in a way that best reflected the wishes of the estate.

So after many years of continual warnings to the wealthy woman--unbeknownst to her, one day while on her yacht, the crew was instructed by her uncle to take the woman to a small, uncharted, and unpopulated island.  This island had no contact with the outside world--there was no electricity, no phones, and no internet. It was the exact opposite of the kind of lifestyle the woman was accustomed to-- there wasn't even indoor plumbing to the small hut that had been adequately stocked with supplies.

She was alone and "unseen" by the rest of the world, and from her perspective she was as good as dead.  Days later her uncle returned in a helicopter and approached her with a laptop in his hands.  He sat down with her and began to show her many recordings of her lifestyle taken by others--of how she abused the servants, and how she mistreated those around her.  It was obvious in the videos of how she openly elevated herself, and looked down her nose on everyone else.

One specific recording displayed how she mistreated an immigrant girl who was part of her kitchen staff.  The uncle then opened another file showing a conference room.  In the middle of the conference room was a large table, and those sitting at the table were all people the woman recognized-- the estate attorneys, her uncle, and the young immigrant girl.

To her horror, all the wealth of the banished woman was being signed over to the young girl. The now no longer wealthy woman began to realize her situation, as if a flashbulb went off in her head, giving her an awareness of what was taking place on the video. The very thought of her wealth and riches being handed over to such a person as this undeserving immigrant girl "tormented" the woman to her very soul.

The "flame of torment" began to burn in her mind about what she had done wrong, so she asked her uncle if she could go back and warn her siblings, so they wouldn't made the same mistake as she. The uncle then showed a file depicting the estate behavioural guidelines, and said like her, all have been adequately warned.

The women then asked if the young girl would be willing to bring her a "small taste" of her wealth-- maybe an heirloom, anything to remind the woman of what she had lost. The uncle explained of the "great divide" of   distance, oceans, and time restraints that wouldn't allow that to happen. Due to her neglect to fulfil the estate goals, there was now a tremendous responsibility placed on the new young heiress to accomplish those goals.

Shortly thereafter the uncle got back on the helicopter and left the island.  He needed to be available to his new ward, and to properly teach her how to best use her new found riches in accordance to the rules established in the estate.  The woman left standing on the beach knew there was nothing she could do about it, because of the "great divide" of ocean that separated her from her previous life.

Just in case you missed it, I will now define each character in "my story" to those of the original parable.

-Uncle Abram is a relative of the wealthy woman, whereas Abraham represents a distant relative of the rich man in the parable.

-The wealthy woman is obviously the rich man.

-The wealthy woman was assigned to represent the wishes of the estate, whereas the rich man represents the Jewish Nation, who were responsible to represent the wishes of God.

-The immigrant girl represents Lazarus.

I considered many things while writing this chapter, such as how I was taught within Christendom, and how my take on the parable of Lazarus and the rich man greatly differs from traditional Christian teaching. My intent isn't to upset or offend anyone, so keep that in mind when reading the next chapter referring to the many other considerations I want to suggest--while reading the Bible.

Chapter 9


Ten Unusual Considerations While Reading the Bible


Before I get into the considerations outline, let me explain the reason why I feel it's necessary to write a no-nonsense, common sense, simplistic approach, of how I now read my Bible. Far too many people read the Bible at face value, not realizing how mankind has put their own thoughts to parchment-- their personal perspective of God, which may or may not be the correct view.  By doing so, it resulted in a corrupted view of God, and this is why there's a need to write a book titled:  In Defense of God's Love. Most likely, people who are willing to read this book will be called, or consider themselves Christian, and most Christians refer to the Bible as the authority for most of their beliefs.  So, it only makes sense to write about how I read my Bible, and what I'm going to call considerations that I apply while doing so.


Webster's defines consideration as:

1:  The act of considering; careful thought or attention; deliberation

2:  Thoughtful or sympathetic regard for others;

3: Something that is, or should be, considered, as in making a decision.

No one is asking you the reader to embrace or believe what is written here, but only to consider it. Have you ever heard it said: Don't confuse me with the facts while my mind is made up? If this is you-- don't continue reading--what is written here may upset you, and that is not my intention.

While reading the Bible most of us make a decision, or jump to a conclusion without a thought of the above definition of "consideration". As you read further, you may be tempted to jump to a conclusion and assume I'm bashing the Bible. No, negatory, nada, not so! I view the Bible as an awesome instrument in the hands of a loving God. I will however step on a few toes by bashing many traditions caused by ignorance, which in turn promotes false assumptions about the Bible. The reader may be wondering why I used the word unusual in my title. Simply put, these considerations are not usually taught. A few of these considerations others have written about, but most have been derived from my personal real life experiences, spanning over 35 years of watching and observing what Christianity likes to call "fruit".

When I quote scripture, I will be using a snapshot style of writing rather than a free-flowing manuscript approach. In other words, I'm not trying to write a book on the subject of considerations when reading the Bible, when a chapter will be sufficient enough. Unless God chooses otherwise, you may find little to no spiritual enlightenment, but you will be entertained, so let's begin.

Consideration One:  Trust

While reading the Bible have you ever considered asking yourself--do I trust myself? My answer used to be yes, for the most part, until I believe God required me to do some self examination. It went like this:  Do I honestly believe a person born with a carnal mind, corrupted by sin, influenced by family, friends, culture and environment, looking through the lens of an American living in the 21st century, can trust himself to read the Bible with accuracy, and later correctly interpret what was read?  If this is you, and you're honest, can you really say you still trust yourself?

The fall-back response I always hear is: God gave us discernment, and a mind for reasoning. Discernment and reasoning still falls within the parameters I previously mentioned. I had to come to grips with the fact that my mind and reasoning capabilities have been corrupted. I have also discovered in this journey that very few are willing to look beyond the corruption, and the above-mentioned influence of family, culture, etc. It scares them to do so.

Why am I writing a book if I don't fully trust myself, and I don't put trust in my opinion? Ironically, that's why it's called an opinion. I don't put my trust in what I'm writing this very moment, and that is why I call it a consideration. What I do trust 100% is the fact, and I do emphasize the fact, that Christ is the Author and Perfecter of our faith. Most believers I've met will agree that He is the Author, while at the same time disbelieve or instigate man-made conditions on how Christ is going to perfect "His" faith in us. His faith rather than our faith? This topic will be addressed and explained in other chapters, so keep your eyes open.

Let's "discerningly" veer off course for a moment, and look closer at the word discernment as in how its been taught within Christendom. I've heard it said God gives us discernment, or people claim they have a gift of discernment! Cover your toes-- there's a need to do some stepping by saying, most people who claim they have this unbiblical gift, thinking it's biblical--use it as a means to elevate how one feels about oneself. It sets them apart from most others, and it gives a feeling of superiority, that they have acquired something special from God. Come on, be honest--my perception could be wrong, but it's my "best guess", and only and "estimation" of what I've seen happen.

Some Christians keep making claims of this gift even though the "gift of discernment" is not mentioned in the Bible as one of the spiritual gifts. Also, there are no examples within scripture of anyone using a "gift of discernment". The next time a Christian colleague approaches you with the claim of possessing such a gift, notice how they speak with an air of certainty, as meaning--all forms of guessing have been eliminated.

Here's the problem...the word "discernment" does not exist in my Strong's Concordance, but as a verb discern and discerning are mentioned. It was easy to look up the Greek meaning of discern, and guess what, it means exactly the opposite of what is taught, believed, and what people claim they have. It simply means:   An ESTIMATION in which we would term as an APPROXIMATION--a BEST GUESS.  Let me reiterate:  A best guess is exactly opposite of certainty, and yet people still hold onto the air of certainty while describing how their gift functions. These people with this supposed gift also claim the Bible is the final authority for their beliefs, yet the scripture and the language disagree with their conclusion of it being a valid gift from God.

I realize this is a petty example, and only touches on the bigger issue of how our American lens is not accurate in relation to the original Greek language.  So that I'm not misunderstood, I truly believe God can give individuals insight and the "word of knowledge", at a specific time for a specific reason, defining a true biblical gift.  Perverting the definition of discernment is one of many examples of how religion has added to, or has twisted what God intended.  Unknowingly, those who twist the meaning of discernment, do so while thinking it's biblical.  This, in part, is the corruption of our mind I'm talking about! I believe we should be totally dependent on God each and every time we open our Bibles.  Defining "discernment" and trusting that discernment needs to be reconsidered while reading the Bible.

## Consideration Two:  Excess Baggage

However God did it, however He drew you, however He opened your eyes of understanding about His love for you--at that very moment did all the memories of the past simply disappear? Did all your previous beliefs vanish?  Did family traditions and other teachings become meaningless?  Was all forgotten--the pain, hurt, sorrow, along with the walls and defense mechanisms they produced--all forgotten?  Did God require repentance of all these traits before He would allow us to become useful vessels?  If your answer is no of course not, then I believe you've come to a wise decision.

A consideration, while reading the Bible:  The people who have written and/or translated the Bible's many versions, brought to the table the same hang-ups and excess baggage that plague us.  The only differences were their culture and technology.  They were people just like us--imperfect, born with the carnal mind, corrupted by sin, influenced by family, friends, culture and environment, looking through the lens of whatever year and place they resided. Either this is true, God giving allowance for human error in scripture, or else He would have put the ancient folk into a zombie like trance and been in total control of their faculties while they put pen to parchment. (But what about "free will"?)


I was traditionally taught a third option that I no longer believe or adhere to, and it goes something like this:  We can trust in a God who would protect what He says by making sure those writing it would be flawless. I was also lead to believe--any writing handed down through the centuries would be preserved and kept accurate. We know this happened for a fact how? This is an example of what I call blind faith, which I term ignorant faith. The Muslims make the claim of how Allah has done the same regarding the Qur'an. Yet, both religions teach of an individual's free will, which would be in direct conflict with a zombie-like state of mind that would be required in keeping perfect accuracy.

Blind faith ignores the free will conundrum, as well as the obvious historical contradictions--, one should be asking the question: Which of the 670 language versions of the Bible are we talking about? Did God protect them all, considering not one version entirely agrees with another? Christendom's answer is along the lines of: Not every word has to be the same, but they are all in unity on important issues. Is hell an important issue? Not one Bible agrees on how many times hell is mentioned! What happened to the other hells, which number of hells is the truth, and which Bible did God protect? You see? It doesn't add up!

I once had a dialogue with an atheist who insisted Christians were mindless puppets. He may not be right, but I understood his perspective. This brings us to my last point of consideration number two: Everything we believe and everything we've been taught has its origin. It all came from somewhere or someone. Do we honestly believe that everything we practice and believe came from and is sanctioned by God, as in every denomination, every ritual, and everything we hold sacred--all came from God? If not, then where??? My search continues.


Consideration Three:  Know Your Teachers


I realize God can use anyone or anything for his purposes, regardless of past or present hang-ups. He has an uncanny way of using the foolish to confound the wise.  I think I've heard that somewhere.  However, all this being true, I'm asking for a consideration in reference to teachers and Bible scholars.  In what way?  By listening to what they say and watching what they do, as well as assessing their character somewhat, and finally determine if you want them to teach you.


Allow me to demonstrate by using three scenarios, three teachers, preaching from a pulpit. My scenarios are fictional, but the stories are an allegory of men who actually existed, and an analogy of what they believed.  They are looked upon with honor as theologians, within Christian seminaries.


Pastor/teacher 1:  He gives a friendly introduction, some Bible references, and a long monologue about how we should be available to minister to others. He stresses the point of self-sacrifice while encouraging the congregation to be willing to do whatever it takes to spread the Gospel. He presses on with the notion to keep all actions clean, above reproach, especially for men. He comments further that it would be better if men didn't minister to women, but be prepared because the sovereign hand of God might plan such an event. "Men, if you think there's even the slightest chance that God might be using you to minister to women, castrate yourself! Being an example of how serious this issue is, I castrated myself. Now with a clear conscience, I can minister to women without the worry of gossip." End.


Now honestly folks, especially men, would you come back the following week? Would you entertain the thought that this teacher is unbalanced in his reasoning? I would strongly think about taking a second look at other doctrines he endorses while at the same time RUN for the door! Let's continue on to our second contestant.


Teacher 2: You are sitting in a local church, music has come to an end, and the preacher walks up to the pulpit to address a congregation. He gives the usual greeting expected from pastors and proceeds to teach on the topic of hell. He tells people the majority of the population from Adam to the end of the world will be there, and he begins to smile at the prospect. He claims that for those who think the blood of Christ is sufficient to save you from hell, you had better think again... And his smile grows. The barrage of conditions and rules to be followed in order to be saved from such a place-- seems to go on forever, and finally he closes with: "I personally know of friends and colleagues who will be in hell. I'm looking forward to the day I'll be able to look down from heaven at them being tortured, burned alive screaming in agony, and I will laugh!" His smile is bigger than ever showing his teeth, and upon a closer look you see a twinkle in his eye. End.

Do you think this sermon sounds preposterous--how about utterly ridiculous? Give me a show of hands; who would be in that church next week? Now for our third and final Bible scholar contestant… .

Teacher 3: In this scenario, this hombre is very well respected and well known. Due to his Latin roots, I mean no offense, nor am I implying a sense of bigotry by calling him a hombre. While sitting in a majestic building, lined with stained glass windows, through two hours of an acquired taste of music-- finally the man of the hour approaches the podium. This man of God begins his sermon about the wonders of creation. Starting from day one to the day God rested, he left out no detail. He emphasized the sinless innocence of the first man and the first woman at that time. He chuckles as he asked the congregation if any of them would know if they were naked--he gets the desired response of light laughter and blushing faces.

205

Then the sermon moves toward the beauty and the splendor of the Garden of Eden.  He describes the importance of the trees, the fruit, and the serpent.  He quickly sums up the conversation between Adam, Eve, the Serpent,  and forges beyond the infamous bite!  This great man of God proceeds to tell the congregation that the disobedient act of eating of the fruit was not the original sin.  He claims that what happened afterwards was the original sin.  Adam and Eve's eyes were opened, and they knew they were naked!  Their new found knowledge produced lust and the desire for sex--this was the original sin.

Sex became evil, and there should be no enjoyment in the act or else you'll be participating in the original sin.  The penalty of enjoyment, even sex between husband and wife--the consequences will be eternal hell.  Sex is for procreation purposes only, however, be aware, the offspring might be the fruit of the original sin. This is why it's so important for babies to be baptized into the church, or they will suffer the same torments of eternal hell.  Take heed to what I say because "fear is the foundation of our salvation!"  End.

Really?  This guy is famous, admired, and respected as a church leader--even today!  How many of my readers would agree with this guy's teaching?  How many of my readers would be back in his church next week?

A consideration while reading your Bible: The three characters in these stories are real people who historically believed and taught what was portrayed in these fictional scenarios. What makes this so important is the person in my first story--his teachings have to be questionable because of his extreme actions (castration). The person in my second story is respected for his beliefs, so much to the degree that they are still being taught in our churches of today (hell). And the third person in my story had a heavy influence on how specific words in the Bible would be translated (sex). Most people would run from these three men today, and yet as a church body of believers--we consider them church fathers, and generally embrace these men's doctrines wholeheartedly.

They were, in order of scenarios: Origen (castrated himself), Tertullian (smiled at people going to hell), and Augustine (original sin). My intent isn't to slander these men, but I'm just stating that we need to be extremely wise in assessing the character of church leaders we glean beliefs from. Since Origen later on regretted castrating himself (ya think?) I'm willing to give some credence to what he believed. Tertullian was also a  lawyer (go figure) who found joy in the eternal suffering of others; this clown has lost all and total credibility with me.

Augustine? Where on Earth did that junk come from--that he promoted? Answer: Before converting to Christianity, Augustine sat under the pagan teaching of a man named Mani.  Mani's teaching was later called the Manichean doctrine.  This guy taught that all flesh was evil and from the devil, and that all things spiritual were good and from God.  I've only supplied a brief summary of why I believe Augustine believed and promoted what he did.

The caveat, the cherry on the top is Augustine's quote of:  "Fear is the foundation of our salvation!"  This guy was clueless about how God's perfect love casts out the kind of fear this ignoramus said is the basis for our foundation.  I think this makes it clear why I felt a need to write a book about defending God's love.  "Consider" re-reading my chapter titled "Perfect Love".

What gets me--there are those today who have the gall to tell me that pagan baggage had no influence on how Augustine translated scripture.  I trust very little of what this guy had to say, and yet I consider him the most influential person in reference to how the church reads and interprets the Bible's of today.  Examples:  He might not have been directly responsible for translating death and grave into the word hell, even though he promoted the action.  However, he was the key reason for translating "a segment of time" into something the exact opposite, as in a time without end, i.e. "eternity".  A consideration, know your teachers.

## Consideration Four:  Garden Precedence


Let's take a journey back to the Garden of Eden where we find Adam and Eve barefoot, along with everything else bare, and I'm assuming no thorns or stickers lying around. God earlier had told Adam, "don't eat from that tree... over there... No, not that one... THAT ONE!"  Did I quote God correctly? Obviously not.


Another consideration while reading the Bible: It's recorded in our Bible that Adam and Eve were together in the garden, having a conversation with the serpent.  When the serpent questioned them about the validity of what God said, Eve told the serpent that she and Adam were not to eat of the fruit and not to touch it!  A precedent was established with this little three letter word... "AND".  God said no such thing as "don't touch it", and yet they said, GOD SAID... .


Let's veer off and chase a rabbit for a moment. You noticed I said "they said".  I question where Eve got the notion of "don't touch it!"  The choices are: From God, a plant, one of the other animals, the serpent, her imagination, or Adam.  Adam was standing there with her and he didn't correct her error.  Why not?  My conjecture is this:  God told Adam first; then Adam passed the info on to Eve with a lie attached for emphasis.  Technically a lie was spoken regardless of who or when, and this

209

happened BEFORE anyone ate or touched the forbidden fruit. I was taught that disobedience by eating the fruit (unless you're Augustine) is what caused sin to enter the world. Is lying a sin? What came first, a lie or disobedience?

Now back to the issue of what is far more important than when sin came into the World--a precedent was established. Consider this--the very first recorded man (or woman) added to what God said. Are we so naive to believe this was the one and only instance where someone added a meaning or words to what God actually intended or said? If this chain of events actually took place, if accurate as recorded in Genesis, then one would have to conclude that God's intent was embellished upon. Accuracy is another issue altogether because it took approximately 1300 years before the Genesis story would be put in writing.

Consideration Five: Scribes

I found it interesting that Webster's Dictionary has a clear understanding of the Jewish culture by defining a "scribe" as: "a person learned in the Jewish law who makes hand written copies of the Torah, a professional penman who copied manuscripts before the invention of printing."

In his own hand, did Moses actually write the Garden of Eden story, or did he use a scribe? I'm not sure anyone knows for sure, but a precedent was established in the forbidden fruit story by putting the blame on Eve. Why is this a precedent? Moses or the scribes ignored the blatant lie perpetrated by Adam as he quoted God as saying something He never said. A consideration while reading the bible:

Jeremiah 8:8 "How can you say, we are wise, for we have the law of the Lord, when actually the **lying** pen of the scribes has **handled it falsely**."

Did I miss something here? Is the law of the Lord considered scripture? The scribes very function was to write, rewrite, and make copies of scripture! My simple approach makes me say, "Hmmm...". A lie was spoken by Adam in The Garden, then the same lie repeated by Eve, and now in Jeremiah God accuses some of the very people who are responsible for scriptural accuracy--LIARS! Again, hmm…

Let me give a couple of other examples which some might deem harmless. Remember what is commonly called The Lord's Prayer? It ends with: "...for thine is the kingdom, and the power, and the glory, forever and ever amen." This comes from Matthew 16:13 out of the King James Version. This portion of scripture was installed in the English Bible by King Henry the 8th around 1525, adding to what Jesus said. This addition obviously took place long after Jesus spoke what is called The Lord's Prayer. Are there any other Bible verses or extra verses that history dictates were later added?  I'm glad you asked; Mark 16:17&18, Luke 24:51, John 7:53&8:12, and 1st John 5:7 were never found within the earliest known manuscripts. (Don't confuse me with the facts while my mind is made up!) These scriptural references along with the entire Bible will be discussed in the next chapter called:  Rightly Dividing The Word of Truth.

Consideration Six:  Describe a  Friend


This is my friend Phil.  He's a good man, a kind man, and he always considers others and their feelings.  He is slow to anger and never abusive.  His wife and children adore him, and the people he works with find his work ethics faultless.  He has always been there for me with kind words of encouragement, and he's a mean person!  What???  Huh???  What did I miss? Does not common sense tell you something is wrong with my last sentence?


A consideration while reading the Bible: Jesus speaking:

"The Spirit of the Lord is on Me, because He has anointed Me to preach good news to the poor.  He has sent Me to proclaim freedom for the prisoners and recovery of sight for the blind, to release the oppressed, to proclaim the year of the Lord's favor,..." (Luke 4: 18&19)

What did Jesus do next?  In mid-sentence, before finishing the remaining quote out of scripture, He closed the book and sat down.

Was Jesus guilty of reading scripture out of context, or how about proof texting?  He didn't finish the verse; after the phrase:  "...to proclaim the year of the Lord's favor." there was an **"AND"**.  Remember my analogy of how I described my friend Phil, and how my last sentence didn't make sense, and how it wasn't in context to what was previously stated about Phil?

Now let's read what Jesus said, but include the second half of the sentence:

"The spirit of the Lord is on me because he has anointed me to preach good news to the poor. He has sent me to proclaim freedom for the prisoners and recovery of sight for the blind, to release the oppressed, to proclaim the year of the Lord's favor, **"AND"** the day of vengeance of our God."

What???  Huh???  What did I miss?  Common sense tells me something is wrong here!  The second half of this verse is not in context to the previous versus, to those that follow it, nor to itself!  How do I know this? Jesus made this quote from Isaiah chapter 61, and immediately after the phrase referencing vengeance--it says:

"...comfort all who mourn, provide for those who grieve, a crown of beauty, oil of gladness, a garment of praise."

LOOK!  See how this verse continues to promote the same theme as the verses before Jesus sat down? Notice how "vengeance, retribution, punishment, or wrath" are not mentioned anywhere else within the context of all the other verses, nor anywhere else within the chapter!  "Vengeance" is in direct opposition and inconsistent to the theme being portrayed in Isaiah 61.  This caused a huge red flag to go up in my thinking.

Why did Jesus close the book and not finish? Traditional Christian teaching tell us that Jesus has fulfilled that portion of prophecy regarding God's vengeance.  So!  What does that mean?  Why didn't He just skip and go on to the other verses that followed.  Did He not fulfill them as well?  Doctrines of men teach us that God beat up Jesus out of "vengeance" for the sins of the world.  To believe that--we must totally disregard Jesus' words in John 12:47:

"I did not come to judge the world but to save the world."

Ah-ha... Jesus didn't judge, but with God that's a whole other matter. Consider John 3:17:

"For God did not send the Son into the world to judge the world, but that the world might be saved through Him."

AND...
"The Father judges no one but has given all judgment to the Son." (John 5:22)


How does God's vengeance fit with everything else Jesus said or did while ministering? I could have sworn Jesus said He and the Father are one, meaning in total agreement. So what could be the problem? Remember that precedent of how Adam included another "God said" in the garden story? Remember the lying scribes? I could be way off base here, but I believe this is yet another example of people adding to what God wanted to be said in Isaiah, and Jesus gave us a real hint of it by refusing to read it. This is only a opinion and a consideration.


Let's continue on with another example of how the ancient Latin church added to scripture by incorporating the phrase: "Wrath of God".

# Consideration Seven:  Ancient Latin Influence

More than a consideration, but accurate--our favorite Bibles were translated from Hebrew and Aramaic to Greek to Latin, then to English. Countless books have been written on the influence of the Latin culture within the early church, so I'll now interject some of my thoughts and opinions on the matter.  With that said; it is not my opinion, but a FACT the phrase:  "Wrath of God" was added into scripture, when it didn't exist in the original Greek manuscripts.

Wrath in our MODERN Culture is how the doctrines of men define the below scripture:

Wrath-noun
1.
strong, stern, or fierce anger; deeply resentful
2.
vengeance or punishment as the consequence of anger.

So, when a person of our day reads Romans 5:8-9, they usually read it with the understanding of the above definition.

"But God demonstrates His own love toward us, in that while we were yet sinners, Christ died for us. Much more then, having now been justified by His blood, we shall be saved from the "wrath of God" through Him."

I must point out a HUGE PROBLEM with this verse folks: "…of God…" does not exist in the Greek text. The words indignation or wrath are used, but it's referring to our own indignation or wrath rather than from God. The first sentence of this verse gives us a clear context by telling us of God's love towards us. Is God's love best defined as being vengeful and deeply resentful? Wrath of God and love of God simply don't jive.

Wrath in the Greek implies an over-the-top, extreme or violent "passion". In this verse, and in context, the proper translation for indignation or wrath is: "Violent Passions". Thus my Greek Bible reads: "…we shall be saved from our (own) violent passions through Him." The wonderful Latins in 440 A.D. via the Latin Vulgate apparently had a better idea by adding "of God" to the end of this verse. I believe this to be intentional as yet another means of controlling the masses using fear--by capitalizing on the term: "Wrath of God".

Since God is good, God is love, and Jesus came to show us the true nature of who God really is, as in "But God demonstrates His own love toward us…", I now ask the question: Which option best represents who God really is as well as compliments what Christ promoted?

1. To save us from God's wrath as in his strong, stern, or fierce anger; deeply resentful vengeance or punishment as the consequence of His anger?

OR...

2. To save us from our own strong, stern, fierce anger we might have for one another-- resulting in having a deep, resentful, violent passion towards our neighbor?

Doesn't number 2 best describe what we as a people need to be saved from?  Is not number two's description the reason for murder and wars?

What the ancient Latins did with these two little words:  "Of God" within verses like Romans 5:8-9-- caused me to research what other baggage they might have added to scripture.  Both history and the Bible tell us of how some pagan practices filtered into the church via the baggage promoted by the pagan Greek beliefs; i.e., Zeus, Apollo, idol worship, etc., but what of the Latin paganistic baggage?

In our modern age, Latin countries like Spain, Italy, Brazil, Mexico, only to mention a few, still celebrate the dead.  We're talking about national holidays here; where you see parades, people dressed like skeletons--carrying coffins. We've all seen it in the movies, television, etc. My point:  If paganistic practices are still going on today, how much more was it prevalent during the time those ancient Latin folk were involved in translating scripture?  If they weren't mindless, zombie puppets of God, then what they believed, wrote, and translated--it had to be clouded with paganism, to one degree or another.  It seems to me that common sense tells me to take a closer look at my Bible, at what they translated, and what I believe and why. Remember, this is only a consideration.

History also tells us of a power and political agenda going on at the time our first Bibles were being translated.  The power agenda of the early Latin Catholic church--of how their government was involved in translating scripture, is definitely something that should be considered.  Have you ever heard of the Dark Ages?  There's a reason it was called the Dark Ages, which I'm not covering here, but during that time is when our first Bibles emerged. Definitely, something to think about!

A consideration:  The "when" should raise a red flag in our thinking--when the Bible was canonized. What kind of red flag am I referring to?  History is clear about how it would benefit the powers-that-be to have a combined pagan and political agenda.  How would this agenda look? Answer:  By keeping the masses of pagan believing peasants ignorant and in fear.  How did the powers-that-be use ignorance and fear?  Answer:  Since most of the peasant's were illiterate, it was easy to keep them ignorant of the true Greek word usage by mistranslating key words from the Greek into Latin.  They only did that to words that would capitalize and complement the peasants fearful pagan beliefs.

Most modern Bibles were translated via some Greek manuscripts, but were very dependent upon the Latin Vulgate. I discovered in most instances, the Latin word usage is a poor substitute for the Greek language. I want to hit on an example of word usage: Assuming sound biblical evidence to support the claims, I'm going to paraphrase a familiar statement a modern evangelist might speak. We've all heard something like this: Brothers and sisters..., you need to **repent** of **sin** or in **hell** you're going to be **tormented** by **fire** for all **eternity**! You have just read 6 little words I want to address, and I realize I might be oversimplifying things as you read further.

Figuratively speaking, our fictional evangelist unknowingly had to be reading his Bible through the eyes of a pagan influenced, ancient Latin translator. As you read further, try to remember how the early Latins influence their pagan believing populace when I ask: Objectively speaking; what kind of picture forms in your mind after reading-- Brothers and sisters..., you need to repent of sin or in hell you're going to be tormented by fire for all eternity? Needless to say, it's not a redeeming picture.

Now, let's eliminate the Latin influence by emphasizing the above example of six words our evangelist used in his statement. Those six words being: "Repent, sin, hell, torment, fire, and eternity". In the original Koine Greek manuscripts those words mean:

Repent: To change one's mind.
Sin: Missing the mark.
Hell: Death or grave.
Torment: To test.
Fire: A method to purify.
Eternity: An age, as in a segment of time.

Having this information, we can now take the example our modern evangelist said, and write it in a way an ancient Greek evangelist might speak.

First, once again--the ancient Latin version:
"Brothers and sisters..., you need to repent of sin or in hell you're going to be tormented by fire for all eternity!"

NOW the Greek version:
"Brothers and sisters, you need to change your mind about missing the mark, or after you die you're going to go through a testing and purification in the age to come."

Judge the fruit! One translation elicits fear, and the other promotes trust. What kind of picture does the Greek version give you, as compared to the statement of our Latin influenced evangelist--totally different right? This is because the words have drastically different meanings than what we've been taught in our modern, Latin influence bibles.

I'm left to wonder, how many more mistranslations and misunderstandings are there? Note: "Age to come" is used throughout scripture, and is not a New Age term. Another point: Why was death, grave, pit, unseen, and Gehenna translated into the word hell, not in every case, but only in context to an unbeliever? Why was the Greek phrase "age to come" translated as eternity or eternal in some places, but not in all verses referring to time? Something is not quite right in Latinville.

To conclude my above language misstep theme, allow me to give an example by telling a true story. Initially, some may view the first line of this story as crude, but after reading the whole story you'll discover there's no reason for offence. I'll start by saying; most men that I've met have heard the crude sounding quote: "It's cold enough to freeze the balls off a brass monkey". This sentence or quote conjures up a vivid picture in the mind of someone listening that is totally contrary to the original intent. Now, let's look into the history of where this particular phrase originated.

About 150 years ago, the U.S. Navy Department still used an old style cannon on the deck of the warships. Positioned on the sides of the cannons were large iron trays called "monkeys". These monkeys were used as a means for the cannonballs to be stacked in a pyramidal fashion for easy access. This became problematic for the Navy, because whenever you stack iron cannon balls on an iron container--everything rusts together.  So, the U.S. Navy came up with a solution by stacking the iron cannon balls on a brass tray instead of one made of iron.  This became problematic as well, because whenever the air temperature dropped to around freezing, the brass tray--the "Brass Monkey" would shrink, and the cannonballs would roll off the tray.  It makes perfect sense for a sailor to say:  "It's cold enough to freeze the balls off a brass monkey".

True or not, Wiktionary claims it came from the Naval Historical Center, so what's my point?  This took place only about a hundred and fifty years ago from people who spoke our same language--from the same culture, but with obvious technological differences.   This history came from a people who generally believed about most things pretty much the same way as we do now.  If I wouldn't have elaborated by giving a context and setting up the story, there is absolutely no doubt that you as a reader would have come to the wrong conclusion about the phrase:  "It's cold enough to freeze the balls off a brass monkey".

A consideration while reading the Bible:  Most readers of this book, or of the Bible, will not admit they do not know the true context of what was written from ancient manuscripts, and later formed and made into our bibles. Most Christians believe context is referring to the before and after verse of whatever scripture is read, yet this is only partially true.  True context requires a study to have a good idea what was going on at the time words were spoken. Not just that, but who was present, what was the possible motive for the dialogue or written instruction, having at least an idea about the cultural implications-- meaning the mindset of the recipients. Then finally after the appropriate research is made, one must ask if what I'm reading in the Bible is applicable for everyone? If not, for who then--what are the instructions, and for what circumstance? Most people who read the Bible don't know what context means much less practice it. I'm as guilty as everyone else, and I know we all could do better in this area.

Consideration Eight: Changing Jesus


So far, in a simplistic way, I pointed out historical evidence and language discrepancies to be considered. As a consideration, I have also given a few examples of why and who added meanings or words to our bibles.


I titled consideration number eight as: "Changing Jesus" in order to use, as an example, word usage versus the intent of what I'm trying to convey. Was I trying to convey that Mary changed Jesus' dirty diapers in changing Jesus? We all know it had to be done in some form or another--I wonder if Joseph helped? Did Jesus change from a boy into a man? Was that what I was referring in my title? After He was baptized and came back from the wilderness, did this experience change Him? Remember, He did start operating with more power and authority after His wilderness experience.  I could have easily made the title, Jesus changed rather than changing Jesus and nothing would have changed... other than Jesus.

Jesus changed my life; how about yours? What I want to discuss has nothing to do with any of the above examples, but you wouldn't have known that if my word usage was written in a different language, or if I didn't clarify it in some way.  Now let's move on to the consideration I am really trying to convey.

Let's play act for a moment and say I'm a Bible college graduate or a pastor who seems to know the Bible well.  You as the reader, will be playing a believer who has done some of your own research, and you want to point out/convey a different perspective than what I believe as a pastor.  As a pastor and teacher, the evidence of my beliefs are founded upon a long history of tradition, my formal education, and what my peers have always said.  As an example of those beliefs I would say to you--the Bible, the inerrant word of God teaches that a person needs to repent of sin, or in hell they're going to be tormented by fire for all eternity.  (sound familiar?) You would respond by saying--no, the Bible does not teach that, rather it teaches... You need to change your mind about missing the mark or after you die you're going to go through a testing and a purification in the age to come.  Your response to my fictional pastor/teacher would be no different than how Jesus responded to the Pharisees/teachers in Matthew

5:38-39, as in: "You have heard it said an eye for an eye and a tooth for a tooth, **but** I tell you...."


A consideration while reading the Bible: In Exodus 21:24, Leviticus 24:20, and in Deuteronomy 19:21--these verses talk about an eye for an eye, and tooth for a tooth. If man didn't influence or add to what God said or intended, then why did Jesus change and disagree with so much of what was written in scripture? The law, the scripture was *"the word"* of His day. Another example and important point; Jesus said **"You have heard it said"**.... He did not say the word of God says, the scripture says, nor does the Torah say! Jesus disagreed with the scripture of His day on a number of occasions, so how can people claim the Bible says all scripture is inspired by God? Jesus certainly could not agree, and on occasion He spoke out against what Christendom considers God's word!


More than any other verse, Christianity has used 2 Timothy 3:16 to prove their claim that the Bible is The Word of God:

"All scripture is inspired of God and profitable for...".

I will prove that 2nd Timothy is NOT really saying that. This verse is a perfect example of how a translation error can change the entire meaning of what was originally intended. I will now repeat the verse above by quoting what it says in most, if not in all of the Latin translated Bibles, 2 Timothy 3:16 claims:

"All scripture is inspired of God and profitable for..." (incorrect translation).

Yet in the Greek; the same verse states: "All scripture inspired of God" **is** profitable (correct translation).

This is stating the **EXACT OPPOSITE** of what it says in the Latin influenced Bible, and it also tells me that not all scripture is inspired by God. You may need to reread the differences a couple more times. This is why Jesus didn't agree with some scripture and felt a need to change it, or had a different perspective of what was written! Let's not forget God called the scribes liars in Jeremiah 8:8 as well.

Christendom can't have it both ways. It just doesn't add up. I see it as two choices:
1: Man is born with a carnal mind, corrupted by sin, influenced by family, friends, culture, and environment--thus influencing what was written in the Bible. Or, think about it.

227

2.  The Bible is the inerrant word of God, even though Jesus on occasion changed or had disagreements about what was stated in it.

The first choice backs up why Jesus disagreed the way He did, and the second choice describes a schizophrenic God that is in conflict with Jesus.

I find it ironic--those same people who demand the belief of free will--will also push the narrative that the Bible is inerrant by implying those who wrote scripture were in an almost zombie-like state, and the Spirit of God took control over what was written.  So much for their free will huh?

Allow me to chase the proverbial rabbit for a moment with this statement:  God knew we couldn't do it, so Jesus fulfilled the law for us by obeying all the rules!  No He didn't; Jesus actually **broke** some of the rules!  There is story after story of Jesus doing this kind of thing, upsetting the cart, and changing what was considered the truth by Pharisees who were required to memorize huge portions of scripture. Yet, Jesus clearly had a different perspective than they did--no wonder these same people were so mad at him, and often looked for an excuse to stone Him.

Yes, Jesus did fulfill the law, but what law or laws are we talking about?  Did Jesus fulfill the written law by following all the rules?  God supposedly gave the commandment about keeping the Sabbath--Jesus was accused of breaking the Sabbath--so, according to me, I guess He didn't fulfill that one!  The law Jesus fulfilled wasn't about the written law of Moses, nor any other written code.  I believe He came to fulfill the law that cannot be written on parchment, but only on the heart--the law of love.

"Love does no harm to a neighbor; therefore **love is the fulfillment of the law** (Romans 13:10).

"Owe no one anything except to love one another, for he who loves another has **fulfilled the law**" (Romans 13:8).

Since Jesus had no disagreements with the law of love, He could fulfill it.  There are laws going on within our church walls that love has nothing to do with.  Do any on this list sound familiar?

The law of adhering to the letter of the written word while ignoring the intent of the Spirit.

- The unspoken laws promoting ignorance.
- The law of making people accountable.
- The law of fear.
- The law of improper judgment.
- The law of the Bible being the inerrant word of God.

- The law that promotes idolatry by calling the Bible the word of God, when the Bible calls Jesus The Word of God.
- The law that pastors have the corner on the market concerning truth.

These laws are not about love, but about power, authority and control--no different of an agenda than what was happening when our bibles were being written and translated. Some Christians view the law of love as weak, without discipline, and permissive. If this is you, read no further; only God has the ability to open the blind eyes of this kind of perverted viewpoint.

To conclude this portion, let's reiterate--what exactly is the consideration I'm asking for? While confronting the people about the "Bible" of their day--Jesus reversed or had a different perspective about much of it. In some cases it was to the extreme, as in 180 degrees out from how the Pharisees believed. Just like some Christians of today, they had available to them the very scripture they believed was of God as well. Yet, this miracle working man who claimed to be the Son of God--He refused to agree with some of it. Jesus knew of the distorted influence of man on scripture, but there are those within Christendom who refuse to see scripture as anything but inerrant.

## Consideration Nine:  Frogs

I was taught that if you put a frog in cold water and slowly turn up the heat to the boiling point, the frog will die without any evidence of danger.  This is precisely my view of the traditions of men within the church.  If there was no danger involved with tradition, then **why did Jesus warn us** of it? (Mark 7:13)  Can leaven be a direct result of tradition?  Jesus speaking: "Take heed and beware of the leaven of the Pharisees and the Sadducees."  (Mark 16:6, Matthew 16:11&12, Mark 8:13, Mark 8:15, Luke 12:1)  Take note of how many verses there are to warns us.

A consideration while reading the Bible:  In the Bible I was using, out of fourteen times the word tradition is mentioned in the New Testament, eleven of those times were dripping with sarcasm, or had a negative view.  And yet, most of us are proud to say I adhere to traditional Christian doctrines, or we are proud to be called a traditional Christian.  If anyone varies from tradition, they would be looked down upon by most Christians, with less respect, and put into a judgmental category...and the heat gets turned up.

Here are a few examples of the traditions I'm talking about.  Don't forget about the frog.  It all starts with... There's a Santa Claus and Easter bunny.  Did our parents and family lie to us as a child?

Harmless?  Probably, but these little things begin to condition us to believe falsehoods...and the heat is turned up.  There's a boogie man that will get you if you're not good...and the heat is turned up.

- The church is defined as a place you go rather than whom you are...and the heat gets turned up.
- Everything that God is saying and doing in the church--it must be cleared through the pastor...and the heat gets turned up.
- All will agree that God cannot be put into a box, and yet if anyone thinks outside the box they are labeled a heretic, New Ager, on the outer fringe of Christianity...and the heat is turned up.
- No discussion that differs from tradition is allowed...and the heat is turned up.
- The Bible states that Christ is called The Word of God, but tradition teaches the Bible--a book is the word of God...and the heat is turned up.
- Jesus died for our sins, but only if you...and the heat is turned up.
- The Bible teaches God will save and reconcile all, but tradition teaches God will only save a few...and the heat is turned up.
- The Bible states no one can thwart God's will, but tradition teaches that man's will is all-powerful...and the heat is turned up.
- The Bible teaches God through Christ paid the ransom for sin, but tradition adds to what God said with a yes, but only if...and the heat is turned up.

- The Bible teaches God has absolute sovereignty to manipulate circumstances to bend the will of man to the will of God, but tradition teaches God is limited by man's free will...and the heat is turned up.
- Tradition does indeed teach that God loves man, yet He gives up most men to endless torture...and the heat is turned up.
- God sent his Son to make the payment for sin for every man, but tradition makes most men pay for their own sins in hell...and the heat is literally turned up.
- Tradition teaches that God allows mankind to fall into sin in the Garden of Eden, with full knowledge that in the end, He would not be able to redeem most of them...and the heat is turned up.
- Tradition teaches that God wants all men to be saved, but will damn most of them...and the heat is turned up.
- God tells us to love and do good to our enemies, but tradition teaches the same God will torment his enemies endlessly...and the heat is turned up.

Where did these Traditions come from? When and where did they originate and how? If you say the Bible, you obviously have not done your homework, because most traditions of men are not in the Bible! It is killing us, slowly boiling away the fruit of the Spirit within us. It's killing our testimony. The world thinks we are nuts and off the deep end.  Guess what? They're right! Some traditions are killing the Good News, i.e., nullifying the work of the cross within the individual.  Obviously nothing can permanently undo what Christ accomplished on the cross.

I'm a firm believer that Christ is the Word of God (1st John 1:1 & Rev. 19:13).  Is the church nullifying the Word of God the working of Christ within the life of a believer, due to the traditions of men? How, you may ask?--by turning up the heat of tradition, and putting people under the burden of religious false teaching.  What I mean by "burden"-- it's taught within TRADITIONAL Christianity, the burden of salvation is entirely on the shoulders of the individual...and the heat is turned up.  What I mean by "religious false teaching"--the free will doctrine is taught in  TRADITIONAL Christian circles, which in turn feeds the individual responsibility narrative...and the heat is turned up.

Don't get me wrong, I'm all for taking responsibility for one's own actions, but not when it "nullifies" the work of the cross.  How does Christendom do this?  Taking responsibility for your own salvation promotes the idea that what Christ accomplished was inefficient--"nullifying".  Another way of putting it--Jesus needs the willingness and help of the sinner in order to redeem them.  For those who believe this way--how much credit does the sinner get as in comparison to the credit Christ gets?

What is the ratio, and is there an example of this ratio within scripture? This is a perfect example of how traditions and doctrines of men have "nullified the work of the cross" within the minds of a believer. What makes matters worse is our church leaders, like the Pharisees, refuse to look beyond traditional teaching and embrace a true Godly paradigm shift, realizing how Christ did a complete, finished work.

Allow me to share a quote from Einstein: "Insanity: Doing the same thing over and over again and expecting different results." I've been a believer in the loving sacrifice of God through Christ for over 40 years, and I have been involved with leading praise and worship for about the same amount of time. My point: I can go to any traditional Christian church and nothing has changed in 40 years, except the style of a few songs. One may experience the same programs, invitations, Bible studies, potlucks, an array of guest speakers, appointed pastors and teachers, and all the while hope for a fresh anointing, something new, something different from God. Doing the same thing over and over, year after year, expecting a different result--is insanity.

Yes, we have a will, but it doesn't overpower God's will, so how is our will involved in order to stop the insanity? My opinion is a person must have a willingness to put aside everything, and let me emphasize everything. Ask God for a hunger for the truth like you never have before, and mean it! Instinctively and out of habit you'll want to pick up all the familiar teachings, all the old religious biases, and all the comforts of where you left off. Don't do it! We all have a tendency to put <u>trust in the things we've learned</u> instead of truly <u>trusting in God</u>. We've been taught that they are one and the same. ***News flash***--they are not!

It is extremely difficult to be patient while waiting on God to speak to us. Sometimes the wait can be months or years, and the whole while you'll feel the pull to get back into the groove of traditional Christianity, because they have something to say that will line up with what you have already been led to believe. To top it all off, you'll be tempted to think it's God doing the pulling. If that happens--take a closer look and you'll realize fear is involved. These considerations sound an awful lot like a formula, and yet I know formulas rarely work. I'm just saying it's how it happened to me. However, I have discovered a common denominator required for this "change", this paradigm shift in thinking to happen--you've got to want it and to ask for it! To want something that is truly different--I warn you--it will shake your foundation to the core! So don't do it unless you're willing to experience the most exciting adventure of a lifetime, but it won't seem like an adventure at first.

Your traditional Christian friends will think you're wack-a-doodle, being led astray, or falling off the deep end. This judgment by others will occur with no regard for the peace you will be exhibiting. You will now have a peace that God has an awesome plan of redemption for all of His creation. They will unknowingly ignore the greater manifestation of the fruit of the Spirit evident in your life. Once you're free from traditions of men, you'll realize religious tradition has blinded your friends and family. Hopefully you'll have empathy towards them, remembering how you've been there and done that. You will be tempted to be angry about the years of deception you've endured, but consider exercising a degree of love and patience instead. Always keep in mind that we all see through a glass dimly to one degree or another, thus, we are all deceived about something to one degree or another.

In conclusion: How we view God is in direct correlation to how we treat other people. Our traditional Christian view of God does not allow us to view everyone equally...and the heat is turned up. Most readers will view this topic as a doctrinal difference, dividing the body of Christ, the church. I do not. I only view it as a consideration, because right, wrong, or indifferent, God will have his way in the end.... period!

Consideration Ten: Idolatry

When a Christian thinks of idolatry the story of Moses and the Ten Commandments come to mind.

For those not familiar with the story let me paraphrase. Moses heads up the mountain to have a talk with God. While he's up there, the folk left behind make an idol out of gold. Where did they get the gold? Was it just lying around with the inscription, don't touch, reserved for future idol worship? No, the gold came with them from Egypt. Anyway...the gold was gathered up from the masses of people who were in total agreement with making an idol. For generations these masses of Hebrews were heavily influenced by the Egyptian culture; it was now a way of life for them. So it was perfectly natural to make a deity, worship it, and to ask it to get them out of that damnable desert.

Was it possible there was a rumor circulating throughout the camp that Pharaoh was angered with Moses and his God, so as a punishment Pharaoh kicked them all out of Egypt? I've often wondered what the motive might have been--why those following Moses were so willing to go against his God by making an idol. I realize this is just a fun conjecture, but if I were in their sandals, I'd be pretty ticked off with Moses.

These folks were not Yahweh loving, God abiding, the cream-of-the-crop, chosen people. I bet most of them didn't even really want to leave Egypt. If this was not the case, then why did they moan, groan, and complain all the time? They had it made in Egypt. Slaves yes, but all their needs and comforts of home were provided. However, our

Western thinking, promoted by Christianity, will tell us that the Israelites were relieved to finally be set free from the bondage of slavery. We would feel that way of course, raised in the free culture of America. This is one of many examples of how we project our thinking and culture on the reality of what might have really been taking place.

Anyway, back to Moses going up the mountain... some of those left behind decided to take matters into their own hands. They had a party, formed a calf made out of gold and proceeded to worship it. The golden calf was made by the hands of men, and in the eyes of journeymen craftsmen it was considered perfect and without flaw. The idol was lifted up and considered holy. It was then worshipped, and finally was given the name God. Take note of the underlined descriptions: "Made by the hands of men, perfect and without flaw, considered holy, worshipped, and given the name of God."

A consideration while reading the Bible: This will no doubt step on a lot of toes, as in what I would call a shocking similarity to what happened in the Moses story. The Bible was made by the hands of men, by journeymen craftsmen called scribes and translators. In the eyes of most Christians, it is taught to be perfect, inerrant, and without flaw. It is described as having the highest of authority, loved by some, and even called holy, which can be perceived as <u>worship</u>.  And finally...finally it's <u>given the name of God</u>, the name given to Christ alone, ie, The Word of God!

I used to believe the same way myself without ever knowing why.  Now I'm no longer afraid to question, to judge, and rightly divide what is written in the Bible.  The way Christendom looks at the Bible is an error in judgment, and will be covered in greater detail in the next chapter.

Chapter 10


Rightly Dividing The Word of Truth (II Tim. 2:15)


      Rightly dividing the word of truth from what? Simply put, from words that are NOT true! Far too much written in the Bible causes me to question God's love. Am I the only one who has been horrified by some of the stories written inside those pages? There is a life applicable, easy to understand, child like answer to the conundrum of how it's been recorded, of an all loving God committing such atrocities.


      This may be a long chapter for obvious reasons. The Bible spans centuries of time, multiple languages, and diverse cultures. There have been a number of considerations I've already addressed in other chapters that included, but not in any order of significance: Exposing mistranslations, language differences, cultural differences, inconsistencies in the various bibles, things that are believed that are not in scripture, yet promoted as if they were.


      The answers are within this chapter if you're willing to put aside the one doctrine of men that has perverted how Christians view and read their bibles. I'm referring to the doctrine of Bible inerrancy. When I discovered errors in the Bible, I had to ask myself; how do I avoid being deceived then latter deceive others due to doctrines of men?  The answer is simple yet profound--I now JUDGE scripture! Doctrines of men will scream:  HERECY!  LUNACY! WHO ARE YOU TO JUDGE SCRIPTURE?  WHO DO YOU THINK YOU ARE?  BY WHAT AUTHORITY?  I have finally escaped the cocoon that kept me from getting my head wrapped around some of those confusing Bible verses and stories.  I'm NO LONGER afraid to judge scriptures... I now "rightly divide" them.

I judge scripture this way:
- Do the verses or stories I read endorse God's character, i.e. love?  By what "authority" do I judge?  LOVE is my authority!
- A child's approach would be:  Do they cause me to trust God more, or to trust Him less?
- Is my understanding of these verses bathed in and does it bring out in me the fruit of God's Spirit,... or the fruit of fear?
- If fear is involved, it is NOT of God, because God's "perfect" love casts out fear.  What kind of fear?  In 1st John it spells it out clearly... FEAR OF PUNISHMENT FROM GOD!

If I read something in the Bible or elsewhere that doesn't compliment God's character, and bring out His fruit--I view it as words from men, i.e. doctrines of men, and NOT words from God. Perhaps it could have been a horrible mistranslation. In all honesty, most people view the words in the Bible through a lens coated with doctrines of men. However, when I "rightly divide" doctrines of men from words from God, I find TREASURE! Simple? You betcha, it's never proven me wrong, and it won't you either.

In addition to judging scripture via the standard of God's character--there's a technical, historical, and cultural side as well in determining the accuracy of some Bible stories.  By looking into ancient Jewish history, one will discover how barbaric and tribal these folks really where.  So, when you come across one of those blood thirsty, cruel sounding Bible stories--think about this:  When a commander of a Hebrew army wanted to conquer a neighbor, in most cases he would simply send out a raiding party to do so.  If they were successful, the scribes would write it down as if God pre-sanctioned the attack and commanded them to do so.  However, if they were unsuccessful in their campaign, that meant God was angry and was using the loss as a punishment for something else they did wrong.  This is one of the reasons it's stated in Jeremiah 8:8 and 23:36:
"How can you say, `We are wise, And the law of the LORD is with us'? But behold, the lying pen of the scribes has made it into a lie." (8:8)
"For ye have perverted the words of the living God, of the LORD of hosts our God." (23:36)

What if the above Bible verses never existed? I would still have all the proof I need that someone is lying to us in scripture. What is that proof? JESUS! He said "if you see Me, you see the Father", and Jesus never behaved the way God has been portrayed in some of the stories in the Old Testament. Everything Jesus said doesn't line up with the actions God has been accused of doing.

Let's be clear--a loving God would never sanction the murder of innocents. Due to the scribes writing bogus scripture, preachers and evangelists for centuries have been making self-righteous claims and giving excuses for why God would slaughter men, women, and children. Also, think about this: The reason God wouldn't allow King David to build a temple was because of the innocent blood spilled in His name. This rejection wasn't about Bathsheba and how David sanctioned the murder of her husband, because David didn't do that in the name of God. It was about all the other atrocities Israel previously did in God's name.

I believe I have "rightly divided the word of truth" within the Bible, from words that are NOT true. I have addressed the falsehood of an inerrant Bible, and how some words take on a different meaning when in context to an "unbeliever" versus a "believer" (example: hell for the unbeliever instead of death/grave for the believer).

In a previous chapter I have pointed out how the Strong's Concordant contradicts itself by defining the English word "eternal" as meaning the same as the Greek word "Aonian", which is NOT correct. However, Aonian is the correct word found in the Greek bibles which means a "segment of time". But, the problem lies in how the Strongs Concordant does indeed define "Aonian" as a "segment of time", but ALSO meaning a "time without end"! Common sense tells you, linguistically it simply can't be both a time without end AND a segment of time.

I've briefly uncovered the major changes the Latins did with the Greek manuscripts when producing the Latin Vulgate in AD 440--how and why they promoted the concept of hell (infernum), thus inserting it into the Bible of their day when it wasn't found within the Jewish writings, nor the Greek manuscripts. Later in future chapters, I want to explore the history of how the concept of hell began.

History. Did I happen to mention history? The argument I hear most is how history is not dependable, because of who might have written it. In some contexts, that may be true, but in the way I'm referring--the actual history does not change, only the perception of it changes. For example, the West was settled here in America, a historical fact. You'll get a different perspective from a white historian than from a Native American historian, but the fact does not change that historically the West was settled. This is the definition and context I'm referring, when I say history.

Every Christian has at his or her fingertips this kind of informational history when discovering who wrote the Bible and when it was written--not only who and when, but what was going on politically and/or socially at the time. There is no excuse for ignorance. The problem I've witnessed within Christendom is how people confuse history with faith. If there's ever a discrepancy between the two, usually a Christian will apply blind faith and ignore history. This is why the average Christian gets so excited when history and science backs up their beliefs. I used to. There is nothing as powerful as a testimony that encompasses an agreement of faith, science, and history, leaving no room for argument.

Do you recall my mentioning in topic number 5 of the previous chapter, how there is historical evidence of many scriptures that were later added to the Bible, because they were never found within the earliest known manuscripts? To refresh your memory they were: Mark 16:17-18, Luke 24:51, John 7:53, John 8:12, and 1st John 5:7. These scriptures carry the burden of major doctrinal beliefs. Many of these beliefs I have adhered to, and yet the knowledge of them being added at a later date causes my intellect to wonder why they were added. I don't have all the answers to why they were later added, and I couldn't care less, because I have the freedom to judge--to "rightly divide" them in the same fashion as I do all others.


However, history does teach at the time of Christ there were many who would use someone else's name when putting quill to parchment.  It wasn't unusual in that day for a person to write letters in another's name.  This was done to gain recognition and notoriety from people they were involved with.  Do we believe con men only exist in our century?  I've been taught from the beginning of my walk that theologians are not sure who exactly wrote the book of Hebrews.  Yet, I never hear pastors, teachers, or theologians red-flag this historical truth--giving them doubt to question its validity.  However, if someone outside their circle of influence (like myself) were to bring to light other historical data that might cause one to question the validity of other Bible passages-- they choose to ignore that data, and usually resort to name calling at the person presenting it.


To conclude this line of reasoning, Jesus offers his thoughts that most will only view as a consideration rather than a warning in Matthew 24:5: "For many will come in my name, saying, I am the Christ, and will deceive many".

I view this verse as meaning:  Many will come claiming to be believers, in full agreement that Jesus is the Christ, and deceive us.  This is a clear warning that should cause us to "... study to show yourself approved..." (2nd Timothy 2:15).  It's not dangerous or bad conduct to question what has been and is presently taught; it's healthy and wise, especially if your discoveries cause you to rely and become more dependent on God.

All these examples are meant as continuing evidence of why there's a problem when blind faith and history collide.  Of course a person has the right and ability to ignore historical evidence and rely on blind faith.  However, I consider hungering for the truth a far better way of doing things than being fattened by deception--the theme of this entire book.

Have you ever played the game of gossip? For those who haven't, it goes like this... Someone writes a short story on a piece of paper.  Only one person is allowed to read it and then verbally whispers the story into the ear of someone else.  This whispered story continues from person to person until everyone in the room has heard it.  The last person compares his or her version with what was actually written on the piece of paper, and shares the discrepancy with the crowd for a good laugh.  There is ALWAYS a discrepancy even though the period of time was short and only a few participants were involved.

This game is an analogy of how the first 11 chapters of our Bible was written. The big difference is we are not referring to just a few people in a room only requiring 5 to 10 minutes of time. I'm trying to clarify the accuracy of the first 11 chapters of our Bibles, that required a countless number of people, spanning over a dozen generations, telling story after story , little to nothing in writing, and then finally getting to Moses. Moses lived sometime between the years of 1300 - 1500 BC. Most of the stories Moses wrote about happened long before he was born. This is history. However, blind faith would have us believe not one story was exaggerated during 1300 years of storytelling from multiple people.

Traditional Christianity wants us to believe everything Moses wrote is completely true, faultless, and inerrant. Christians need to be better educated about the history of their faith. **News Flash** We can have faith and be intelligent at the same time. I have no problem putting my trust in an awesome God rather than stories based on hear-say. I agree, portions of these stories are based upon truth, and some may very well be true. I'm just stating--the Bible is not inerrant. **Well!... how do you know? You can't just pick and choose which parts of the Bible are true!** Why not! You do! However, there's a correct way to choose, by rightly dividing.  What we both can do is be educated as well as putting complete trust in God's character, and use that character as a measuring rod to judge what we're reading in the Bible.


Rabbit chasing time again... the very people who accuse others of picking and choosing which parts of the Bible are true are guilty of consistently doing the same thing themselves. Everyone does, to some degree or another; no one is exempt. However, traditional Christian teaching actually encourages and endorses the pick and choose technique.  How?  By ignoring dozens of scriptures that follow the same theme while picking and choosing just a handful of scriptures to support their tradition.  The next paragraph lines up perfectly with what I define as following a theme.


In the below examples, I will only be using five out of the 73 scriptures I used in chapter 5 to show how traditionalists will accuse me of promoting a particular doctrine over another.  I am not!  In this case I simply choose to believe what was written, because it lines up beautifully with the character of God, with the actions of Christ, and is confirmed by over six dozen comparable verses.  In perfect context to God's will and the purpose of the cross--those five examples are:

- 1st Timothy 2:4 - God will have all to be saved
  1st Timothy 2:6 - Salvation of all is testified in due time
- Ephesians 1:10 - All come into Him at the fullness of times
- John 4:42 - Jesus is savior of the world
- Philippians 2:9 every tongue will confess Jesus is Lord

If you research these verses and the other 68 like them mentioned in chapter five, you'll notice there are no conditions attached to them like: "Only if you believe," or, "you must first confess," or, "you must repent", or, "it's only a gift if you receive it". When speaking to a Christian traditionalist, they will add these phrases as prerequisites to validate the above scriptures. Then, for their conditions to be relevant, they have to pull verses from elsewhere in scripture, out of context, to justify a man-made, perverted doctrine. Remember the precedent of Adam adding to what God said in the Garden of Eden, by telling Eve that God said not to touch the fruit? This kind of thing is still going on in every Christian church of our day.

It becomes problematic when most Christians don't know or believe the Bible's of our day are copies of copies of copies of translations upon translations upon translations upon copies of translations, spanning many years. Not one book (letter) in our Bible was translated from the hand of an original author that we've all read about. Not only that, but some of the ancient manuscripts could have been penned by forgers. The canonization process had concerns about how some men practiced identity theft of their day by representing themselves as Peter, Paul, John, etc. Unfortunately there seems to be more secular people who know this as truth than the average believer, and this simple example of ignorance is often used as a weapon by people, against those who are believers.

Our ignorance in the form of blind faith is a terrible witness, giving the world cause to ignore our message. I've heard teaching that being shunned by the world is a good sign you're doing something right. What a load of bullshit! Being separate from the world doesn't mean we're supposed to be stupid and ignorant. I don't know how many times I've heard a person accuse Christians of coming across as holier-than-thou. Why do some Christians give an impression like that? Answer: Because they've been led to believe they are above the average person of the world due to their acts of obedience. In reality-- this is called self-righteousness. We're viewed as just religious kooks that historically have been proven wrong, over and over again. This shouldn't be. We need to be on top of things, well educated and honest rather than doling out multiple forms of deception. What kind of deception? Deceiving the church and trying to deceive the world into believing that the Bible is inerrant. It only takes the tiniest amount of historical research to disprove such an erroneous belief.

Far too much in the Bible will not add up until we come to a conclusion that men's intentions and their words are deeply married and mixed into the purposes of God. Basic reasoning and simple logic dictate that the Bible is fallible as long as man is involved, because man is fallible.

Where is it written in the Bible that scripture is inerrant? In the previous chapter I proved that not all scripture is inspired by God, so where did that notion--that doctrine of men come from? I suggest putting blind faith aside and use the Bible as a tool I believe it was meant to be. Nowhere is it written in the Bible that scripture or the Bible is called or considered The Word of God. Nowhere in the Bible is the Bible or scripture called Holy. God is Holy, not a book!

The Islamic Qur'an is considered holy by Muslims, and look on the evening news at what they do when people come against their "holy" book. As a side note, can one perceive their actions as worshiping the Qur'an? Perception can be wrong, but from the outside looking in--it can understandably be viewed as worship! Is it possible the world perceives the scary Bible-thumping Christian on the corner with the same trepidation as that of a radical Muslim? **Well!... How dare you! We don't cut**

**people's heads off for not believing in our Bible!**
No, not today we don't, but historically there was a time we did, as well as disemboweling someone until they died. How about torture and burning people alive when they disagreed with the established view of the Bible? The only reason we don't act that barbaric any longer is because we're content, fat and sassy. In my opinion, we're still the same religious people at heart. Only the laws of the land have changed.

You don't think we're still the same religiously cruel people at heart? Generally speaking, with a few exceptions, instead of disemboweling someone, we now cut to shreds a persons integrity and invalidate anything they have to say. Instead of burning someone alive, we now burn bridges between people who have different perspectives, and then claim they're going to burn in hell for all eternity. We as a church torture people with slanderous names such as heretic, New Ager, out there, and being on the fringe. With the same breath, members of the church will say "come to Jesus just as you are, He will never reject you", then we as the church do the rejecting! It's followed up with "God is love and requires us to love people, even our enemies!" We then shun, ostracize, and call people our enemies when they don't agree with us, and then we expect those same people to believe the Christian church is on the side of a loving God.(?) Yes, I believe the church is trying to be, but a major paradigm shift in thinking is necessary along with an honest, fearless desire for the truth. We can no longer be mindless puppets the atheists claim we are.


Scriptures have to be inerrant in order to be considered the word of God. BINGO! That's the crux of the whole problem isn't it? Religion has produced a conundrum. I often wondered, when and where did the term "word of God" come from in defining our Bible? I've been involved with many churches with diverse denominational ties, and I can't remember anyone in the early seventies calling the Bible the word of God. But, of course, I was a mid-teen at the time and could have been oblivious to it. However, as an adult, this particular phrase and definition of our Bible has grown into a Christian fad.


Why does the Christian community call the Bible the word of God? It seems that suddenly it became a fad when it wasn't always called the word of God. Shortly, you'll understand why it happened, when I quote my friend Jim who will be answering where that phrase came from. I grew up hearing it called "The Good Book, The Scripture, or simply The Bible", but it changed in my short lifetime and became a fad calling the Bible "The Word of God".

Prior to the sixties, if you opened any literature or walked into a park and greeted a perfect stranger and said: "It's a beautiful day--are you gay"? At that time in history they would have answered with something like: "Yes, it is a beautiful day. It makes me happy, so I have a reason to be gay." Today, if you were to approach a total stranger in the park and ask: "Are you gay?" That person would respond with a yes or a no about being homosexual. Yes, language and word meanings can change over time, but what I personally observed in the gay community was not a change of meaning over time. The movement started as a dynamic "fad" to be called "gay" within the homosexual community. Then much later the new meaning for the word gay became culturally acceptable within society as a whole.

Likewise, it became a "fad" to call the Bible The Word of God, and now it's culturally acceptable within Christendom to do so. Yet, it's very clear in the Bible **Who** is the Word of God. It is not a thing, it is not a book, it is a person--the person of Christ--"the One whose robe was dipped in blood and His name is called the Word of God". (Rev. 19:13)

During my lifetime I've witnessed this Christian fad spread like wildfire. It crosses all denominational lines when it never used to. You who are middle-aged and older--think about it... I think you'll agree with the timing of all of this. My Bible doesn't teach or endorse this fad, so I felt it necessary to research it. I came up empty-handed until my friend Jim gave me a possible answer he had learned in seminary. I asked him to email me a brief summary along with his thoughts on the matter.  Other than not using my real name, I'll quote Jim as he wrote:

Why Guy

"Here are my thoughts I shared about the Bible as word of God:

Sometime in the late 150 years or so, the modernist world started emphasizing that science would start bringing us to the place of certainty about everything, and that maybe we wouldn't need faith anymore.  Christianity responded to this idea by firming up their idea about the Bible and its certainty-- making it into the very "word of God", inerrant, infallible, without fault often in its originals.

However, this is not the stated purpose of the Bible.  It is a book that is written by 40 different authors, coming from various points of view and cultures.  Sometimes, it is difficult to understand exactly what to do with certain passages, and how they fit together with other passages.  So, since Christianity was becoming certain about the Bible being the word of God, the only answer to this problem was that we would need experts on the Bible to tell us how to interpret it, how to read it. No two of these "experts" ever came up with the very same answer; this led to the biggest explosion of denominations, the dividing of Christianity, in the history of the church, each sect following its expert in each bound to hold to the incorrectness of the experts of the other denominations. This was the very fruit of the doctrine of the Bible as the word of God.

Personally, I believe that move was one of the greatest mistakes the church ever made, and the damage from that doctrine's wake is the proof. Even now, as the modernist era is over and we have moved past the demand for certainty, the divide between Christians is very deep. Even between Christians who have left the system."


I'm sure Jim would agree, the history about it should be considered, even though it doesn't encompass every reason for why the term "Word of God" became popular. Jim also referred to the organized church as "the system", which brought to my mind an additional motive for why the Bible is being taught as infallible, inerrant, holy, the word, and the word of God. Who do we have in the church system? People! Do any of these people depend on the church system for advancement in their careers? Oh big time! We're talking big business here: Seminaries, Bible colleges, professors, Bible scholars, pastors, teachers; an array of paid staff such as secretaries, accountants, and janitors.

Some within the system have become famous, world-renowned, televised, mega institutions. Think about this... what is the foundational **tool** of their trade? The Bible of course! Naturally it needs to be infallible and inerrant. You wouldn't want to use a faulty tool in your trade would you? What if you were an accountant with an adding machine that didn't add correctly, or a mechanic trying to use a wrench that didn't fit? The list goes on and on; the Bible is no different.

Having an infallible Bible would give the career-minded person within the system more authority and credibility. We all have to understand; the Bible has been MADE--it was created purposely and was progressively morphed into a tool to fit into and complement the church system. Historically it was designed that way and for that exact purpose. Most people were illiterate at the time of its conception. It's not the other way around; the church system did not come from the Bible, or because of the Bible, but instead the Bible was birthed out of the church system.  This is the reason behind the division and madness between denominations.

The division is obvious, but what do I mean by "madness"?  Why else would so many God-loving, Christ believing, grace promoting people, be so willing and eager to commit idolatry?  How so?  Of course, none of these wonderful people will believe they're being idolaters, because the brainwashing is complete.  What "brainwashing"?  I've heard it said: If you repeat a lie often enough, it will become truth in the mind of a listener, as in:  The Bible is the inerrant Word of God!  From the perspective of a lot of people, it appears that quite a few Christians hold their Bibles up to the level of God.  Why not, it's viewed as His actual word.  I've seen people clutch to their Bibles as if they were holding God Himself in their hands.  Un-admitted idolatry!

I have a goofy sounding analogy to describe what I believe has happened within Christendom regarding the Bible.  Let's say I have a problem with my toilet.  **(Here he goes again Myrtle... now he's comparing the Bible to a toilet!)**  Anyway, I call a plumber.  The plumber shows up and brings in a large tool box. He fiddles with the toilet for a moment and then opens his toolbox, pushing aside the majority of his tools until he finds the exact tool needed.  I am amazed at how easy it was for him to reach this hard to get to area, with that tool.  I asked him about it and he responds with, "It's a special tool made only for this specific problem that I'm having with the toilet."  Those who know me know that I'm kind of a tool nut, so after he leaves I call all my friends and family just to tell them about this marvelous tool I've seen.  I later run out and buy one and set it on my fireplace mantel for all to see.  As time goes on I begin to infatuate about it and to be quite honest... I go off the deep end.  I begin to worship the thing!  I don't stop there... I consider it holy!

Folks, listen up.  The Bible is nothing more, nothing less than a wonderful tool in God's tool box.  Let me emphasize the following two points: No other tool can accomplish what it can; no other tool can replace it--IN THE HANDS OF A LOVING GOD, while we're being led by His Spirit!  In our hands alone it's a self-righteous, divisive weapon!

One day when I was out having lunch, thinking about the Bible as a wonderful tool--I asked God what was his favorite tool?  I believe He answered me with, you are... and him, and her, and them, as I was reviewing people within the restaurant.

In conclusion to this chapter I must encourage my reader not to be fearful about judging the Bible, but instead look at it as if it was a marriage. The Bible often talks about our relationship with one another, and our relationship with God. There are passages that refer to a relationship with Him that uses the metaphor of a bride and groom, i.e., a marriage. Like any marriage, reading and understanding the Bible is a learning process.


The Bible is a wonderful, beautiful marriage story between God and mankind--between the thoughts of man and the thoughts of God--the history of man and an extremely limited history of God. It's a marriage of words--words of man and words of God. A wonderful tool called the Bible that instructs us to "rightly divide the word of truth". Divide which words are of men and which words are of "The Way, The Truth, and The Life", to be sure which words are truly the words from God. I wholeheartedly agree that when God's Spirit reveals something true to you, through that book, that wonderful tool called the Bible--at that point in time for you specifically and personally--it becomes the word of God. I guarantee as a "fact", when God does so--what is revealed as truth will ALWAYS compliment His character of love, and NEVER... EVER cause fear! Speaking of facts-- the next chapter will delve into a few.

# Chapter 11

## Fun Facts Just For the Hell of It!

When I say "fact", I'm basing this chapter on history, language, and culture.  Fun?  Now, that might be another story.  I find it extremely fun to learn of cultures other than my own, how they describe things, and how they view their world around them.  If a culture is on the scale of "ancient", or has died out, then obviously recorded history is all we have at our disposal.  I understand that "history" is relative and I do consider that "fact" in my research.  I'm one of those who loves to delve into what might have been going through the mind of an individual, living within the ancient culture I'm investigating.  I also realize I'll be applying a certain amount of conjecture to my conclusions, but without a time machine, I have no other alternative.

One thing I know for sure is people are people, and generally speaking, all people are more alike than different--regardless of time and cultural differences. Even though people are people, I DO NOT view a different culture through my own lens as being an American living in the 21st Century. The problem I do see is how the vast majority of Christians who read their bibles--read them through the lens of their own time, language, and culture. This is a huge mistake! (Don't confuse me with the facts when my mind is made up) With all this said-- there may be a few readers of this chapter who may not agree with what I view as a "fact". If you happen to fall within this category of readers--I highly doubt you'll have much fun either, so let's begin... .

**Fact:** There is no mention within scripture of hell ever being created. So what, you might be thinking? What is mentioned in "the creation story", is everything from the Sun and stars to plants and bugs. Christendom refuses to see a problem as I do with the creation story! We are expected to believe God cares more about informing us of when and how bugs were created, than a place where countless souls would be tortured and/or separated from Him for an eternity?

**Fact:** There is no mention of hell in the Old Testament, nor the Jewish Torah, or the Talmud. Some will claim there most certainly is--at least in the Old Testament of their version of the Bible. Think about this for a moment... your version of the Bible? This will be addressed in an upcoming "fact".

**Fact:** No mention of hell in the Greek Septuagint (Greek Old Testament) circa 132 BC, yet there is mention of hell in the King James Old Testament circa 1611 AD. When and where did the hells and Hades come from in all those 1,743 years, since God never claimed to have created it in the Genesis story? Of course you won't find the word hell in the Greek, because it's not a Greek word-- right? That would mean the writers of the Greek Septuagint wouldn't use the Hebrew word of Sheol either--also right? So, what word did they use instead of Sheol--they used Hades 65 times. How's your math? The Greeks translated Sheol into Hades 65 times, yet that same Old Testament, the King James translated Sheol into hell only 31 times. What happened to all those other 34 Sheols or hells? Someone is wrong--they both can't be right. My claim is they BOTH are wrong due to the fact Sheol doesn't mean Hades or hell.

**Fact:** There is no word in the Hebrew language for an after-life in an underworld/netherword. Some will claim: "Oh yes there is, and that word is Sheol." If that is true then why didn't the Jewish religion; Judaism ever teach about a hell or an existence of an underworld/netherword?

**Fact:** Sheol is a Hebrew word for death, grave or a pit. Culturally, Sheol was never a place--it was seen as a period of time while people are dead and waiting to be **resurrected**. When describing the characteristics of Sheol, the Hebrew scriptures explain it this way:

"Whatever your hands find to do, do with all your strength, because there is no work, planning, knowledge, or wisdom in Sheol where you are going." (Ecclesiastes 9:10)

"For the living know that they will die, but the dead don't know anything. There is no longer a reward for them because the memory of them is forgotten. Their love, their hate, and their envy have already disappeared, and there is no longer a portion for them in all that is done under the sun." (Ecclesiastes 9:5-6)

The above verses explain the ancient Jewish mindset about death. It's similar to how the common person who hasn't been indoctrinated by Christianity would describe their dead, as in buried, "unseen" by the living, usually under the ground or in a crypt, having no consciousness, and no knowledge of joy or pain.

**Fact:**  Jews in general didn't believe in hell; Jesus was a Jew, so why is it a stretch to say Jesus didn't believe in an underworld or a netherworld, i.e. hell?  Jesus was considered a Rabbi by his followers, because at the beginning of His ministry, the people didn't quite understand who He was, nor His purpose for being there.  A logical conclusion would have to be reached that a Rabbi would never use a pagan word like hell or Hades, representing a pagan place, that promotes pagan beliefs of a pagan kingdom, ruled by a pagan god, from a different language and culture--while talking to Jews.

**Fact:**  Jesus never spoke the word hell, according to most historians and people who have researched language.  It is assumed Jesus spoke Aramaic and Hebrew, and that He did not speak Greek or Latin to those around Him considering the average Jew spoke Aramaic and Hebrew and not Latin.  It's not a stretch for historians to come to their language conclusion considering the sandal wearing Jesus Himself said--He came only for the house of Israel, and not for the house of Greek or Latin.

**Fact:** Even though proclaimed otherwise by Christendom, Jesus never warned anyone of hell in all His ministry. His admonitions were always referring to a real place--a trash heap called Gehenna. Once the trash was taken to the dump, they did what most cultures did and still do--they burned it. As long as they kept feeding the fire with trash, the fire wouldn't go out. This is why it states in Mk 9:22, and Mk 43-44: "... AND THE FIRE IS NOT QUENCHED".

Jesus also warned of what would happen if your eye or hand offended you. It's better to pluck it out, or cut it off rather than having either cause you to end up on this trash heap. How would your eye or hand cause such a thing? How about looking at something or someone who didn't belong to you. Then your hand would follow up by grasping what doesn't belong to you, you get caught, put to death, and your body eventually would get burned along with the rest of the trash, but in the mean time the worms would feast. As long as you keep feeding the worms carcasses--guess what happens? "... THEIR WORM DOES NOT DIE". This explains what is meant by: "... AND THE FIRE IS NOT QUENCHED and THEIR WORM DOES NOT DIE".

But NOooo!  The ancient Latin translators had a better idea.  Let's take the word Gehenna and change it to infernum (hell), and since the fire isn't "quenched", that obviously means it's eternal.  So, in some passages they added the word "eternal" to the word fire, so it would all sound like Jesus is warning everyone about ending up in an eternal, fiery hell, rather than allowing Jesus to be a practical Rabbi who wanted to warn people, if they didn't change their ways, there would be a possible and pragmatic outcome IN THEIR PRESENT LIFETIME!

What about the "worms"?  Apparently, according to the ancient Latins, God must love worms more than people.  God is going to give eternal life to worms, since they never die, and give them an endless supply of food for an eternity.  WOW!

Gehenna still exists today.  It's outside the walls of Jerusalem, and has been changed into a park.  The fire is not eternal, but has been out for over 2000 years.  The worms residing underground might actually be the descendants of those that once fed on the criminals of Jesus' day.

**Fact:**  The ancient Scandinavian tribes kept invading what would later be known as (Latin) Italy.  These invasions took place on and off again for over 300 years starting right around 9 BC, and continued to around 300 AD.  If you invade and occupy a country, are you not going to influence the country's culture--especially spanning over 300 years?  The invaders were an ancient Germanic people who were all part of Scandinavia back then.

For survival, most Scandinavian tribes were allied with one another, and they all shared the same belief in a pagan underworld/netherworld.  The ruler of their version of hell was run by a goddess who went by the name of Hel.  A coincidence?  Possibly, but I don't think so.  "Hel" is pronounced the exact same way as "hell" in English.  When reading ancient history, it became evident to me how the ancient Greeks and Latins would cannibalize each other's pagan beliefs in an afterlife.  So, I submit this hypotheses--at least a portion of the populace of ancient Italy did the same cannibalization of Scandinavian beliefs in an underworld/netherworld.

**Fact:**  Both Hel and Hades are names of a pagan god & goddess.

**Fact:** Hades was the name of a Greek pagan god of the underworld/netherworld. When reading about the ancient Greek culture, it was said that most people who believed in the afterlife were not comfortable uttering the name of Hades, so they often used the nickname of Pluto. Yet, they were still willing to use the word Hades in describing the actual place of the dead. It was all in their mind and held onto as a belief--with no basis of reality. Christians of our day are doing the same thing when they read the word Hades in their Bible.

**Fact:** Even though most cultures had their own versions of a hellish afterlife, none took hold and has influenced modern Christianity like this one: A society based on a place, later translated as hell, is a Latin invention and made into a comedy play called: Dante's Inferno.

**Fact:** The 1st commandment: "There shall be no other gods before Me", yet unknowingly, Christendom promotes the existence of Hades, named after a pagan god, and the existence of hell, named after a pagan goddess, and both places are deemed as one and the same, ruled by a god of evil known as the devil, a.k.a. satan, a.k.a. Lucifer.

**Fact:** The Apostle Paul warned of preaching a different gospel than the one he preached in Galatians 1:8-9:

"But even if we, or an angel from heaven, should preach to you a gospel contrary to what we have preached to you, he is to be accursed! As we have said before, so I say again now, if any man is preaching to you a gospel contrary to what you received, he is to be accursed!"

Notice the double emphasis of Paul's warning by mentioning the word "accursed" twice! The point: Paul never mentioned nor included the hell doctrine in all of his thirteen letters which became about 2/3rds of the New Testament. Christendom either needs to eliminate the majority of the N.T., or eliminate the hell doctrine.

Now, I will double emphasize Paul's point by saying... If you are including the hell doctrine in the gospel message--YOU ARE ACCURSED! If anyone proclaiming salvation is in reference to being saved from hell--THEY ARE ACCURSED! If you don't agree, your argument is not with me, but with the Apostle Paul.

**Fact:** By including hell, the Christian religion preaches a different gospel than Paul. I'll now expose the irony, if not the hypocrisy, within

Christendom concerning being "accursed". Christianity uses the verse in Matthew 25:41 as a means to prop up and confirm their belief in hell by sharing:

"Then He will also say to those on His left, depart from Me, accursed ones, into the eternal fire which has been prepared for the devil and his angels".

So, ironically speaking... let me get this right... "Accursed ones" are destined to hang out with the devil and his angels, in a fiery hell for all eternity? Yet, are not Christians who promote and believe in a different gospel than the one Paul preached are not destined for the same outcome?

In reference to the verse in Matthew:

First: "Eternal" is NOT in the Greek manuscripts! The correct word is "Aonian", which means a segment of time.

Second: Within scripture, "fire" is often used as a metaphor for God's intense presence. That intensity usually implies a judgment. God is love so it's not a stretch to assume His judgment is based on love, and His judgments have always been used as a means to purify.

Conclusion: The "accused ones" spoken about in Matthew are in store for an intense time of purification from a loving God.

Back to Paul and his view of "accursed": Paul explains beautifully what accursed really means as he himself wanted to be accursed on many occasions. What? Accursed is a figure of speech to mean a separating from God or Christ, not literally, but in attitude or thought--best explained in Romans 9:3:

"For I (Paul) could wish that I myself were accursed, separated from Christ for the sake of my brethren, my kinsmen according to the flesh"

Being separated from God in thought or attitude makes complete sense, as explained in 1st Corinthians 16:22:

"If anyone does not love the Lord, he is to be accursed."

My point and conclusion in all this... Christians who include the hell doctrine are mentally or intellectually separated from the character of God, which is love. Love would never create a place like hell, thus anyone who believes such a thing is separated from the very nature of God by slandering His character in regard to this belief--they are accursed!

**Fact:** The Bible speaks of lies and slander written within its pages, so how can it be inerrant?

Jeremiah 23:36: (speaking to the scribes, the ones who wrote scripture which later became the Bible) "For ye have perverted the words of the living God, of the LORD of hosts our God."

Jeremiah 8:8: "How can you say, `We are wise, And the law of the LORD is with us'? But behold, the lying pen of the scribes has made it into a lie."

But I thought "all scripture IS inspired of God and is profitable..."? (2 Timothy 3:16) Wouldn't this mean the verses in Jeremiah are wrong and NOT inspired by God? I know I've explained this conundrum in a previous chapter, but I will now reiterate once again by using the CORRECT translation of:

"All scripture inspired of God" **is** profitable..." It is clear some scripture is inspired by God when others are not. How do we know the difference between what is inspired of God and what isn't? 2nd Timothy 2:15 has the answer:

"Study to show thyself approved unto God, a workman that needs not to be ashamed, rightly dividing the word of truth."

Rightly dividing the words that are true from the words that are not!  How do we go about doing that?  In answering, again I will reiterate what I've previously written by saying I "rightly divide" scripture this way:

Do the verses and stories I read endorse God's character, i.e. love?

Do they cause me to trust God more, or to trust Him less?

Is my understanding of these verses bathed in and does it bring out in me the fruit of God's Spirit,... or the fruit of fear?

If fear is involved, it is NOT of God because God's "perfect" love casts out fear.  What kind of fear?  In 1st John it spells it out clearly... FEAR OF PUNISHMENT FROM GOD!

If I read something in the Bible or elsewhere that doesn't compliment God's character, and bring out His fruit--I view it as words from men, i.e. doctrines of men, and NOT words from God (possibly a horrible mistranslation).

In all honesty, most people view the words in the Bible through a lens coated with doctrines of men.  However, when I "rightly divide" doctrines of men from words from God, I find TREASURE!

Simple?  You betcha, it's never proven me wrong, and it won't you either.

**Fact:**  Very few Bible translations agree with how many times the word hell should be in them.

| Number of times "Hell" appears in the text in English Bible Translations | | | |
|---|---|---|---|
| Bible Translations | Old Testament | New Testament | Total |
| Douay-Rheims (Roman Catholic) | 86 | 24 | 110 |
| Bishops Bible 1568 | 35 | 24 | 59 |
| Original 1611 King James with Apocrypha | 41 | 23 | 64 |
| "Authorized" King James Version | 31 | 23 | 54 |
| Geneva Bible 1599 | 21 | 21 | 42 |
| New King James Version | 19 | 13 | 32 |
| The Voice | 0 | 17 | 17 |
| New Living Translation | 1 | 16 | 17 |
| American Standard Version (Revision of KJV) | 0 | 13 | 13 |
| New American Standard Bible | 0 | 13 | 13 |
| Revised Standard Version (Revision of KJV) | 0 | 12 | 12 |
| New Revised Standard Version | 0 | 12 | 12 |
| Revised English Bible | 0 | 13 | 13 |
| New Living Translation | 0 | 13 | 13 |

| | | | |
|---|---|---|---|
| Amplified | 0 | 13 | 13 |
| English Standard Version (ESV)***** | 0 | 14 | 14 |
| New International Version, first edition (best-selling English Bible)<br><br>New International Version (later editions)*** | 0<br><br>0 | 14<br><br>13 | 14<br><br>13 |
| New English Bible (NET) | 0 | 13 | 13 |
| Darby | 0 | 12 | 12 |
| New Century Version | 0 | 12 | 12 |
| Holman Christian Standard Bible (Southern Baptist) | 0 | 11 | 11 |
| Wesley's New Testament (1755) | | 0 | 0 |
| Scarlett's N.T. (1798) | | 0 | 0 |
| The New Testament in Greek and English (Kneeland, 1823) | | 0 | 0 |
| Young's Literal Translation (1891) | 0 | 0 | 0 |
| Twentieth Century New Testament (1900) | | 0 | 0 |
| Rotherham's Emphasized Bible (reprinted, 1902) | 0 | 0 | 0 |

| | | | |
|---|---|---|---|
| Fenton's Holy Bible in Modern English (1903) | 0 | 0 | 0 |
| Weymouth's New Testament in Modern Speech (1903) | | 0 | 0 |
| The New Testament, James Moffat, (1917) | | 0 | 0 |
| Jewish Publication Society Bible Old Testament (1917) | 0 | | 0 |
| Panin's Numeric English New Testament (1914) | | 0 | 0 |
| The New Testament, Charles B. Williams, 1937 | | 0 | 0 |
| The People's New Covenant (Overbury, 1925) | | 0 | 0 |
| Hanson's New Covenant (1884) | | 0 | 0 |
| Western N.T. (1926) | | 0 | 0 |
| NT of our Lord and Savior Anointed (Tomanek, 1958) | | 0 | 0 |
| Concordant Literal NT (1983) | | 0 | 0 |
| The N.T., A Translation (Clementson, 1938) | | 0 | 0 |

| | | | |
|---|---|---|---|
| Emphatic Diaglott, Greek/English Interlinear (Wilson, 1942) | | 0 | 0 |
| New American Bible (1970) | 0 | 0 | 0 |
| Restoration of Original Sacred Name Bible (1976) | 0 | 0 | 0 |
| Tanakh, The Holy Scriptures, Old Testament (1985) | 0 | | 0 |
| The New Testament, A New Translation (Greber, 1980) | | 0 | 0 |
| Christian Bible (1991) | 0 | 0 | 0 |
| World English Bible (in progress) | 0 | 0 | 0 |
| Orthodox Jewish Brit Chadasha [NT Only] | | 0 | 0 |
| Original Bible Project (Dr. James Tabor, still in translation) | 0 | 0 | 0 |
| Zondervan Parallel N.T. in Greek and English (1975)** | | 0 | 0 |
| Int. NASB-NIV Parallel N.T. in Greek and English | | 0 | 0 |

| | | | |
|---|---|---|---|
| (1993)** | | | |
| A Critical Paraphrase of the N.T. by Vincent T. Roth (1960) | | 0 | 0 |
| New Testament, Recovery Version, Living Stream Ministry, 1991 | | 0 | 0 |
| New American Bible Revised Edition (NABRE) Roman Catholic | 0 | 0 | 0 |
| Holy Bible In Its Original Order, Fred R. Coulter, 2007 | 0 | 0 | 0 |
| Etymological N.T. (An Ultra Literal Translation, 2011, Michael Wine) | | 0 | 0 |
| Aramaic Peshitta New Testament, 2006, Janet M. Magiera | | 0 | 0 |
| MirrorWord N.T. (Francois du Toit) still in translation | | 0 | 0 |
| Victorious Gospel of Jesus Christ, Electronic Ver. (Tentmaker Ministries) | | 0 | 0 |
| The Source N.T. (Dr. Ann Nyland), 2004, 2007 | | 0 | 0 |
| Jonathan Mitchell N.T. (Jonathan Mitchell) 2009 | | 0 | 0 |
| Tree of Life Version, Baker Bookhouse, 2016****** | 0 | 0 | 0 |

| The New Testament (David Bentley Hart) Yale University Press, 2017 | | 0 | 0 |
|---|---|---|---|
| The Message Paraphrase (Eugene Peterson, Navpress)**** | 44 | 24 | 68 |

How many hells are there?  Which bibles are right and which ones are wrong?  They all can't be correct!  Doesn't this conundrum bring up a red flag in your thinking, or are you one of those who ignore facts? (Don't confuse me with facts when they go against my beliefs) Please, don't make the same mistake I made for so many years in fearing everything you've believed is wrong!  How does any of this information disprove God is Love, and Love has a plan to reconcile all of creation to His love?  If anything, this all endorses what you as a Christian should believe about God.

At this point I feel I must address another belief in the sentiment that God miraculously protected the Bible from error.  This belief is nothing more than another perversion of trust and requires a form of blind faith.  One is led to believe they are trusting God to protect something He never said He would, by using this out of context scripture:

"Isaiah 55:11 - So will My word be which goes forth from My mouth; It will not return to Me empty, without accomplishing what I desire, and without succeeding in the matter for which I sent it."

Notice how it specifies "from My mouth", rather than from a book!? Doctrines of men will claim everything written within a book (Bible) actually came from God's mouth! Yet, in Jeremiah is plainly states that some of those words are a LIE! Technically, wouldn't that make God a liar, or double minded? People who believe this way can't have it both ways. The "book" cannot be exclusive words from a God who does not lie, when in that "book" it is written that some words written in it are a lie. If the Bible is indeed protected as some claim, this all would mean God protects those portions that He considers lies. That wouldn't make sense.

The very question, did God protect the Bible, is so important in the mind of so many Christians. Why? Because so many are putting their trust in something tangible, something they can feel and touch and hold in their hands. They can use their eyes to view a God they love so much through words written on paper. I understand that--I really do, but it's wrong, it's dangerous, and causes nothing but division in the body of Christ.

Far too many substitute their trust in God with trusting in the Bible. Why did I earlier call it dangerous? Think about it... you're trusting in the accuracy of man when interpreting, translating, writing and rewriting through a mind that has been corrupted and influenced by their own culture and personal beliefs. Blind faith is required, and blind faith in and of itself is dangerous.

Did God protect what he wanted to protect in the various Bibles--those "words" that really were from Him that we're supposed to "rightly divide" from those words that are lies? Yes, I think so because of so much good fruit in our lives that has come from His words. Why did He allow so much perversion, lies, and slander to take place in something as valuable as the Bible? Simple answer: Grace and mercy has always allowed circumstances for people to make mistakes.

Another reason I don't I believe the Bible in its entirety has been protected by God, is because there are far too many discrepancies in the various translations. Usually the reasoning I hear from Christendom is... "The general theme throughout the Bible has been protected by God.". I'm sorry to say that I've already proven that statement is not true. There's a huge theme of hell that was erroneously introduce into scripture. The very fact that no Bible agrees with how many hells or Hades they will permit, proves a major theme has not been protected by God. So, the million dollar question again is... which Bible, much less "theme", did God protect?

I will now address one last issue I've heard used to further divide an already divided body of believers. "The King James is the only true version of the Bible"! That would make the wife(s) murdering King Henry the VIII an instrument of God, because Mr. Henry added his own words to the King James Bible. But, let's ignore this historical fact along with so many other issues requiring us to use blind faith. We'll also need to ignore how the King James lost or misplaced dozens of Sheols when translating it to the word to hell.

I've been told by the "King James only" crowd that the New King James version is the same, but it only left out the "thees, thous, iths, and eths", thus making it easier for some to read. I've discovered a little problem--the New King James also left out 22 hells as well by only mentioning hell 32 times instead of the 54 times written about before. What happened to those other 22 hells?

To conclude this portion, I'm just trying to get to the point that there is no way, other than through an act of blind faith, that anyone can claim that God has protected the Bible, thus making it the inerrant Word of God. I'm not trying to discourage anyone about the Bible--why would I--it is a treasure book full of treasure. It's full of words (plural) from God, however it is not The Word of God. The Bible has been horribly idolatrize by Christendom, because the only real Word of God that is valid, according to the Bible, is Christ Himself. Jesus is The Word of God--not a book, as in, not the Bible. I'm sorry if this offends you, but if you believe otherwise--much like the Muslims and their Qu'ran, you have been bamboozled, brainwashed, and indoctrinated.


**Fact:** Christians don't agree on what sin or sins are required for one to end up in hell. I feel it necessary to address some points in case a "hell believer" happens to come across this book, and had the guts to proceed reading it! All I ask is: THINK before you believe!


Every Christian I've had the pleasure of fellowshipping with claim Jesus paid the debt of sin, but only if you believe it. They go on to claim that hell is the debt that the individual must pay themselves for the sin of unbelief. Huh? Shouldn't Jesus be suffering in eternal torment right now for all the unbelief since He paid the debt of sin? Another way of putting it: If unbelief is a sin, and hell is the place that people go when they don't believe, and Jesus paid for that sin--then logically that payment must be Jesus in hell right now--this very moment, because He's paying for the sin of unbelief.


What most of my friends believe doesn't make sense. We know of course that Jesus is not in hell, so I have to come to the conclusion hell is not a place that people go when they don't believe, because if it was--Jesus would have to be there to pay the debt. It has to be this way or He didn't pay the debt after all.


Because Christianity is constantly telling people to make the right choices, I'm going to give my reader four questions to think about, and to choose which one best fits their belief.

- Is Jesus in hell right now paying for the sin including the sin of unbelief?
- Did Jesus not pay the debt for all sin, including the sin of unbelief?
- If Jesus really did pay for the sins of all men, then why is there a need for hell?
- If hell is not the debt, not the ransom, then what did Jesus pay for when spoken about in 1st Timothy 2:6: "Who gave himself a ransom for all, to be testified in due time."


Ransom, payment, and dept for what? As an angry child or teen, did you ever blame your parents for your birth? If not, consider the fact that many have. Along this same vein of thinking--who's responsible for your existence--you or God? Is it your own fault that you were born with a desire to sin? A parent never has to teach their children to do wrong--it seems to come "naturally" to them as if it was in their nature. Consider Ephesians 2:3:

"Among them we too all formerly lived in the lusts of our flesh, indulging the desires of the flesh and of the mind, and were by NATURE children of wrath...".

Side note: "Wrath" in the Greek means violent passions, so we're all by nature children of our own violent passions. So when someone vomits the idea that "being saved" means to be saved from hell-- apparently they're clueless of their own violent passions they need to be saved from. Are we starting to get the hint of why Jesus came?

When it comes to taking responsibility for how we were born, even the Apostle Paul wouldn't put the blame on himself in Romans 7:20:

" But if I am doing the very thing I do not want, I am no longer the one doing it, but sin which dwells in me."

But how does this answer the "debt", the "payment" Jesus made on our behalf? The answer would be so simple if only a person would be willing to stop looking at scripture through a hell lens. The next paragraph contains the real answer to what Jesus paid for, as in, something else had ownership of us, we all had been sold into slavery.

Who was it, or better stated, what owned us before Christ purchased us, before the ransom was paid? Simple... WE DID! Our "wrath" owns us. Our violent passions own us. Our bad decisions own us. The ramification for all those bad decisions have been paid for. Christ purchased us from ourselves by paying for any and all wrongs that our passions wanted to commit. Not just us individually, but for the whole world, and all of creation. Paul obviously understood this when he wrote in Romans 7:14:

"... but I am of flesh, SOLD INTO BONDAGE to sin."

Being saved from myself has opened my blind eyes, and I now have been given the ability to love God and my fellow man--this is GREAT news! The flesh still wants what the flesh wants, but it no longer has the power to condemn us. This is why Paul refused to take responsibility for what the flesh wants by saying in Romans: 7:15:

" For what I am doing, I do not understand; for I am not practicing what I *would* like to *do,* but I am doing the very thing I hate." Then two verses later in 17:

"So now, no longer am I the one doing it, but sin which dwells in me."

Here's a thought that will tweak most Christians--God created mankind, God created the Garden of Eden, God set up the scenario in the Garden, and God created us with the ability to choose. Is there anyone besides God with the ability to create something that never existed before? Who created sin, and who created the ability to choose sin? Now my final question is: Who's really responsible for it all? You guessed right, and guess what--He took the responsibility onto Himself through Christ on the cross. So, what is our responsibility in all this mess? Simple, swallow some pride, and acknowledge our helplessness without Him.

**Fact:** A person only has a choice if they know what they're choosing. Christianity is constantly telling people to make the right choices. The right choice, in the context of this writing, means to choose Christ--which is legit. So you might think that if someone doesn't choose Christ--what then? Generally speaking, we as "believers" are putting all the responsibility on the shoulders of an individual to choose correctly. Thus, it's concluded by Christendom one must pay the ultimate eternal price if one chooses incorrectly.

Don't get me wrong, it's extremely important to choose Christ, but it's even more important to acknowledge who it is that enables a person to make the right choice. Who is it that gives a person the gift of faith in the first place so they can make the right choice? Christians are continually "boasting" about how they made the right choice. Note, there is nothing wrong with feeling good about your decision to follow Christ, but to take the credit for that decision is stripping God of the glory as well as making yourself the focus of your admiration rather than Christ.

"Deed" is defined as "an action that is performed intentionally or consciously, as in doing a good deed". Is it a "deed" to choose Christ? Was it an intentional and conscious act on your part? Most Christian would give a resounding YES! Did you feel righteous about performing the deed? If so, you have boasted according to Titus 3:5:

"He saved us, not on the basis of deeds which we have done in righteousness, but according to His mercy, by the washing of regeneration and renewing by the Holy Spirit".

"Works" is defined as an "activity involving mental or physical effort done in order to achieve a purpose or result." Most Christians I know claim they made the mental, physical, often times emotional effort to respond to an "alter call", or as a reciprocation to a strong sense of hopelessness in making a choice to follow Christ. On the surface it all sounds wonderful, but if you're taking the credit for it-- you just boasted according to 2nd Timothy 1:9:

" ...who has saved us and called us with a holy calling, not according to our works, but according to His own purpose and grace which was granted us in Christ Jesus...".

The word "yourself" is used to emphasize the person being addressed--is it not?  A dictionary example states:  "Yourself" is defined as "you personally are going to have to do it yourself".  Now combine this definition with "works" and you'll essentially get:  "You personally will have to do it yourself by actively making an effort to achieve a result."  The result is obtaining a salvation according to Christian preconceptions.  Doesn't this describe what Christianity claims you have to do in order to be saved?  Some denominations will add even more hoops you'll be required to jump through as well.  Usually what happens next is the person making this effort will boast about it.  These beliefs are the EXACT OPPOSITE of what it states in Ephesians 2:8-9:

"For by grace you have been saved through faith; and that NOT OF YOURSELVES, it is the gift of God; NOT AS A RESULT OF WORKS, so that no one may boast."


Also, when the above verse states "saved through faith", this is NOT your own faith that it's referring to, otherwise the faith would NOT be a "gift", but instead it would be a faith of "yourselves", and would be "a result of works".   The "faith" this verse is alluding to is described in Galatians 2:16:

"Knowing that a man is not justified by the works of the law, but by the faith "OF" Jesus Christ". (not IN Christ)

Also in Philippians 3:9:

"And be found in him, not having mine own righteousness, which is of the law, but that which is through the faith "OF" Christ". (not IN Christ)

**Redundant Fact:** As a matter of fact, all of the above facts are not simply beliefs, but can be proven linguistically and with historical FACTS!

**Last Fact:** The word hell never existed in all the letters and manuscripts that later became the Bible, yet it is NOW in most Bibles. Why? The whens and hows will be brought to light in the next chapter.

Chapter 12

Who Put Hell Into The Bible?

Before I write about how, what, and when the word hell was inserted into scripture, I first want to address a few of the many beliefs Christendom has in order to legitimize, or justify the reason for such a place.

I've know my friend Scott M. for about 30 years, and another good friend (more like a slightly older brother) Dave V. for 47 years. I can give an historical account of their lives whenever it involved me. (no duh--right?) Like all friendships we had our share of bumps and bruises, but that's not the point. In their interactions with me, they both have been honorable in every way, and in every circumstance.

If I wrote a blog, an article, or a historical essay, spanning 30 to 47 years of my experiences with these men--as a witness, obviously this gives me more credibility than someone who has never met them. What if someone else came along--someone who's never met my friends, and started writing derogatory and slandering comments about their character? Most Christians I know would take my side, my view of these men over what these others had written, yet...


Written by someone who was actually there, witnessed or was in contact with a person who was involved--the book of Acts gives an early account of how the "Christian" church was established.  It was a narrative depicting about 35 years.  In those recorded 35 years, there were 27 occurrences when the Gospel message was preached, and in all of those times, hell was never mentioned.  Doesn't this piece of historical fact raise a red flag in the mind of a hell believer, and cause one to question the legitimacy of hell?


Christendom considers and calls God their "Heavenly Father".  It has been taught and assumed God is NOT a Heavenly Father to anyone until that person is adopted. How is a child adopted--by the child's act of obedience?  I was adopted by my dad, and all three of my siblings were adopted by both my parents.  So... was it my act of obedience that caused me to acquire my dad's last name?  As toddlers, did my two sisters and brother gain acceptance from their future parents by any action on their part?


There are five verses in the New Testament that mention "adoption" in reference to becoming "a son".  In not one instance within the context of these verses, has a prerequisite been placed on the person described as the one being adopted. There are two perspectives when reading these verses--the Adopter, versus the adoptee. From God's perspective (Adopter), we are ALL His children, but not all children know it yet. Once the "adoptee" (child), comes to the understanding they truly are God's child, then in their mind only--they become adopted--they become what they always were from God's perspective. Charlatans, dressed as men of God will twist those five verses to place and keep people in fear or bondage. However, in response to how the doctrines of men have perverted these verses, the below self-contextualizing verse states:

"...one God and FATHER OF ALL who is over all and through all and in all." (Ephesians 4:6)


Consider rereading chapter 5 " When Did "All" Become A "Select Few"?" There are four "all's" in the above Ephesians verse, and every one is a "passive" all in the Greek--meaning no action is required to be part of the all--no actions on the part of a child to be "adopted"--no exclusions, meaning EVERYONE!

If God is only a Heavenly Father to a select few, conditional upon the actions of those few, then He's not a good father--heavenly, earthly, or otherwise. So what does "adoption" have to do with how hell got into the Bible? Technically it doesn't, but I propose this reasoning to my reader--according to Christian beliefs, what is the final outcome of someone who has not been adopted? Is hell that outcome, and is that outcome legit in the first place? If it's not legit in the first place then why is it in the Bible? By the time this chapter is finished, I'll prove that neither a perverted doctrine of "adoption", nor the even more perverted doctrine of "hell" is legitimate.

If a person perceives in their mind that they have been adopted by God, and it gives a person a peace that they are now a child of God--GO FOR IT! A correct understanding of adoption is moot considering God is the creator of all, and the Father of all according to the verse in Ephesians. This means we have a Father that is omniscient, omnipotent, and omnipresent who loves each and every child equally.

According to Jeremiah 7:31, it's recorded as saying it would never enter the mind of our Father to burn His children. So then, would a Father like the One in Jeremiah create a place of eternal fiery torture for any of His children? Would a Heavenly Father, since He is in all, throw Himself, along with anyone else who didn't obey the rules, into a place of fiery hell that Christians claim is true?

Would a Heavenly Father who loves all equally, create a being who apparently doesn't love all--giving this created being the authority and power to circumvent the creator of His own authority and power? Since this Heavenly Father was and is " omniscient", would He create a being that He knew would rebel and trick the vast majority of His children into not loving Him? Then for those who were tricked, hold them responsible for being tricked, so He could justifiably abandon them to a torturous place for all eternity!? To those reading... if any of these questions offend you, ask yourself why, and then try to answer these questions within your own heart and mind.

Now it's time to address "faith", but from an unusual angle, as in: I'm beginning to believe the modern Christian has more faith in hell, than they do in the saving power of Christ.

I'm going to reiterate a few key points from Chapter 3 "Does Death Stop God?". Jesus spoke of faith quite a bit, and the occasion that stands out over all the rest is when He spoke about having the faith of a mustard seed. With that kind of faith you can tell the mountain to go into the sea and it would happen. Let me propose that the story wasn't about the size of a mustard seed after all, nor how big the mountain was, but instead I believe it was all about how powerful faith is. I rarely hear this angle, and I never hear it mentioned how faith is "unbiased".

Christians have been taught to think faith is all about their faith, and how it operates in and through them. That wouldn't make it unbiased--would it? Hey Why Guy, we never claimed it was unbiased-- you're the only one saying that. I get my reasoning this way... contextually, as well as a consideration, who was Jesus speaking to at the time He was speaking the parable about faith? The masses of people were His fellow countrymen--the Jewish people. Since there was no such thing as Christians at the time, I have to conclude that faith is not only about Christians. This tells me that faith is unbiased, and it is not a respecter of persons.

I believe faith is a power in and of itself that God created for all mankind. This power can operate within a person regardless of them being Jew, Christian, believer, or unbeliever. Since not all people are good--this tells me that faith can be used for good or bad purposes. The crux of why I now believe Christians have faith in hell is because of Hebrews 11:1:

"Now faith is the assurance of things hoped for and the conviction of things not seen".

This verse states "now faith"--notice how it doesn't say your faith, good faith, or bad faith, or faith in God, or faith in Christ... it just says faith! Let's take the next phrase of: "assurances of things hoped for". Do you know how many people have a hope for the existence of hell? There are hundreds of quotes, and thousands upon thousands of people who feel justified in their hope for a hell, and I used to be one of them. Even though there are hundreds of quotes to choose from in proving how many people "hope" for hell, I offer only these three below quotes:

Here's a quote from an early church Theologian by the name of Tertullian: "At that greatest of all spectacles, that last and eternal judgment; how shall I admire, how laugh, how rejoice, how exult, when I behold so many proud monarchs groaning in the lowest abyss of darkness; so many magistrates liquefying in fiercer flames..." "...so many sages philosophers blushing in red-hot fires...".

Let's fast forward about 1400 years to a guy named John Calvin. This clown had some of his theological enemies slowly burned to death in green slow-burning wood.

"Forever harassed with a dreadful tempest, they shall feel themselves torn asunder by an angry God, and transfixed and penetrated by mortal stings, terrified by the thunderbolts of God, and broken by the weight of his hand, so that to sink into any gulf would be more tolerable than to stand for a moment in these terrors"

About 150 years later, a guy pops up by the name of Jonathan Edwards, and to no surprise he was a "Calvinist" of the "Great Awakening" era. I'm not going to veer off and explain the "Great Awakening", but let's just say newspapers at that time reported of how people leaving his sermons had committed suicide from the fear he instilled in them by saying things like: "...they shall be tossed to and fro, having no rest day and night, vast waves and billows of fire continually rolling over their heads, of which they shall forever be full of a quick sense within and without; their heads, their eyes, their tongues, their hands, their feet, their loins and their vitals, shall forever be full of a flowing, melting fire, fierce enough to melt the very rocks and elements; and also, they shall eternally be full of the most quick and lively sense to feel the torments; not for one minute, not for one day, not for one age, not for two ages, not for a hundred ages, nor for ten thousand millions of ages, one after another, but forever and ever, without any end at all, and never to be delivered."

Notice the evidence of things hoped for, but not yet seen in these testimonies. Are any of these men promoting the fruit of God's Spirit, as in love, joy, peace, etc? Hmmm... let's see: Laughing and rejoicing at the thought of someone suffering--not for a time, but for an eternity (Tertullian). How about slowly burning someone alive (Calvin)? Their god (who they claim is our God) will tear people to pieces because of his anger. Is it considered a fruit of God's Spirit if someone commits suicide due to something you've said (Edwards)? If you're a hell believer who agrees with these quotes--from the deepest parts of my soul I pity you. If you're a hell believer who might be disgusted by the words and behavior of these men--how are you any different, considering you believe the eternal end result is the same as what they all claim?

Again: "Now faith is the assurance of things hoped for and the conviction of things not seen". The above quotes have proven how people seem to have an assurance of things hoped for, and that "thing" happens to be hell.

What initially gave Tertullian this assurance of the existence of hell? There were no bibles at the time, and the only thing available to him might have been a few copies of copies of copies of letters written in Greek, rather than his native tongue of Latin. So, I ask the question again... why was he assured (so sure) of the existence of hell? Answer:

HIS FAITH IN HELL, due to his pagan beliefs, and not just him, but anyone else who believed in hell at the time!

It didn't take as much faith for Calvin and Edwards to believe in hell--they had the "evidence of things not seen", and their evidence was something they could hold in their hand--the hell they've not seen was now in print form in their BIBLES--they could see it! It takes even less faith for the modern Christian to believe in hell, because of over 1578 years of mistranslations, superstitions, ignorance, doctrines of men, tradition, brain washing, indoctrination, and the fear inducing deception in believing that hell exists. The evidence is not only in the Bible, but now Christians have even taken it a step further by claiming it's in "The Inerrant Word of God", and they have a full "conviction" that it is true, thus putting the final nail in the coffin of deceit about hell.

To stress my point, I will now paraphrase the "faith is" verse by saying: Now "faith" in hell is the "assurance" that it exists, "hoping" people will get what they deserve. Even though it's "not yet seen", I don't have to see it due to a "conviction" it exists, because it says so in the inerrant Word of God.

It's going to take a lot of honesty while looking in the mirror reflecting your faith. The power--we all have the power to believe what ever we want, and often times we'll see evidence of our faith, even if it's manifested in a bad way. I call it fear based faith rather than love based faith. If this were not true then why is it that the vast majority of Christians have more faith in the existence of hell than they do in the love of God? God is love, and love doesn't separate Himself from his creation for an eternity! If separation isn't bad enough, how about including never ending torture and pain? Either love is perverted, an understanding of love is perverted, God is perverted, or the teaching of hell is perverted and hell doesn't exist. If you're reading this book now, you're going to need to make a choice on what is perverted. I used to be right where you're at and I understand your trepidation.

If you don't think that believing in hell is perverted, then explain to me, why the vast majority of Christians who have personally witnessed the fruit of God's Spirit operating within my wife and I, while being involved in church, street, prison, and music ministry--from their perspective, we are going to hell simply because we no longer believe in it? They ignore the fruit expressing itself before their very eyes. How can that be? They have proven to me that they have such a strong faith in the existence of hell that it has blinded them to see the Godly evidence operating in our lives. Ironically, that evidence also happens to be the exact opposite of what they claim is required to go to hell in the first place. None of it makes sense, but their fear based faith is telling them that it does.

It's all quite a conundrum.  Some people can't understand how I can possibly love God without believing in hell, and I can't see how they can love God BECAUSE of a belief in hell.
Usually the answer I get to justify hell is--some people are just so wicked and evil, and what you're telling us is they're going to get away with it, if there is no hell.  My answer is:  Do you honesty think that hell, that petty little pagan place known by a number of different names, in a variety of pagan cultures and religions is the only option God has?  Do you think God is limited to a pagan belief in order to get rid of the existence of evil?  Is God really that small and limited?


For those of you who are parents--if you heard of your child doing something evil or wicked to themselves or to others around them--are you going to cast that child away forever and ever?  Does the love of a parent reach a point where they never want to see that child again?  (don't answer that.  haha) Would you sanction an authority to take them away, for the sole purpose of continuously torturing them with no end in sight?  Is that the kind of love you have for your child, and would torment be your only option?


What if you had an option to witness your child's heart break over what they've done wrong, to realize the harm they've caused, and to learn from their mistakes?  Does this option sound like love to you?  Only you can answer that.  What makes this option so feasible is because God is God, and He's not limited to this lifetime nor the issue of time at all.  He's got all time and eternity at his disposal to teach people, and we know from previous chapters that death does not stop God.  This actually makes sense, and explains how evil and wicked people won't get away with anything--love doesn't allow evil to get away with anything.

In reference to the potential evil of mankind, 1st Timothy 4:10 states:

"For it is for this we labor and strive, because we have fixed our hope on the living God, who is the Savior of all men, especially of believers."

Let's dissect this verse:  "We have fixed our hope"-- remember what faith is, as in something hoped for.  "On the living God who is the savior of ALL men".  All men?  This would include evil men would it not?  And not just the evil men only, but then the verse goes on to say...
"Especially (Greek-malista) of believers."  In a moment, I want to come back to that Greek word "malista", and prove it does not mean "exclusively of believers".

This verse in Timothy is addressing both believers and unbelievers regardless of them being evil or not!  What?  Believers can't be evil!  To me, it's pure evil to look forward to a day when you can look upon your enemies and laugh at their eternal suffering. (Tertullian)

You don't think it's evil for a preacher to portray "that God could toss a sinful human into hell with as little thought, let alone remorse, as a human would exhibit while stepping on a worm or crushing an annoying insect. God has not the least bit of pity for sinners--He finds them to be abhorrent and abominable.  A sinner asking God for mercy will only make an already wrathful God even angrier."?  This quote is from a book titled:  Sinners in the Hands of an Angry God, by Jonathan Edwards.

To slander God in this fashion--this is how I define evil--every bit as much as any other evil, but with a different mask.  How about Calvin who slowly burned "other believers" alive?  This is only three out of hundreds of examples of a "believer" saying or doing evil deeds.  I have to conclude "savior of ALL men" would include believers and unbelievers alike, regardless of how evil they are.

Previously I wrote how I wanted to come back to that Greek word "malista".  Another example of how that word is used can be found in Galatians 6:10 which states:

"So then, as we have opportunity, let us do good to everyone, and "especially" (malista) to those who are of the household of faith."

If we are to believe the phrase "especially of believers" in 1st Timothy actually means exclusively of believers, then that would mean this verse in Galatians is telling us to only (exclusively) do good to those who are of the household of faith. Does this mean we're not supposed to do good to anyone else? To do so would mean ignoring how it says "everyone". Yet, isn't this exactly what Christendom is doing in the 1st Timothy verse by pushing aside and ignoring the "all men" statement?

I've discovered Christianity is far more divided in beliefs than I could have ever imagined. Beliefs are as many and as diverse as there are people within Christendom. Future chapters will address even more of those beliefs, however in this chapter I zeroed in on a belief in hell--mitigated by a faith that has been manipulated by unscrupulous men.

I will address one more widely viewed and established belief about hell before concluding this chapter about the history of why it was inserted in the Bible. I know I approached the topic of "separation" in a previous chapter, but I thought a little more information would be appropriate. I'm going to give this a sub-title of: Love Goes to Hell

Let's look at the separation idea that some hold onto as a definition of hell. Let's put aside the torture aspect for a moment and only address the belief of how God will be separated from the vast majority of people for an eternity. Are there Bible verses that confirm or deny such a notion? As covered in a previous chapter we know the word Sheol was later translated by the Greeks into the word Hades.

Then hundreds of years later, both Sheol and Hades were horribly translated into infernum (hell) by the ancient Latin people. We all know how Christians have been led to believe that Sheol, Hades, and hell are all one and the same. I'll will restate how the Hebrew people never believed in hell--it's not part of their culture. As I've said many times before--Sheol only meant death or grave as in a place for the dead.

The Greeks then came along and they produced the Septuagint. A certain percentage of the Greeks realized that Hades would only mean death or grave to the Jews even though it represented an underworld to a portion of their populist. Then the Latins got into the mix with their own version of an underworld. Yes, the Latins and Greeks cannibalized off of each other's pagan beliefs about an underworld, so it wasn't unusual for the Latins to add their pagan baggage to the belief in Hades, and then incorporate the word Sheol into the mix while producing the Latin Vulgate. Christendom has completely fallen for this unholy 3-way pagan marriage ceremony.

Just for the sake of argument, let's say Sheol means Hades and/or hell as Christians believe.  If this is true, then I can righteously paraphrase Psalms 139:8 to read:  If I ascend to Heaven you are there, if I make my bed in Sheol or, if I make my bed in Hades, or if I make my bed in hell YOU ARE THERE! How does this jive with hell representing an eternal separation from God?

Ah-ha... what about the infamous "Lake of Fire"?  Some claim the Lake of Fire is hell even though that's impossible.  How can hell be thrown into itself, because according to some Bible translations, hell is thrown into the Lake of Fire.  That would mean Hades is thrown into the Lake of Fire, and Sheol is thrown into the Lake of Fire. Regardless of the mistranslations and perversions of words--this verse in reality is actually saying death and the grave are thrown into the Lake of Fire--this represents the purification of death, the second death, the death of death, as in the END of death!  It doesn't get any better than that.

The metaphoric Lake of Fire is a wonderful PROCESS to purify whatever, or whomever is symbolically thrown into it.   Christianity has turned this process--what God intended for good, into a slanderous, horrible perversion of His love.  You're still not convinced?  Are you still saying the Lake of Fire is hell and represents being separated from God?  How can something be separated from God and be in His presence at the same time?  In Rev. 20:10 & 11 reports of a "Great White Throne" (the presence of God), and it speaks of how the devil and the false prophet are going to be tossed into the lake. Verse 10 ends with forever and ever, even though it doesn't say that in the original Greek manuscripts-- the Latins inserted the phrase "forever and ever". So, even if you want to consider the Lake of Fire as hell--God is right there with them.

If a person wants to believe in hell as a place of separation and/or torture--oxymoronically sounding-- God is there, and if God is there--that means love is there--if love is there--that would mean that patience is there, and so forth.  I could go on by including how the fruit of the Spirit is operating in hell, and/or how the love chapter in 1st Cor. 13 would describe the kind of love found in hell, considering it's all in God's presence, but I think you're getting the point.  None of it would add up and none of it would make sense for a loving God to be involved with eternal separation, torture, or torment.  Don't be like I used to be!  STOP assuming the worse case scenario when God only has the best outcome for all of creation.

So far, I've explained what I believe and why I believe--concerning the doctrine of hell.  Depending on who you are I've also explained what you believe and why you believe the doctrine of hell is true.  I will continue along these lines in future chapters, but in concluding this chapter, I believe it's now time to answer the question of "Who Put Hell Into the Bible"?

Historically, at the time the first "official" Bible known as the Latin Vulgate was written, the mainstream Latin government and the state run religion were essentially one and the same. By teaching the folklore of hell, this religious government combo used fear to manipulate and control the peasants who couldn't read or write. Our very constitution here in the U.S. separates church and State for reasons similar to what took place in many European societies. As a child I remember reading in my history book about why some people came to America--they were fleeing persecution from their "religious" governments. I believe it was from the Tentmaker website that I once read quotes from early Latin church leaders of how they would talk and laugh amongst themselves about how easy it was to manipulate the peasants--using fear about a place in the afterlife that they themselves didn't believe in.

Initially, you may think of my next story as being goofy and absurd, but in reality, nothing is more absurd than a loving God creating a place to torture people for an eternity. With that said, I will now tell you what might be viewed by some as a ridiculous story, but in my defense, it's a decent analogy of what happened when the Latin Vulgate was written. I entertained myself in writing this, so I hope it entertains you as well. I call my story: "Broccoli"

Would it be acceptable to the Christians of our day--if I were to put together a group of influential people and scientists--who had unlimited funds at their disposal--who later manipulated the DNA of broccoli, resulting in a cure for all cancers, heart disease, and slowed the aging process down dramatically?  Christendom would embrace it, because it would be seen as "good news" for humanity, and probably worthy of the Nobel Peace Prize.  The world would look at broccoli in a whole new light--wouldn't they?  It would be as if broccoli was the "savior of the world".

Would it also be acceptable to those within Christianity, if a conglomerate group of influential people and scientists wanted to print their own version of the Bible?  Furthermore, what if in their Bible, they wanted to substitute the name of Jesus for the word broccoli, so religiously speaking--broccoli became the new savior of the world?  Pictures would be painted with children sitting on Broccoli's lap, and new churches would be built depicting a man-size cluster of broccoli in a test tube, mounted high in the front of the sanctuary.

At first it was not received, and there was an uproar, but over time this new religion grew and grew into a massive system that continued for a long time. Generations came and went, resulting in fewer and fewer people willing to fight these religious beliefs, because the church system gained so much power. They had the law and the military on their side, followed by a thousand years of persecution for those who didn't believe in Broccoli the way they did.

After the "dark age" of violence and persecution ended, the leadership in the church system realized there was no need for violence any longer, because the vast majority (who used to be the minority) believed that Broccoli was the true savior of the world. Of course there were the agnostics who could care less one way or the other if Broccoli was a deity, and naturally there were atheists that didn't believe at all in a god called Broccoli.

Even after all these changes to the Bible happened, there was still a minority of people who were trying to proclaim--"NO! NO!" What you have been led to believe isn't true! Something has happened in history--just look in your actual history, and you'll see that a group of powerful men changed scripture. They changed the name of Jesus to the word Broccoli! This minority of people making the accusation of error within scripture were usually ignored, scoffed at, ridiculed, ostracized, and called names, because the majority agree that Broccoli is a deity. As centuries go by, as they naturally do, these changes in the Bible became acceptable as truth and orthodoxy by mainstream Christianity, or better known as "Brocclianity"!

Yes, I agree--this story is ridiculous and absurd--but why? Because you know the truth! Exactly!

What is far more ridiculous and absurd to those like me--is how such an enormous amount of people, spanning over 2000 years have been duped--myself included at one point in time.  It's so easy to find the truth in church history, and the only thing holding most people back is FEAR!

My story represents what actually took place around 400 AD.  A very powerful, and influential group of men took the lead from the writings of hell believing theologians like Tertullian and Augustine-- they then incorporated the Greek and Hebrew manuscripts of that day, (what was considered scripture) and then rewrote them by making their own Bible called The Latin Vulgate.  They took key words, just like the people did in my broccoli story, and changed them.

These men took the Hebrew word Sheol, and the Greek word Hades--which only meant death or grave to the Jew and early Christians, and changed it to the word "infernum" (hell) which represented torture and torment. Did they do that each and every time they came across the words death or grave? Hell no! (pun intended) They only changed those words to hell when in context to an unbeliever. Out of the 111 times within the Latin Vugate, the Latin Church took the words like death, grave, pit, Gehenna, and unseen, and translated them into the word: "infernum". Why didn't they use the word infernum each and every time they came across the words death, grave, etc.?


For a moment, let's take the words "death and grave", and ask: Why use infernum, and why not "sepulchrum", which in Latin means: grave or burial place? And why not the Latin word "tumulus", which can mean: grave, hill, mound, knoll, or heights? Last but not least, how about the Latin word "tumba", translated into English as: grave, tomb, mausoleum, or sepulchre? The translators had all these words available, but they chose to use the word infernum for grave. What the infernum is wrong with this picture?

Here's one example of many within scripture of how the word "grave" in Rev. 20:14 has been perverted: "Then death and hell were thrown into the lake of fire." Yet, in the Koine Greek manuscripts it says death and the grave (or unseen) were cast into the lake. Something else to consider... death and grave are in context to one another--not only within scripture, but within all cultures--eons past to present day.

It makes complete sense to state how the process of both death and the grave will be eliminated in the lake of fire. Now think about this... by changing the word grave into hell--not only is death and hell non-contextual with one another within all aspects concerning death, but "a place" being cast into "another place" makes no sense! Whereas, death and the grave are like a hand in a glove scenario.

The verse continues by saying "this is the second death". "Second death" doesn't confirm a hell, but instead it confirms "the death of death"! The action of God eliminating both death and the grave in the lake of fire--it becomes a wondrous birthing of "eternal life" for all of creation--the exact opposite of eternal death that Christendom proclaims. I intentionally use this kind of reasoning to prove how there is no point for anyone to use the word hell in this verse!

I've "covered" the topic of grave (pun intended), so what about the word death?  The Latin word "mors" means:  decease/deadness/depart.

The Lain word "obitu" means:  death.

And finally the Lain word "moriuntur" means:  dead.


We are being led by Christendom to believe the word infernum means hell, and hell is the same as the Hebrew word Sheol as a place for the dead.  Where is a place for the dead--sitting on your sofa, in their hospital bed, where ever they happened to fall?  No, of course not, but in the Jewish mindset, "the place" was a grave, awaiting a resurrection, and according to Jesus--asleep.  Most Jews, as well as people throughout the world that were not cremated--they couldn't afford an above the ground tomb, so naturally they were buried "underground".  (ya think?)

When one asks for a definition of infernum, in most cases you'll simply get the word "hell", but depending on the site you're using, you might get the word "underground" as well. I don't find this deduction valid. The reason? Using a Latin translation tool--if you type in the word "hell" and ask for a translation, you'll get "infernum". Reversely, if you type in the word infernum, you'll get the word hell in English. So, one would think if you did the same with the word "underground", the same thing would happen--right? Wrong, you get the words metropolitiana or sottoterra instead of infernum. To believe "infernum" means "underground", one would have to assume there was a large hot fire underground. Maybe they were thinking of a volcano, or magma--so I checked on those words to find infernum, and you guessed it--no such luck.

My point: Inferno is defined as a large fire that is dangerously out of control. It originally came from the Latin word infernum, but when asking for an English translation of the Latin word infernum, you'll get "hell" instead of "a large fire that is...". Are you catching this? Do you see a manipulation of language for a specific purpose? This was NOT an act of innocence and ignorance, or a mistake in translation. This lie was well thought out and intentionally promoted as truth!

The Vulgate took the word "unseen" in Lazarus and the rich man parable, and changed it into the word infernum. However, when you ask for a translation of unseen from English to Latin, you'll discover:

"inaspectus" - wondrous, out of sight
"inobservatus" - unobserved, <u>unperceived</u>
"caecus" - blind, obscure, aimless
"indeprehesus" - undetected, unnoticed

Latin based Bibles state in Luke 16:23:

"In hell he lifted up his eyes, being in torment, and saw Abraham far away and Lazarus in his bosom.

Yet in my Greek Bible the same verse reads:

"And in the unseen, lifting up his eyes, existing in torments, he is seeing Abraham from afar and Lazarus in his bosom."

WAIT A "DAMNED" MINUTE, I thought the Greek word for hell was Hades, so why doesn't it say Hades in this verse? What the Hades happened? If your Bible uses Hades instead of hell or unseen, then it further proves it's actually a Latin influenced Bible, only pretending to use a Greek word, because they often shared each others pagan beliefs in an underworld/netherworld. But what about the oldest manuscript we have available known as The Emphatic Diaglott, and it says Hades? Let me also point out, it too came from the Latin Vatican--it's based on copies of copies of numerous copies of letters, and one would have to believe that Jesus would use a Greek word representing a pagan place to teach Aramaic and Hebrew speaking people. Is this why the Latins didn't use: "inaspectus, inobservatus, caecus, orindeprehesus" instead of infernum, since they all mean "unseen" in Latin? NO! They knew exactly what they were doing when they pulled a word out of their vocabulary of "infernum" (hell) to better fit their agenda. I cannot believe it was just a mistake and we're only dealing with a misconception.

Some still believe there was no insidious intent on the part of those who translated scripture.  But instead, it is believed the word infernum got turned into a teaching of hell, and it was only done by a select few whose minds believed in pagan myths going back thousands of years.  This doesn't explain why they would use the word infernum ( large or hot fire ), when they already had at their disposal the actual words for death, grave, and unseen in their vocabulary, and they chose not to use them.

Augustine's writings were very influential in producing the Vulgate.  He also was notorious for taking the Greek word aion (eon-a segment of time), and changing it into the word eternal!  It was extremely effective to the Latin agenda to combine the two words of hell and eternal to further promote the deception.  This method was manipulative, deceptive, inconsistent, and obviously NOT the way to translate anything.

The persecution that went on in my broccoli story was mild compared to what the ancient Latin church system did to people who didn't agree with them.  For over a thousand years, the church at that time persecuted and prosecuted people by means of burning them alive, disembowelment, beheadings, drowning, and torture in far more ways than what I've listed here.  Think about this--if you were a person in a society that threatened you or your family like this--

wouldn't you submit to the mainstream belief system? The average person did, and the emotional torture and the threat of eternal torment is continuing today, but thanks to Christianity, now the threat is actually coming from God rather than a government. Ironically, these same people still call their God-- Love! (sarcasm intended)


For over a thousand years, circa 400 to 1530 AD, the Latin Vulgate was the only Bible respected within Western European society, so for Christians who could read at that time--this was the only Bible available. But what about the King James Bible? Over social media I've been ridiculed for making the claim that for the most part, the King James version came from The Latin Vulgate. Okay, I'll admit it wasn't a direct translation word for word, but follow my reasoning. One must ask which Bibles existed between The Latin Vulgate and the King James?

Answer: The Great Bible circa 1539, which was authorized and promoted by the wife murdering Henry the 8th. This Bible was indeed translated directly from the Vulgate.

After that came the Geneva Bible circa 1557 which was translated using the previously mentioned: The Great Bible.

Then, along came the The Douay–Rheims Bible circa 1582 that used both: The Great Bible and the Geneva Bible as a template.

Finally, the King James Bible smacked Christianity in the face in 1611, which used all the previously mentioned English Bibles as its template. So, did the King James Bible come from The Latin Vulgate? Directly and exclusively no, but since "The Great Bible" did come directly FROM the Vulgate, and all those that followed was from The Great Bible--I believe it to be accurate to claim the King James Bible came from the Latin Vulgate!

The Church of England was established in 1534 and was in direct competition with the Church of Rome. Competition? Why? The rulers in England could clearly see how the ruling class in Rome had united and subjugated their population. Those cathedrals in Rome, along with works of art, and religious icons brought people together under one umbrella like no political party could ever do. How were all those enormous buildings and exquisite works of art paid for? Answer: Promote a fear based religion that required large sums of money to keep an offender out of hell. It was well established how one could buy forgiveness, thus it was also assumed the vast majority of hell occupants came from the poor section of town in their earthly lives.

So, who was the king in 1534 when The Church of England was established? You guessed it--King Henry VIII. Who was it that authorized the first English Bible called: The Great Bible? You're right again-- King Henry the 8th. Who wanted the kind of power and prestige that the Pope of Rome was

receiving from his followers?  You get the door prize--
King Henry the 8th.  He established himself as the
"Supreme Head of The Church of England".  Even
though he wasn't called a Pope, his title sure sounds
like a "Pope" kind-of-guy to me.  Because of his self
proclaimed authority--naturally he felt he had the right
to add his own thoughts and words to scripture, and
guess what... he did so.  "For thine is the kingdom,
and the power, and the glory for ever and ever -
Amen", are words from one of the worst, most blood
thirsty, murderous kings in England's history.

Why is all this "junk" about The Church of
England important to how the word hell found its way
into our Bible?  I'm simply trying to point out how
political corruption was the basis for why The Church
of Rome inserted the word "infernum" into scripture,
then how The Church of England followed suit by
using the English version of the word infernum (hell)--
resulting in both church systems obtaining the
desired effect of controlling the masses thru the
means of fear.  The King James Bible is nothing
more than a corrupted Latin based Bible, almost as
much as the Latin Vulgate itself.  Everything I've
written explains why the word hell is in the English
Bibles.

Imagine how it would have been if our English
Bible was actually translated directly from the Greek
and Hebrew, rather than being filtered through the
Latin language.  Hell, Hades, and infernum wouldn't
be in our Bibles, but would have been left where

those words originated--in the minds and imaginations of those who hold on to their pagan beliefs.

Now, in our present time, those of us who no longer believe in hell are considered on the fringe of Christianity. What's worse, is a large percentage of Christians don't even consider people like myself Christian at all. We're nothing more than deceivers and heretics in their eyes--all because we no longer believe in hell. Jesus? Who's that? What importance does He have in the mix? He's irrelevant! What is most important is one must believe in hell to be saved! Will the true deceivers and heretics please stand up?

I know how it may bore some readers, but later in this chapter I'll supply a number of quotes I obtained from the Tentmaker site about how early church leaders never believed in hell. What gets me is--the vast majority of Christians between 300 and 400 AD didn't believe in the Latin agenda. The agenda of building a religious empire through the means of fear and intimidation. About a hundred years before that time, Tertullian was considered a theologian on the fringe of orthodox teaching, and wasn't taken seriously. Why? BECAUSE HE BELIEVED AND PROMOTED THE HELL DOCTRINE!

I will end this chapter now with a number of quotes from early church leaders who didn't believe in hell. The best research tool on the internet can be found at Tentmaker.org. This is the site where I obtained the below quotes--consider visiting this site. If anyone has a hard time swallowing what was written in this chapter as truth, then try to do as Jesus suggested, and swallow a camel instead, which I'll address in the next chapter. "Finally, whatever is true, whatever is honorable, whatever is right, whatever is pure, whatever is lovely, whatever is good, whatever has good repute; a good reputation; is there any excellence, and if anything worthy of praise; dwell on these things" (Philippians 4:8) You know what? Hell doesn't fit in this verse!

Quotes:
For the wicked there are punishments, not perpetual, however, lest the immortality prepared for them should be a disadvantage, but they are to be purified for a brief period according to the amount of malice in their works. They shall therefore suffer punishment for a short space, but immortal blessedness having no end awaits them...the penalties to be inflicted for their many and grave sins are very far surpassed by the magnitude of the mercy to be showed to them. -- Diodore of Tarsus, 320-394 A.D.

And God showed great kindness to man, in this, that He did not suffer him to continue being in sin forever; but as it were, by a kind of banishment, cast him out of paradise in order that, having punishment expiated within an appointed time, and having been disciplined, he should afterwards be recalled...just as a vessel, when one being fashioned it has some flaw, is remolded or remade that it may become new and entire; so also it happens to man by death. For he is broken up by force, that in the resurrection he may be found whole; I mean spotless, righteous and immortal. --Theophilus of Antioch (168 A.D.)

These, if they will, may go Christ's way, but if not let them go their way. In another place perhaps they shall be baptized with fire, that last baptism, which is not only painful, but enduring also; which eats up, as if it were hay, all defiled matter, and consumes all vanity and vice. --Gregory of Nazianzeu, Bishop of Constantinople. (330 to 390 A.D.) Oracles 39:19

The Word seems to me to lay down the doctrine of the perfect obliteration of wickedness, for if God shall be in all things that are, obviously wickedness shall not be in them. For it is necessary that at some time evil should be removed utterly and entirely from the realm of being.—St. Macrina the Blessed

For it is evident that God will in truth be all in all when there shall be no evil in existence, when every created being is at harmony with itself and every tongue shall confess that Jesus Christ is Lord; when every creature shall have been made one body. -- Gregory of Nyssa, 335-390

The wicked who have committed evil the whole period of their lives shall be punished till they learn that, by continuing in sin, they only continue in misery. And when, by this means, they shall have been brought to fear God, and to regard Him with good will, they shall obtain the enjoyment of His grace. --Theodore of Mopsuestia, 350-428

We can set no limits to the agency of the Redeemer to redeem, to rescue, to discipline in his work, and so will he continue to operate after this life. –Clement of Alexandria

Do not suppose that the soul is punished for endless eons (apeirou aionas) in Tartarus. Very properly, the soul is not punished to gratify the revenge of the divinity, but for the sake of healing. But we say that the soul is punished for an aionion period (aionios) calling its life and its allotted period of punishment, its aeon. --Olnmpiodorus (AD 550)

Wherefore, that at the same time liberty of free-will should be left to nature and yet the evil be purged away, the wisdom of God discovered this plan; to suffer man to do what he would, that having tasted the evil which he desired, and learning by experience for what wretchedness he had bartered away the blessings he had, he might of his own will hasten back with desire to the first blessedness ...either being purged in this life through prayer and discipline, or after his departure hence through the furnace of cleansing fire.--Gregory of Nyssa (332-398 A.D.)

That in the world to come, those who have done evil all their life long, will be made worthy of the sweetness of the Divine bounty. For never would Christ have said, "You will never get out until you have paid the last penny" unless it were possible for us to get cleansed when we paid the debt. --Peter Chrysologus, 435

I know that most persons understand by the story of Nineveh and its king, the ultimate forgiveness of the devil and all rational creatures. --St. Jerome

"In the end or consummation of things, all shall be restored to their original state, and be again united in one body. We cannot be ignorant that Christ's blood benefited the angels and those who are in hell; though we know not the manner in which it produced such effects. The apostate angels shall become such as they were created; and man, who has been cast out of paradise, shall be restored thither again. And this shall be accomplished in such a way, that all shall be united together by mutual charity, so that the members will delight in each other, and rejoice in each other's promotion. The apostate angels, and the prince of this world, though now ungovernable, plunging themselves into the depths of sin, shall, in the end, embrace the happy dominion of Christ and His saints." – COMMENTARY ON THE NEW TESTAMENT – Jerome (347-420 A.D.)

Our Lord is the One who delivers man [all men], and who heals the inventor of evil himself. -- Gregory of Nyssa (332-398 A.D.), leading theologian of the Eastern Church

# Chapter 13

## Swallowing Camels

Was Jesus ever sarcastic?

Jesus said in Matt 23:24 - "You blind guides, who strain out a gnat and swallow a camel!"

Below is a list of 73 "GNAT" Bible verses referencing how God will have ALL, EVERY PERSON, the WORLD, ALL of CREATION, ALL to be RECONCILED, and how He is going to do it!

Christianity "strains out" or ignores everyone one of these verses while swallowing the many camels I'll expose in this chapter.

GNATS: Matt 18:13 --- Luke 2:10 --- Luke 3:6 - Luke 9:56 –Luke 15:4 - Jn 1:29 --- Jn 3:35 --- Jn 4:42 --- Jn 5:25 --- Jn 5:28 –Jn 6:37-- Jn 6:39 --- Jn 6:44 –Jn 12:32 --- Jn 12:40 - Jn 17:2 --- Jn 12:47 – Acts 3:20-21 --- Rm 3:3-4 --- Rm 5:15 –Rm 5:18 --- Rm 8:19-21 --- Rm 8:38-39 --- Rm 11:15 –Rm 11:32 ---1 Cor 3:15 –1 Cor 15:22-28 --- 2 Cor 5:15 --- 2 Cor 5:19 --- Gal 2:16-- Eph 1:10 –Eph 1:11 --- Eph 1:22 - Eph 4:10 --- Phil 2:9-11 --- Phil 2:13 –Col 1: 19-20 --- 1 Tim 2:4-6 --- 1 Tim 4:10 --- Titus 2:11-12 --- Heb 2:9 --- Heb 7:25 –Heb 8:11 -- II Peter 3:9 - 1 Jn 2:2 --- 1 Jn 3:8 --- 1 Jn 4:14 --- Rev 5:13 --- Rev 21:4-5 -- Gen 12:3 ---Gen 22:18 --- Sam 14:14 – Job 42:2 - Ps22:27 --- Ps 33:15 –Ps 65:2 --- Ps 86:9 --- Ps 103:8-9 --- Ps 145:9-10 --- Ps145:13-14 --- Ps 145:14 --- Prov 16:9 –Prov 19:21 – Isa 25:6-8 --- Isa 45:22-23 --- Isa 49:6 --- Isa 54:8 --- Isa 57:16-18 --- Jer 7:31-- Jer 31:33-34 --- Jer 32:35 – Lam 3:31-33 --- Micah 7:18

This might be the third time I've mentioned this, but whenever the word "all" is used within the above verses--it is a "passive all" in the Greek.  Meaning, there is nothing a person can do or not do to be included as a member of the inclusively redundant "all" group.  As an example from the above "gnat" list, let's use Romans 5:18:
"Therefore just as one man's trespass led to condemnation for ALL, so one man's act of righteousness leads to justification and life for ALL."

There is nothing written within the chapter that one must believe, confess, repent, or obey for this statement in Romans to be true!

Before I go any further, let's look at the word "condemnation" in this verse, because in some Christian circles, it is taught that condemnation is synonymous with going to hell.  In this case in Romans, it only means death, die, etc.  The exact same Greek word for condemnation can be found in 1 Cor 15:22 – "In Adam ALL die (condemned)...".  The word condemnation has never been used in scripture within the context of anything of a spiritual nature, nor has it ever applied anytime to the eternal (hell).  It is always used to describe a corporeal matter, for example:

"...for that which you judge another, you condemn yourself" (Rm 2:1).  Is this saying you kill yourself, or you die, or you're going to hell because of judging another?   It's nothing more than a strong figure of speech implying a "death" to your conscience, attitude, or the way you view life.

"...by your words you'll be condemned" (Matt. 12:37).  Literally, are you going to die, or you're going to hell because of words?  Again, it's only speaking of a possible ramification of a temporary "death" to those things in life that give you peace.

"he who has disbelieved shall be condemned" (Mk 16:16). Jesus promises a vivified life to those who believe. A life full of the fruit of God's Spirit, so without believing, one is "dead" to those attributes of God. Move along... nothing eternal here.

Jesus said to the adulterous women: "I do not condemn you..." (Jn 8:11). Was Jesus saying I do not kill you, or I do not sentence you to an eternal torture chamber? I think you're getting the point.

Back to...
"Therefore just as one man's trespass led to condemnation for ALL, so one man's act of righteousness leads to justification and life for ALL."

Obviously the word condemnation in Romans 5:18, means "death", as in we're all going to die someday. Everyone born is going to die. In this present age, no amount of free will, confessing, believing, repenting, or obeying God is going to stop the death process! This is why it's a passive all when it states "condemnation for all"--there is nothing you can do about it. It's almost common sense if you think about it.

Christians are willing to accept the "all" death scenario, because they know they have no choice. Yet, the exact same Greek word "all" is used in the same verse stating all will be justified and live. In using this verse, Christendom pushes the narrative that we are given a choice to live and not a choice to die, even though it's the exact same word "all". In this context, Christian theology doesn't make any sense! This is a perfect example of religious carnal thinking, that it's acceptable to strain out a gnat by ignoring what this verse is actually saying, and later swallow a camel in the form of the man-made doctrine that being made alive in Christ is conditional on the willingness of the individual rather than "the act of righteousness" performed by Christ.

Remember the proper use of the word "all" if you decide to strain any other verses in the above list. Consider rereading chapter 5: When Did "All" Become A "Select Few"? Applicable to every verse in my list--the Greek root word for "all" is "pan" as in: Panton, Pantes, Pantas, or Panta. When cross referencing these words in a Koine Greek Bible, the Greek dictionaries usually display symbols representing "passive, neutered (neutral), active" as : "pas", "neu", or "act".

An "active all" looks like this in Matthew 14:20: "...and they "all" (act.) ate and were satisfied." They ate--an action required on the part of "the all" in order for "the all" to be satisfied. So, when you see a verse like the one in 1st Tim 2:4: "God will have "ALL" (pantas) to be saved...", you will not find anywhere within the context, an action of believing, confessing, repenting, or obeying, for God to save all. I know this is going against everything some people have been taught, but it's the truth and not a camel.

How do I know it's the truth and not a camel? As cute as those camel faces are, they are not the face of God. Even if I didn't know what I now know of how the Greek defines the meaning of the word "all" in my list of gnats, I still have eyes to see, and a brain to use to notice there are no conditions attached to any of the above "gnat" verses. In other words a person cannot contextually apply a "one must first...", or an "only if...", or "true--but...", because there is no "first, only, or buts" to validate any of these verses. They are all self-contextualizing, as in they are speaking truth to every circumstance, to all people, and for all time. Also, in every case, they compliment God's character of love, as well as what His end goal is. It's easier for the carnal mind to believe the worst outcome, and maybe hope for the best, than it is to trust God for the best outcome for "all". I do completely understand, because when a carnal mind watches the carnal news broadcast--one can't help but to think the worst outcome for humanity.

Let's now look at a few more camels Christianity is feeding its members. I'll be painting with a broad brush, so you as a reader may not be participating in my camel Tourtière (meat pie) at this time in your walk.

There is a camel by the name of Gehenna: Every Latin translated Bible calls Gehenna--hell! Christians believe this translation to be accurate, thus swallowing a camel of ignorance. At the time of Jesus' day, Gehenna was a practical, real place, as in a garbage dump. Christians would rather swallow a camel by calling it hell rather than what it historically was, and still is today. I'm only half right, it's no longer a garbage dump, but it most certainly exists today. So, according to Christian thinking, am I assuming wrong, if someone were to tell me to go to hell--I could book a flight to Jerusalem? The garbage dump has been turned into a pristine park near the southeastern corner of the old city.

I met two camels once, who went by the names of Lazarus and the rich man. As covered in detail in a previous chapter, we should know the rich man wasn't in hell. Jesus was recorded as calling the place: "the unseen". However, the ancient Latin church fed a camel of hell to the illiterate peasants of their day, and Christians of today are still swallowing that same damn camel.

I thought it was a camel instead of a sheep or a goat. The parable of the sheep and the goats begins by saying in Matthew 25:32:

"All the NATIONS will be gathered before Him; and He will separate them from one another, as the shepherd separates the sheep from the goats."

Did I miss something or did Jesus say He was going to gather ALL THE NATIONS? However, Christians are swallowing the camel of believing it's all about the individual, describing the goats as unbelievers, and the sheep as believers, rather than referring to the sheep and goats as nations.

Later on, how does Matthew 25:40 fit into all this? "Truly I say to you, to the extent that you did it to one of these brothers of Mine, even the least of them, you did it to Me." ' So, what does "... one of these brothers of Mine, even the least of them..." mean? Who were His "brothers"? When addressing the "goats", Jesus metaphorically points out what the goats have done, or are going to do to His brothers. His "brothers" represents a nation. Can you guess which one? Since Christians didn't exist at the time when Jesus spoke these words, and there was no such thing as a Christian nation, then contextually this verse isn't for or about Christians. Who are the goat nations? I'll answer with a question--how often have we read or watched on the news about the nations of Iran, Syria, Lebanon, Iraq, Jordan, or Egypt coming to Israel's aid?

When did any of these nations aid Israel when they were hungry, thirsty, welcome them in as a stranger--clothe them when they were naked, or visit them in prison?  All my life, I've watched on the news how some of these countries did the exact opposite of feeding, giving drink, etc.  The goats are the nations that persecuted, or are going to afflict His brothers", versus the NATIONS (the sheep) that have supported Israel.  I was taught for years that "the sheep" in this verse was referring to a group of people... that didn't even exist yet..., i.e. the Christians.  Gulp!  One more camel bites the dust.

When it comes to the Lake of fire, Christians are swallowing a smorgasbord of camels with this one.

Camel 1:  The lake of fire is hell, yet poorly translated bibles claim death and hell are going to be thrown into it.  The correct translation is "death and the grave" are going to be thrown into the lake of fire... this is the second death, as in the death of death.

Camel 2:  The lake of fire is a real place that is eternal, torturous, and is separated from God, yet the Bible states it's in the presence of God.

Camel 3:  It's God's justice to torture people for an eternity, even though this goes directly against the character of God.  God's "loving justice" is to purify those things listed as being thrown into the lake.  God is good.  His purposes are for the good.  The lake of fire is for the good.  The lake of fire is a symbolic PROCESS to PURIFY--it's NOT a real place!  To believe so requires a camel to be swallowed.

Have you heard about a camel that promoted ancient pagan mythology?  Did Jesus promote ancient pagan mythology?  Apparently He must have according to Christian beliefs, since Jesus has been accused of using both Hades and hell in His teachings.

Everyone seems to practice some form of paganism exemplified by the names of the days of our week.  There are numerous things Christians practice; from lighting candles to celebrating Christmas and Easter--they all have their roots in ancient paganism.  My opinion is:  So what!  Who cares--no harm is being done--no one is being hurt by these practices, especially in celebrating Christmas and Easter.  Yet, we do have those people within Christendom, who are referred to as "legalists" or "purists", who act somewhat self-righteously in the way they judge others for enjoying things like Christmas and Easter.

Ironically and hypocritically, those very same people who make that judgment call--showing very little love and grace to their fellow members in the family of God--these very same people practice, believe, and actually promote ancient pagan mythologies themselves by promoting the doctrine of hell! And because they're so legalistic, ironically, they'll threaten you with pagan hell fire for practicing pagan holidays like Christmas and Easter. Knowing how they feel about paganism, would it be offensive to them, or to you as my reader, to say: "For Zeus so loved the world that he gave his only begotten son Hercules; that whosoever believes...". Again, would that be offensive to you--it would be extremely offensive to most people within Christendom.

I think it would okay to assume that most Christians would be aghast at the thought of paying sacred homage to Zeus and Hercules. Me being the smart ass that I am, I would have to ask what is wrong with giving this kind of tribute to Zeus and Hercules? I would have to assume they would chastise me for substituting God with Zeus, and swapping Christ for Hercules. Those offended would further defend their position by making the claim that Zeus and Hercules came from ancient pagan Greek mythology, and we as Christians don't believe in, and shouldn't promote those kinds of things! Oh really?

I would have to respond by claiming I still don't see a problem with it, because Christendom claims most people are going to end up in Hades, yet Hades is the name of Zeus's brother, so why not include

Zeus if you're going to involve his brother?  Not only is Christianity elevating another god by incorporating pagan mythology, but they're basing one-third of their gospel story on a lie.  Two-thirds of Christian theology might be based on truth, but, to add a third element of Hades into the mix leavens the whole loaf.  How so?  The modern gospel story claims how God sent His only begotten Son (truth) to save us from Hades (hell--a lie).

Along this same vein of pagan thinking, I need to ask of Christian men:  Do you believe in Liber, a Roman god of male fertility?  I don't want to leave out Christian women, so I'll ask if they, or their men believe in Cupid, a Roman god of love?  Do you both believe you're going to Valhalla in Asgard after you die, to sit down at a banquet table with your god Odin?  WHAT?  NO?  WHY NOT?  I'll answer the questions for you--it's because those gods came from ancient Latin and Scandinavian paganism--right?

I'm a bit confused, (not really) because Christianity believes and promotes a Latin pagan place called infernum, later called hell in English, which was named after a pagan Scandinavian goddess of the underworld--who's name was Hel. To make matters worse, they claim there is a god of that underworld. They're quite divided within their church system on what his name was. Was it Lucifer, satan, snake, devil, the dragon, Morning Star, Angel of light, or Beelzebub?

And the cherry on the cake that's on the camel's back is this: They claim this god of their Christian underworld can supersede--override God's will, and can be everywhere, tempting everyone all at the same time. Not only that--he will end up defeating God in the long run, because the vast majority of people will end up in his pagan fiery underworld rather than in Heaven. Wow... a created being having more power than its creator! If you're reading this, and you're a hell believer--I used to believe the same as you until I tried to prove someone wrong about this, so now I'm asking you to prove me wrong.

All pagan beliefs deny a one true God, so that would leave God out in the cold when praying to a multiple of deities. Since Jesus is known to be God's only Son and only did what God told Him--He wouldn't be admonished in a pagan feast either. On the other hand, both Hades and hell are welcomed guests as an intricate part of the multi-god pagan practice, so of course you'll find writings of such places within pagan sacred texts. Neither place, nor the concept of hell or Hades can be found within the Hebrew texts, so it takes a huge camel to swallow to think that pagan words are a derivative of the Hebrew word Sheol.

A camel once told me that both hell and Hades was in its Bible!

New American: 10 Hades and 13 hells.

NIV: 5 Hades and 13 hells.

Revised Standard: 9 Hades and 13 hells.

King James: 0 Hades and 54 hells.
But I thought they used the Greek manuscripts to translate the King James? What the Hades?

New King James: 11 Hades and 32 hells.
How's your math? Add 11 plus 32, and you get 43. King James claims there are 54 hells, so what the hell happened to the missing 11 Hades or hells?

Some will make the claim that Hades and hell are one and the same, yet they come from two different languages, and from two different cultures that believed in two different pagan practices. Yes, but they both came from the one word Sheol! What? Now you're adding a third different language and a third different culture into the mix.(?) Only the ignorant would fall for such a hoax. So, if I'm not allowed to change God or Jehovah to Zeus, and Jesus to Hercules, then why is Christianity allowed to change the word Sheol, that simply means death or grave, into an ancient pagan belief of Hades or hell?

I have a story for the people who claim the King James version is the most accurate. I had a friend in law enforcement, and he teaches interrogation classes--he teaches other officers how to interrogate people. I called him one day and I reiterated to him how he has a suspect write stuff down over and over again--giving the same testimony over and over again, and sometimes as a interrogator, you would ask the same questions over and over again. If you get different answers, you would then bring in a different interrogator to do the same line of questioning. If you still get different answers to what was originally written down or verbally spoken, then you'd know something is wrong, something is inconsistent--you know that something is false, and they must be lying--requiring further investigation!

He told me I was on the right track and that's exactly how it was usually done. Since he was a

King James only guy--I pointed out to him how hell was mentioned in the King James 54 times, and none of the other Bibles agree with it. Not only that, but none of the other Bible versions agreed with the King James, nor with each other--don't you think that discrepancy requires an investigation on your part? He didn't feel a need to investigate the discrepancies. This man was an articulate police officer, yet his blind faith, i.e. the camel that he swallowed told him the King James Bible was the most accurate. He didn't even follow his own guidance and teaching methods.

My cop friend's reasoning on why the King James Bible was more trustworthy was BECAUSE it has the most hells in it! Sad, but due to my questioning, our friendship didn't last too much longer after that. If he was still my friend, I would ask him why his KJ is accurate due to hell being mention 54 times as compared to other versions? I would follow up by informing him of how the King James was translated by the means of using three other English speaking Bibles--one directly and two indirectly were translated from the Latin Vulgate. And the Vulgate mentioned infernum (hell) 111 times, yet the King James only listed it 54--so what happed to those other 57 hells when the King James was published?

If the number of hells is the criteria for accuracy, then shouldn't we all be using the Vulgate? This same kind of reasoning should be applied to the word Hades as well.  Both word usages of hell and Hades are never consistent with each other.  What I mean by that--if they mean the exact same thing, why use both within scripture rather than just one or the other?  At least the KJ only used the word hell, even though it's claimed to be translated from the Greek.  None of it adds up, and it requires a bit of camel swallowing to believe the accuracy of any of it.

By applying what I've learned from law enforcement to my conundrum of hell and/or Hades-- what we're getting in scripture are many different answers to what people claim was originally written down or verbally spoken.  This tells me something is wrong, the way the words are used is inconsistent-- the number of times the words are being used is inconsistent--something has to be false, and someone is lying!  Don't be like my ex-friend cop buddy by ignoring the inconsistencies--all I'm asking of my reader is to investigate.

It would be easy to swallow a camel if Jesus encouraged it--right?  One of my preacher buddies once told me of how Jesus warned us of hell more than anyone else within the entire New Testament!  At the time I shook my head in agreement, but if I knew then what I know now--I would have grabbed my friend's shirt collar, pulled his face close to mine and say that's not true.  Jesus didn't speak English-- are you inferring He spoke Latin as well?

The excuse (the camel) is:  The "concept" of hell was His warning, regardless of what word was being used.  I want to make it clear--Jesus warned of Gehanna more than anyone else within scripture--He never warned anyone of hell, concept or otherwise.  Let's examine the idea of "concept" for a moment, and reflect by asking the question:  Do you think you have it good by being a Christian?  If the above "concept of hell" is true, then I would have rather lived in the Old Testament times.  What?  Are you crazy--why?  According to the writers of the Old Testament--death to them only meant sleep, but since Jesus came, death can now mean hellish eternal punishment!

If Christianity is correct, and they expect the rest of us to swallow the "concept" camel, then that would mean Jesus brought BAD NEWS for the majority of mankind. Wouldn't it have been better for the world if Jesus never came in the first place? Think about it! I have to conclude that the "Good News" message brought by Christianity has been grossly perverted. By the way... Jesus never mentioned hell or Hades when referencing the Good News message, so why do Christians?

The early Christians, as in the very first Christians--before "the message" got to Rome--were Jewish. Jews didn't believe in hell, concept or otherwise, and they would have never promoted pagan words that would promote pagan mythology. That's why I believe those words of hell or Hades were never in their original letters that later became the Gospels. The rest of the New Testament was written by Paul, and he never mentioned either hell or Hades in his thirteen letters, yet he spoke fluent Greek.

However, the Septuagint used the word Hades as a "concept" of a Hebrew grave, but when the Latins got hold of it--they applied their pagan concepts to the letters and the Septuagint--changing it all to hell (infernum). Why the hell not? About 700 years earlier, the Greeks laid the foundation made of leaven, by applying a pagan underworld word known as Hades to replace the word Sheol.  Yes, Hades might have meant nothing more than a grave to those Jewish captives in Greece, but to anyone else reading the Septuagint--the word Hades obviously brought to mind a tortuous place that they thought was true--that actually existed, even though it's all based on myths and folklore from early pagan practices.

To conclude this chapter I want to point out that Jesus and the early Christians must have promoted ancient pagan mythology, or something is horribly wrong with scripture.  Fearlessly puke out those camels and start afresh with a clean slate while doing your research.  You have a choice--you can keep swallowing camels sautéed in a broth of ignorance, by continuing to strain my list of 73 "gnats", or you can see how these 73 verses clearly proclaim God's awesome love, power, and authority to exercise His will for all creation to be reconciled.

In closing, it's so easy while researching to put the cart before the horse.  My next chapter will expose the numerous ways Christendom puts the cart before the horse.

# Chapter 14

## Putting The Cart Before The Horse

Who is responsible for your salvation? I can easily follow up with a second question of: What is our part to play in the process? The combination of these two questions are quite thought provoking-- don't you agree? Possibly not, but this chapter is going to be loaded with questions for the purpose of making a person think, rather than just believe. Don't get me wrong, believing is extremely important, but Christendom has a nasty habit of expecting its members to believe whatever the church system promotes. I, on the other hand want you as my reader to question why do you believe what you believe, and where did the information come from that you consider truth?

I get it, I really do. People within your church walls are kind and loving people for the most part, and they wouldn't lie to you--right? So it's natural to conclude that everything they have told you about God is the truth. Being human, that's impossible, and I would think reasonable people would agree that some things taught in church are blatantly wrong. A lot of what they say might be the truth, but often times it's a backward kind of truth. What I mean by that is, they will teach you something that is based on truth, but approach it from the wrong side of things.


Some teachings use all the right words, find the right scriptures, but end up "putting the cart before the horse" in applying scripture. I'll be giving examples in depth of how this is done within Christendom. But, as an analogy it would be like me warning you of a deep hole in the ground after you've already fallen into the hole. It's all based on truth-- the ground, the hole, its depth, and then sadly--I hold you responsible for falling into it even though I knew it was there all along.


In my attempt to reveal how Christian theology puts the cart before the horse, I'll be using well known Bible verses that are self-contextualizing. First, let my clarify what I mean by the term "self-contextualizing". I try to avoid sounding ultra religious, but in this case I have to say it this way: I never saw it in my previous 35 years of walking with God, so I can't help but to believe His Spirit has recently revealed to me that there are a number of scriptures that are truth for all people, every time, and in every circumstance. I don't think I'll get much flack once you see which scriptures I'll be using.

As an author of my book, am I not responsible for what is written within these pages? However, what if someone gave me credit for writing a book I intended to write, but I've not yet written? I'm sure one would agree this is "jumping the gun", or better said as, "Putting the cart before the horse". Let's take a step further into the bizarre and say a group of people took you to court for simply reading the remarks in my book that they considered slanderous to them, and they held you liable.

There are two points I'm trying to make.

- First: An author is the one who is responsible for the content of his or her book.
- Second: Would it be right to hold someone responsible for the actions of another?

Holding someone responsible for the actions of another is precisely what is promoted as good Christian theology. "No", they will claim. "We believe everyone should be responsible for their own actions, and if those actions result in spending an eternity in hell, then the person only has to blame themselves". This is absolutely true--to a carnal mind, but this kind of thinking ignores grace completely.

I want to come back to how it's considered good Christian theology to hold someone responsible for the actions of another, but first we need to hit on the idea that people should be held eternally responsible for their short lifetime of actions, by quoting Romans 5:20: "...but where sin increased, grace abounded all the more." Why do most Christian leaders hate this verse? Sure, they won't admit it, but they know how to dance around it.

The whole chapter in Romans 5 is talking about the "actions" of people labeled as: "helpless, ungodly, sinners, enemies of God, condemned, and transgressors". Does God hold them eternally responsible, much like Christianity holds all mankind responsible for their actions? Hell no--better put, no hell. Nowhere within this entire chapter does it mention believing or repenting as a prerequisite to reap the benefits of God's grace. Also, nowhere within this chapter is there a hint of the existence of hell.

Let me get this straight... doesn't a person who is "helpless" as an "ungodly sinner", and an "enemy of God" that's "condemned" to die as a "transgressor", best define someone who is unbelieving and unrepentant? (ya think?!) Is this not the exact profile of an individual who should be held responsible for their own actions--resulting in a judgment of eternal torment for those actions? Yet, that judgment can't be found in the same chapter that mentions the offenses, but instead, all we read is how grace abounds! If you disagree, your argument is not with me--I can't see any other way to interpret this chapter! I know I specifically covered verse 9 in a previous chapter, but once again I want to point out that "wrath of God" does not exist in the Greek texts. The context of why grace abounds is due to our personal wrath towards others--defined in the Greek as our own violent passions.

So, how does Christian theology hold someone responsible for the actions of another? I'm sure, since you've read this question three times, you're probably assuming I'm insinuating something negative. What I mean by that is, someone did something bad and someone else is getting the blame for it--right? No, I'm implying how someone did something GREAT, but what they did was incomplete, insufficient, and someone else must be held responsible to complete the task. I hope that made sense. Read on, and I'll make it clear.

Christian theology expects and teaches that the individual is responsible to complete and accomplish what Christ has already accomplished. Again, that doesn't make sense, yet the opposite way of thinking is described in Hebrews 12:2: "Looking unto Jesus the author and finisher of our faith...". Some Bible versions use the phrase "perfecter of our faith", rather than finisher. Imagine, having your faith in God perfected--I like that idea. So, according to this self-contextualizing verse--who is the Author, and who is responsible for your faith? Yet, Christendom teaches people are to be held responsible for gaining faith and later on perfecting it through an obedient walk. This is wrong teaching and it is putting the cart before the horse!

Christ is the Author! Just like the author of a book is responsible for the content of that book, the Author of your faith is responsible for the content of your faith. Noticed how this verse doesn't say your free will is the author, nor the confession of your mouth is the author, nor believing in your heart is the author, nor some teacher or preacher is the author, it doesn't even say having faith in Christ is the author, and especially it doesn't claim how you personally are the author.

Christianity puts the cart before the horse with the above Hebrew verse, by claiming it's YOU FIRST who must believe!  They hold you responsible for the COMPLETED actions of Christ, but in an bass-ackwards kind of way.  It's agreed that Christ is the Author of your faith, but it's all on you to make or allow Him to be the Author--you're responsible for making Him responsible.  Who in the hell, I no longer believe in, does that make sense to?  As in my above analogy, it would be like holding you as my reader, responsible for what I write.

If it takes believing, then how can one believe without faith, and where does that faith come from?  The verse in Hebrews 12:2 beautifully answers those questions.  So, who is really responsible for you having enough faith to believe--you or Christ?  Do you know what else is so cool... the cherry on the top?  Not only does Christ instill/install that faith in us--He also PERFECTS it!  What is the end result of that perfection?  You guessed it!  SALVATION!  Now it's worth asking the most important question of all--who is the real One responsible for your salvation--you or Christ?  Also remember, salvation has nothing to do with hell, but it's all about being made whole so one can encompass a vivified life.

It should now be obvious where I'm going with this chapter, so the following examples of scripture I'll be using may seem a little redundant.  In other words, I'll be repeating myself a lot to make a point of how Christianity puts the cart before the horse.

"For I am confident of this very thing, that He who began a good work in you will perfect it until the day of Christ Jesus". (Philippians 1:6 )

Who began a good work in you?  Did you just one day look into a mirror and say:  "Know what?  I'm confident this will be the day I'll start walking with God"?  Redundant time... Notice how this verse doesn't say it was your decision that began a good work in you, nor the confession of your mouth that began a good work, nor believing in your heart that began a good work, nor some teacher or preacher who began a good work (even though some will want to take the credit), not even does it say having faith in Christ is what began a good work, and especially it doesn't say you personally, as in your free will is what began a good work.

Yet, Christendom teaches the exact opposite by putting the cart before the horse.
How so?  By insisting it is YOU who begins a good work in you through your act of obedience by way of believing.  But, how can one believe something without the gift of faith--the inner awareness, the enlightenment--all describing the conviction of the Spirit of God--to do so?  (Note:  Conviction in the Greek simply implies a bridging of God's thoughts to your own.)

"He who began a good work in you will complete it...". Will complete it? This is great news and should give us hope, a confidence, and a trust in God's love and competence. It is written: "The adversary (the satan) comes to steal, kill, and destroy...". In this case "the church" is "the satan"! Why? Because the same One who "began" a work in you will "COMPLETE" it, but the church denies this truth by stealing, killing, and destroying the trust and confidence people have in God's ability to "complete" what He "began"! Ending up in hell sure doesn't sound like a completion to me. The point: The Beginner and the Completer (Perfecter) is the One responsible for "the good work in you"--resulting in? You guessed right again-- SALVATION! Again--who is the real One responsible for your salvation--you or God?

"No one can come to Him UNLESS HE DRAWS THEM". (Jn 6:44)

Who is the "He" in this verse? Your confession doesn't initially draw you--your confession happens after you've already been drawn! Your believing doesn't initially draw you--your believing is what takes place after the Spirit of God draws you to Himself. Are you sensing the cart before horse syndrome? We all should share the love of God to everyone around us, in our everyday lives, and if necessary-- doing so as a teacher or preacher. Even so, the above verse is not saying that the sharing, teaching or preaching is what drew you.  It certainly wasn't you who drew yourself, so who is responsible for drawing you, resulting in your SALVATION--you or God?  Your answer doesn't change the truth, nor will your belief change the fact that it is God who is responsible for your salvation.


The below example is one of the best paragons of how Christianity puts the cart before the horse.  As I've written before, but worth repeating again--it's extremely important to confess, believe, and repent, but these important things happen AFTER God authors, draws, begins, and gives His gift of faith.  So there's no way it could be your faith in Christ that started anything, because in your mind you were an enemy of God.


Christendom somehow reasons how a person (who by their very nature desires to be their own god in every aspect of their lives) will suddenly yield to someone they have never had any knowledge of.  Not only that, but that specific someone they never knew--happens to be invisible, and rarely if not ever speaks to them.  Somehow a sinful individual obtains the ability on their own to gain their own faith to believe in something they never thought of before.  Who could do that without God's initial power, that some misconstrue as an invitation?  "Invitation" is yet another doctrine of man, because the word "invite" is never in context within scripture to accepting or receiving salvation.  What happened to Paul?  Was that an invitation?  If you call being knocked off your ass--on your ass, and then blinded as an invitation then....  I think you get my point.

"Therefore just as one man's trespass led to condemnation for ALL, so one man's act of righteousness leads to justification and life for ALL." (Rm 5:18)  In this verse, who is the "One" who did such an act of righteousness that lead to justification and life for some"?  OOPS... I mean "ALL".  In the same fashion as I mischievously inserted the word "some" in order to replace the word "all", Christian theology changes the "One"--who represents Christ in this verse, into an individual, thus making mankind responsible for their own justification.  The deception reads like this:  "... so the individual's act of believing leads to justification and life for him or herself", or how about:  "... so the one whose act of repenting leads to justification and life for him or herself."

You get the point.  Yes, I twisted this scripture to expose the underlying tone perpetuated by most within the Christian church.  NOT SO!  We are not doing that!... some may shout.  If I'm wrong, then answer this:  How does a person become a member of the "all being justified" group that Christ's act of righteousness provided?  I know for a fact your answer will require, to one degree or another, some action from the individual to believe, confess, and repent.

This is probably the third time I've felt forced to mention this in my book, but the word "all" in this passage is a "passive all" in the Greek.  Meaning, there are no prerequisites to being part of the "all"-- there are no requirements or actions from an individual to be justified!  The exact same "passive all" in the Greek was applied to:  "Therefore just as one man's trespass led to condemnation for ALL...".  If the "passive all" was not true, then it would require each and every individual to perform the same disobedient act of Adam to be condemned--to die.  Otherwise, we'd already have eternal life until we did what Adam did.

Who is responsible for your justification that leads to salvation?  Do you still believe it was your confession that leads to your justification?  Was it because you believed or was it One man's act of righteousness that lead to that?  You're going to have to decide to stop putting the cart before the horse in regard to this.  I'll explain it this way--the bottom line is we NOW confess with our mouths, and we NOW believe in our hearts **because** of that "One man's act of righteousness".

Our acts of believing, confessing and repenting, are all after-effects of "One man's act of righteousness".  Our believing, confessing and repenting didn't cause Jesus to do what He did for us.  "But while we were yet sinners, Christ...".  We have been enabled to do all these "acts" because of His faith--given to us as a gift so we can't boast about how we believed, confessed, and repented.  Who is responsible for salvation--you or God?  It's simple and it's not rocket science folks, but unfortunately Christianity has put the cart before the horse by saying we're the ones responsible.

I'm going to continue along this stream of redundant thinking by saying the same thing, but in different ways.  Which came first, the chicken or the egg?  What?  Which came first, believing or salvation?  Christianity has a nasty habit of putting far too many responsibilities on the shoulders of the believer--of their members, that actually belong to God so He can get the glory!  But, for some reason man's ego and pride (the true Adversary) have a tendency to feel if we don't do out part--it somehow cheapens it.  Don't get me wrong, I'm not coming against being responsible--I'm coming against a deception when it comes to responsibilities.

If someone believes the doctrine that you must first believe before you can obtain salvation, I've got to ask what happens to those countless billions of people throughout history who have never heard of the name of Jesus? They've never been given the chance to "believe".  How does "you must first believe" apply to them?   It's far too easy for us as an American or Western indoctrinated Christian to simply ignore that question, considering there's not even a city anywhere in this country where there isn't some fanatical Bible thumper screaming: "Turn or burn!" We take it for granted--we hear Jesus-Jesus-Jesus everywhere. In reality, it's not like that everywhere in the world, and especially in times past.

So again, I ask what comes first--believing or salvation? Was it the accomplishments of Jesus that best defines your salvation, or was it your believing that clinched it. Some will say both--a fifty-fifty kind of a scenario. Are you sure you don't want to give Jesus at least 51% of the credit? This kind of thinking--this kind of doctrine of men is one of the most corrupt self-righteous beliefs to infect Christendom. How is it "self-righteous"? Whatever percentage you choose--that percentage is due to something you accomplished, so if you give Jesus 51% because of His righteous acts, and then keep 49%--you're 49% self-righteous. The Bible teaches the exact opposite of a cooperative salvation!

The Greek word soteria covers a variety of words such as: salvation, save, saved, etc.. You can attach several meanings of: preservation, protection, healing or health, prosperity, but the one English word that best describes "soteria" is wholeness.

There are six verses in the New Testament that talk about believing to receive salvation. (Mk 16:16, Lk 8:12, Acts 15:11, Acts 16:31, Ro 10:9, 1 Cor 1: 1) One of them requires a baptism, along with believing in order to receive salvation. However, in every case within those six verses, salvation is "soteria"-- meaning, being made whole in whatever circumstances the verses were referring in context. Let me reiterate--in every case where "believing" is required for salvation, the Greek word for salvation is "soteria". In every case, being saved was pertaining to life in general, meaning a daily issue, as in a practical day-to-day struggle. All the above scriptures are about being made whole from being sick, or being saved from death, but mostly they were about obtaining a vivified life that would make a person whole no matter what the circumstance.

Within the context of the verses I found, soteria has nothing to do with anything spiritual or eternal. As an example, let me provide a modern day, practical scenario of how "believing" is a prerequisite to being saved (soteria). If someone warns me that a bridge is out and if I choose to not believe them, and plunge into the river--the ramifications and responsibility are all mine to bear. Using this same scenario, if I change my mind (repent) and believe what I'm being told, then I would be "saved" from that accident. There is nothing eternal about this.

There is absolutely no Bible verse about being saved spiritually--as being saved from hell. To assign verses to that belief requires an assumption to be made, because if translated properly, the words hell nor eternal can't be found anywhere within the context. So technically it is true we must believe to be saved, but not in the cart before the horse way Christendom teaches. Simply being alive, teaches us all that in most cases in life we must believe there is a problem for us to be saved from that problem. If the problem is illness, don't you think it's important to "first believe" you have an illness in order to be saved from the illness?

I don't know about you, but there's been plenty of instances, and probably more to come, where I didn't trust God! Wow, shocker... I know. If I chose not to repent--change my mind about trusting God-- my life would be miserable. One could call this a spiritual issue--I don't see it that way--I see it as pragmatic. My point: God, in His great kindness, will hound us and keep on us until we believe Him, resulting in our repentance for not trusting Him-- succeeding in an eventual salvation from whatever the circumstance presented. Contextually, believing before receiving salvation unto wholeness is exactly right, but NOT in the way Christendom teaches it.

So, if Jesus didn't save us from hell, then what did He save us from?  Is it a "saved from" issue, or is it being "saved in order to" scenario?  Both, as in we all need to be saved from our own violent passions, which metaphorically can be a hell for us as well as those around us.  But technically most Bible verses are referring to being "saved in order to" have a "vivified life".  But, once again the Christian church has it all backwards--putting the cart before the horse.

They teach about how Jesus saves mankind to have "eternal life", versus what they consider an eternal death in hell.  To make matters worse, even though they claim Jesus saves, it later is oxymoronically understood that it's not up to Jesus to do the saving, but it requires your decision to save yourself.  Poorly translated Latin agenda bibles imply that theme for sure, but in the Greek--Jesus never offered anyone eternal life.  WHAT?  No eternal life?  I didn't say that.  What I am saying is Jesus offers something so much greater than just eternal life!

Jesus saved us to have an aonian life, a quality of life, a vivified life that will last an eternity. In this case we need to be saved from our ignorance rather than being saved from hell. Ignorant to having a vivified life that starts right here and now, in this lifetime, as in a renewed life--that is endowed with the fruit of God's Spirit. By exhibiting and walking "in the Spirit", also known as "love, joy, peace," etc., one brings a new excitement, adding a quality of energy to life that one never had before. Your life becomes a union between you and God with a quality and meaning like it never had before. And guess what? It lasts for an eternity!

Yes, generally speaking Christianity promotes these things I wrote above, but in a half-assed sort of way by including hell in the mix. It all comes down to you're going to live what you believe. Jesus offered a vivified life that encompasses the fruit of the Spirit. How does a threat of eternal destruction, hanging over your heads, add to and compliment a vivified life, much less bring out the fruit of the Spirit? Does this kind of threat give you "peace"?

This is what being saved is all about--defined as being saved from ourselves in whatever way needed to overcome wrongful temptations.  Jesus was a perfect example of how to do that.  However, on the other hand, if you believe being saved is referring to being saved from hell--this "saved" offers no vivified life that Christ offers for this lifetime or in the ages to come.  The best it will offer is a fake eternal life.  What good is an eternal life if it's not vivified, and how can it be vivified if many of your friends and family are suffering in hell?

Someone might be thinking... If what you're writing is true, of how the Christian church is putting the cart before the horse in requiring its future members to "believe first" to be saved--then what about someone who chooses not to believe?  Simply, they're missing out BIG TIME, but only in this lifetime!  Frankly, all of us are missing out in this lifetime, because we are refusing to "believe" certain things that are true in order to live a full vivified life.  I suppose none of us are "fully saved" as long as "we see through a glass dimly".  (1 Cor. 13:12)

God has an answer to everyone's unbelief in Romans 3:3:  "If some did not believe, their unbelief will not notify the faithfulness of God".  I might add how this verse is self contextualizing as in God is faithful no matter what.  Also interestingly, this verse actually is in context to what Christians consider "the unbeliever".  I completely understand why Christianity teaches the importance of how an "unbeliever" in Christ needs to believe in Jesus, but they want people to do so for all the wrong reasons.  Their primary  reason is to escape hell, then secondary, if you happen to exhibit the character of God--all the better.  Doesn't this best describe someone who has a self-preserving, self-satisfying priority in mind?

Yes, we've got to believe in most cases, and yes, repentance is critical, but again, NOT in the way Christian theology promotes repentance.  They claim it means to turn from what you believe you are doing, and do the opposite.  On the surface this sounds pretty legit even though it's a doctrine of men.  Repentance simply means to change your mind-- PERIOD!  What do your actions usually do once you've change your mind about something?  They eventually turn and do the opposite.  Okay, I get where they're coming from--I used to teach it as well, but what should we be promoting people to repent--to change their mind about?

Christians need to change their mind and repent as much if not more than anyone else!

- Repent of:  Polluting the Good News message.

- Repent of:  Believing in hell.

- Repent of: Not trusting God for all humanity.

- Repent of: Not believing in the finished work of Christ.

- Repent of: Fear!

- Repent of: Believing everything you've been taught is true.

- Repent of: Thinking the Bible is inerrant.

- Repent of: Believing a person's "free will" can determine an eternal outcome of Heaven or hell.

- Repent of: Giving man's free will more power than that of God's will.

- Repent of: Doctrines of men.

- Repent of: Threatening people while thinking you're loving them.

- Repent of: Slandering God.

- Repent of: Thinking the Bible is The Word of God rather than words "from" God mixed with words from men.

- Repent of: Trusting in the Bible more than trusting in the character of God.

- Repent of:  Perverting love - perverting God

- Repent of:  Not "rightly dividing the word of truth" from words that are not true.

- Repent of:  Being gullible.

- Repent of:  Being lazy and not "studying to show yourself approved".

- Repent of:  Sitting on God's throne by judging others of not being worthy of His grace, because they didn't believe, repent, or confess as you did.

- Repent of:  Limiting God's love and power over someone's choices to only this short lifetime.

- Repent of:  Not willing to admit... you might have been taught wrong about some things.


From God's perspective, salvation for all happened before the foundation of the Earth was laid.  Which one of my readers was there, "believing", so all that could happen?  "For it is God who is at work in you, both to will and to act according to his good purposes." (Phil 2:13)  Is it "believing" that works in you, or does it say for it is God that works in you?  Since God in the One who enables us to believe in the first place--it's putting the cart before the horse to put the responsibility of "believing first" on an individual. This verse sure sounds like God is responsible for salvation rather than a believing person.

Let me be clear, I'm referring to the "initial salvation" that God completed before any of us were born. I'm not talking about being saved daily which I'll address shortly, but I'm referring to the true salvation that God has offered and has supplied to all mankind. The salvation that gives a person a vivified life, before they even knew it was available. A person can't "repent" from not having a vivified life if they don't even know it exists or it's available, and why don't people know it's available? Because the Christian church is preaching a "damned" message that slanders God's character--so why would a person want to turn to God or even believe a god like that would offer a vivified life?

What happens to those billions upon billions of people throughout history who reject what they deemed as a false god of Christianity? If believing first is the most important issue and they didn't believe at all--"will this nullify the faithfulness of God? May it never be! Let God be found faithful, and let all men (some Christian doctrines) be found liars!" (Ro. 3:3) I'm trying to encourage people to trust God alone, because you can't always trust man--no kidding, right? I'm not asking you to not love the people that you fellowship with, but don't put your trust in them. Most of them would agree with that, but unfortunately if you disagree with some of their doctrines that they put their trust in--they're going to take that as a personal affront and you're going to be judged for it.

These next few paragraphs are going to deal with a lot of doctrines, more accurately called doctrines of men that people hold tight to their vest. I'm going to share one of those major doctrines with you, and I hope you catch this.

I'm going to use Luke 11:10: (Jesus speaking) "For everyone who asks receives, and he who seeks finds, and to him who knocks it will be opened." What happens when the doctrines of men get hold of this--they twist this verse. They put the cart before the horse by wanting you to believe this verse is stating that you must ask FIRST even though it doesn't say that--then they apply it to receiving salvation even though salvation isn't mentioned! The word save, saved, or salvation is nowhere in the chapter, yet look at how this verse is used, or better put--abused. Actually, what it does say contextually is: It's giving us the RESULT of when we do ask, seek, or knock, rather than a prerequisite for salvation. In this case, "the result" is the horse, and "the prerequisite" is the cart. See what I mean?

I'm going to get a little more "gritty" with this next section, so my passion may come across as being feisty.

People didn't save themselves through the power of their own belief, nor even having faith "in" Christ, but rather Christ has saved (past, present, future tense) people first--already, through the power of His faith. Having faith in Christ sounds spiritual and oh so religious. It's good to have faith in Christ, but Christendom takes the idea and twists it by making it a requirement which slanders or nullifies grace. By doing so, having faith in Christ becomes nothing more than boasting. Do these statements sound familiar?: "I" have faith in Christ, "My" faith in Christ, Do "you" have faith in Christ? Now wait…before you get your panties in a knot and start defending your position, please consider the following:

I've done my research so let the reader do some research and prove me wrong. The simplest Greek dictionary points out there is a huge difference between the word "IN" and the word "OF". By misrepresenting or mistranslating these two simple words--Christian theology has been lead down a deceptive path of major proportions.

In reference to the two scriptures below, the word "in" puts the burden of faith upon the shoulders of man--the total opposite of the "light burden" Jesus promised in the Beattitudes. The word "in" is not the correct translation, and does not describe the gift of faith FROM God--if anything, it's describing some form of faith FROM us. What I find interesting is how the New King James Version uses the "in" translation which disagrees with the King James version that uses the word "of". Who does that make sense to-- they both can't be right, so which one is correct? If your translation has "in" instead of "of"…it is wrong!

**Galatians 2:16** - Knowing that a man is not justified by the works of the law, but by the faith "OF" Jesus Christ

**Philippians 3:9** - And be found in him, not having mine own righteousness, which is of the law, but that which is through the faith "OF" Christ

Folks… it's all about Christ! His faith! The same faith that created the universe. The gift of faith that kicks our boasting in the ass. If you drown, and someone gives you C.P.R., it's their breath that saves you--NOT YOUR OWN. Christians think their faith saves them, i.e., their faith "in" Christ. Not so! It is a free gift that is called "THE FAITH OF CHRIST" that saves all from sin (missing the mark), so no one can boast about having their own faith "in" Christ.

Has anyone ever heard the plea: "Come to Jesus"? It's not a bad thing to ask of people, but biblically it's another example of how Christendom puts the cart before the horse. How so? In Jn 6:44 it states: "No one can come to Christ UNLESS HE DRAWS THEM". Did you get that word "UNLESS"? Where's the boasting? I hear people all the time quote the verse in Ephesians 2:8: "For by grace are you saved through faith; and that not of yourselves: it is the gift of God." Yet, they turn right around and claim it's YOUR FAITH in Christ that grace has bestowed upon you. If it was your faith to begin with, then you bestowed it upon yourself, and grace wouldn't be needed! Did they forget about the second half of the verse that states: "...that not of yourselves..."? Did I miss something? Isn't the word "your" in the word "yourselves", yet it's taught that it's "your" faith? Another thing... the phrase "that faith" is referencing someone else's faith, rather than your own... "...saved through faith; and that faith is not of yourselves...".

To confirm where I'm going with this theme, I'll quote Romans 12:3: "For I say, through the grace given to me, to everyone who is among you, not to think of himself (or his faith) more highly than he ought to think, but to think soberly, as GOD HAS DEALT to each one the measure of faith." Who "dealt to each one"? What measure and by whose standard is it measured? Answer: The measure and standard that was set by Christ--that's why the two scriptures in Ga. 2:16 and Phil. 3:9 can proclaim it's the faith "of" Christ! Let's not forget, according to Ro.12:3, it states that "God has dealt to each the measure of faith." To me, this sure doesn't sound like He's left anyone out.

Christianity promotes carnal thinking in regard to faith, because they make God carnal by limiting His "measure of faith" to this temporal lifetime. This measure of faith that God gives is a necessary tool for the purpose of walking according to the fruit of His Spirit. That same tool is His gift to all humanity so we can have the ability to ask, seek, knock, and find--so we can eventually receive, as spoken about in Lk.11:9. All of this is for what purpose? To be saved from hell? How absurd and ridiculous! How about for the purpose of knocking and to keep knocking so "it" will be opened unto us, and that "it" is defined as having an amazing relationship with God.

Again, any and all belief pertaining to God is through the power of the Faith of Christ, so no one can boast that it is their own ability. The blind are not going to seek sight if they don't know they're blind in the first place. Christ's gift of faith is what opens the eyes of the blind--this is what being saved is all about, having our eyes opened to who we truly are. Just as Jesus asked the adulterous woman: (paraphrased) "Where are your accusers? I don't accuse you either. Now go and no longer do this adulterous sin." In the same manner I believe Jesus is telling mankind: The accuser is standing day and night accusing you, but I stand in intercession on your behalf. Now go and walk, knowing you can trust Me.

So technically, contextually, spiritually, and scripturally--the only difference between a believer and an unbeliever is a change of the mind, which in the Greek means repentance. It's not a change of sonship or daughtership as doctrines of men claim-- it's simply a change of mind. But, I want to give this warning; the doctrines of men want to add to the definition of repentance by inventing hoops a person needs to jump through to qualify as being a son or daughter. When they do that, they're putting people back under the law, eliminating grace from the equation, and giving themselves something to boast about.

The million dollar question is how do you get someone to change their mind?  The answer is, you don't!  None of us have that ability and only the Spirit of God can change minds through the gift of Christ's faith.  This is why earlier in this chapter, I used a verse that distinctly claims that Jesus is the Author (the beginner--not me--not you) and finisher of our faith.  So what can the average Christian do to help rather than hinder? STOP slandering God's character by trying to scare people with that false doctrine of hell!  You're actually scaring most people away from God thinking you're scaring them towards Him!

There's a minority of Christians that say if it wasn't for the threat of hell, they would have never turned to God.  Think about how horrible that motive is by putting yourself in the shoes of a loving Father. God doesn't work that way, grace doesn't work that way, and love doesn't use threats.  So, let's say you're not one of those who turned to God because of the threat of hell (which is nothing more than a perversion of love).  As long as you continue to see God and others through the lens of hell glasses, rather than through the lens of love, you're slandering God and you're not truly loving other people.  I also might add, you don't have a clue what grace is!  The doctrine of hell and the doctrine of grace don't mix. They both can't be true!

Has any of my readers heard of a Christian oxymoron called "deserved grace"? Probably not, because it's one of my originals. Grace! Grace! Grace! Christians shout it and claim it as their own. I've been told by Christians that grace means unmerited favor, or in layman's terms, God's favor towards them even though they didn't or couldn't do anything to deserve it.

So, let me understand this right. You as a Christian didn't or couldn't do anything to receive God's favor as in the way He perceives you, in His acceptance of you, or in the love from Him you claim to enjoy.

I'm confused. So, what did you do to receive this grace that you've claimed you couldn't do anything to receive? A better question would be: What makes you any different in God's eyes than an Atheist or a Buddhist? The answer always given is: "Because I believed". WAIT! Your "believing" is something you could do, is it not? Yet, you claimed you couldn't do anything in order to deserve or to receive God's grace. I plead with you to think about this conundrum. You can't have it both ways. You can't say you believed in order for grace to take effect!

The Christian doctrine of it being necessary to believe first, while at the same time claiming you were saved because of grace, just doesn't add up. Everyone, but the indoctrinated Christian, can see there's a con somewhere in the mix--as in a deception somewhere, or else a bald face lie. In my opinion, the only thing different that happened to you, dear Christian, is--in God's timing and purpose He gave you, as a gift, the exact measure of Christ's faith that you needed.

And, as I wrote earlier, but worth repeating--it's not your faith God gave you, but instead it's "The Faith of Christ, so you couldn't boast about believing—as you so quickly and always have been taught to do. So you see… since death is no hindrance to God, He can bestow His gift of grace to anyone, any time, in any age, thus making everyone equally loved in regard to how He perceives everyone in His love and acceptance. To me, this is GRACE!

If believing is necessary first--before salvation, and if you still don't think that's putting the cart before the horse, then let's explore an analogy to see if it makes sense.

What if you had a distant relative who happened to be millionaire? Unbeknownst to you, this relative passed away and left you millions of dollars. Would you be a millionaire? You may not know about it but according to the information recorded with the various authorities--they would claim you were a millionaire. What if you were out of touch with the authorities and their reality--either due to being incognito, or mentally ill? Would you still be considered a millionaire?

Even though you didn't know it for any reason-- would you still be considered a millionaire? By using every degree of reasonable standard that exists in modern society, I would have to answer the question with a resounding YES--you absolutely were a millionaire! But what if you never found out about it for your whole life time, and you died not knowing it-- would you still be a millionaire?

Technically, does it take you acknowledging or the authorities to contact you for you to be a millionaire? By every legal and reasonable standard- -you are a millionaire. If you're living out of your car, or living on the street, experiencing a harsh lifestyle (that I'm very familiar with)--you would still be considered a millionaire. What is the difference between you acknowledging it and not acknowledging it--does that change the amount that is sitting in the bank? Regardless of you receiving the money that's sitting in the bank, or rejecting that money--none of it changes the fact that you're a millionaire.  If you chose to live a lifestyle of a pauper because someone convinced you to fear money--you would still be a millionaire.  The only place you're not a millionaire is in YOUR MIND, due to ignorance or fear.  Even if you died in your ignorance of being a millionaire--you'd be a dead millionaire.

My point is this:  Jesus the Christ--He was slain before the foundation of the world, so from God's perspective you are saved--you're a millionaire.  "Saved" is a relative word that has been abused horribly by Christendom.  Being saved in biblical context has never been applied to the word "eternity", yet that's how it's applied in about every sermon referring to "being saved".

The people of the world are all reconciled to God--they just don't know it, just like that millionaire who never knew he or she was a millionaire.  Just because the people in the world don't know that God loves them, it doesn't mean God does not love them.  Just because they don't know that they have been reconciled to have a relationship with God, doesn't mean they're not reconciled to have a relationship with Him.  They have been saved whether they acknowledge it or not!

How many people throughout the centuries have passed and never heard the name of Christ? All that I've written above answers that conundrum, because we should know that death doesn't stop God--as you've read in a previous chapter. Yes, I will say that all are saved and reconciled! I used to reject it, but now I will boldly say that you are saved whether you know it or not, whether you believe it or not, whether you receive it or not, because it's not based on you receiving it.

"You've got to receive it!" I used to say the same thing as what I hear now from various camps within Christendom. "You've got to receive it! Sure it's a free gift from God--yes salvation is a free gift from God, but you have the responsibility to reach out and take it. It would be like me coming up and offering you a Christmas present, and if you didn't receive it then it wouldn't be yours." I looked back and wondered where did that crap come from? Now I know exactly where it came from--it comes from the carnal mind and promoted through doctrines of men.

"Your responsibility"? "You must reach out and take the gift"? Both of these scenarios sound correct, but they are an affront to grace. Remember "nothing of yourselves"? "Your responsibility and reaching out to take it"--is an action "of yourself". What is our responsibility? Phil. 4:8 answers it with: "Finally, brethren, whatever is true, whatever is honorable, whatever is right, whatever is pure, whatever is lovely, whatever is of good repute, if there is any excellence and if anything worthy of praise, dwell on these things." This results in us having a vivified life-- showing the world what is available with God-- effective before the foundations of the Earth were laid--long before any of us had any responsibilities, or opportunities to "reach out".

I'm not forgetting about "repentance". Understand something--repentance, changing your mind is critical to enjoy the lifestyle that God has for us. Let's call it a salvation lifestyle. One must change their mind about its existence in order to reap the benefits--right? Gaining knowledge is still considered "a change of mind", is it not? The millionaire needed to change his or her mind in order to reap the benefits of having millions of dollars--also correct. Changing one's mind, i.e. repenting, is all for the purpose of enjoying a Godly lifestyle, rather than a prerequisite to being accepted by God. Scriptures that refer to repentance are in context to the temporal, because God has got all the eternal "stuff" sewn up! The plan of salvation for all of creation is wonderful Good News!

In conclusion to this chapter I'll ask again--who is responsible for salvation? I think I've made it quite clear that it was NOT YOU! As many songs and hymns proclaim: "Jesus did it all", so I'll be asking in the next chapter--which Jesus are we talking about?

Chapter 15


Will The Real Jesus Please Stand Up!


What do I mean by "real Jesus" and by implying that, am I suggesting there's a fake Jesus? Obviously there is only One true Christ, but religion has a tendency to create God in the image of their religion, so wouldn't it be understandable to envision a Jesus as something or someone He was not? In this chapter I'm going to compare the Jesus of the Bible to the Jesus of Christianity and there is a shocking dichotomy. Doesn't Christendom use the same Bible as I do, so how can that be?


Years ago there was a Christian campaign called WWJD (What Would Jesus Do?). There were all sorts of jewelry and bracelets made--mostly worn by young people, and promoted by church youth groups. All in all I think it was harmless, because I believe anything that might remind a person of Jesus couldn't be all bad--right? The letters WWJD were designed to remind people and encourage them to consider what Jesus would do in any given circumstance. I personally was involved with it, so I understood the noble purpose of the slogan WWJD. Since I've discovered so many inconsistencies in what Christians believe and promote, I now have a nagging question I must ask about "What Would Jesus Do"? Which Jesus are we talking about?

What causes a red flag to go up for me is this rhetorical question: Am I the only one who senses a problem with judging my actions or the actions of others based on the lens of how I personally perceive Jesus? I believe there's something a little off with that notion, and some wisdom needs to be applied. What Jesus had to say about future perceptions of Him was best described in Matthew 24:5 (paraphrasing) where Jesus warns everyone that many people would come in His name (agreeing that He is the Christ), and deceive and lead many astray.

The important point of this verse is how the deception is actually coming from those who follow Jesus, as in those who declare He is the Christ, rather than from unbelievers. With that warning, think about the promotion of the WWJD campaign. Are not all those who were involved in instigating and following the WWJD movement in agreement that "He is the Christ"? I think so, don't you? What about the pastor or priest you hold at high esteem? What about the book you're reading this moment? I am not here to judge the motive of those who promoted the WWJD campaign, nor any church leader, or denomination, but at least consider "judging the fruit" of what you read, hear, and believe. As an example of fruit, if fear of retribution from God is involved, then it's not of God.

No matter who is proclaiming Jesus as Lord, and that He is the Christ, we all must take heed to the warning He gave in Matthew 24, and consider asking the question: Which Jesus are we talking about? Is He the homogenized, pasteurized, westernized, folkloreized, traditionalized, doctrines of manized white Jesus? Is this the Jesus that WWJD movement promoted, or your church leaders talk about? Is it the Jesus that has been created and recreated over and over again due to the winds of change from different denominations within Christianity over centuries of time?

Is He the traditional Jesus? Because of changes in time and what is socially acceptable, is He what was considered the traditional Jesus or is He the new Jesus that is now traditionally taught? Perception! This is what I meant when I earlier stated my concerns about judging my actions or the actions of others based on the lens of how I personally perceive Jesus. Most people now perceive the traditional Jesus as the One who indeed died for the sins of the world, but will make the world pay for their own sins through the wrath and the judgment of His father--of God. That Jesus? They also claim their Jesus sanctions how the world has to pay for their own sins, but they could escape that payment (that was already paid?) if they would only believe, confess, repent, so on and so forth, even though none of that was ever contextually said within scripture. Will the real Jesus please stand up, because one Jesus paid in full for the sins of the world, yet the other Jesus requires some form of payment from mankind.

Which Jesus?  Is it the Jesus who has the false good news message of saving people from a horrible place where there is no written record of it ever being created?  Yet, it's  believed to exist, and the existence of that place slanders the very character of God's love--His Father--that Jesus?  I had a pastor friend who once told me that Jesus warned of hell more than anyone else.  Is your Jesus the one who has been credited for that, or is He the One who warned of Gehenna more than anyone else?  By now my reader should know that Gehenna and hell are not one and the same.  According to my friend, wasn't the Jesus of Christendom the one who spoke and taught of eternal hell?  If that is true, then why can't the two words "eternal" and "hell" be found side-by-side anywhere within scripture?

To find out if the Jesus that I used to believe in, which seemed at the time to be the same Jesus championed by the vast majority of pastors, priests, and teachers, is the same as the One I believe in today--I'll need to look into the lens of history rather than just what I've been taught all those years.  Even though I would be looking at history using my personal perception, my goal is to always be objective when looking into a different culture, time, and language.  This is what true context is all about, rather than simply reading a verse or two ahead of the scripture I'm researching.

While doing so, I found it appropriate to change the idea of WWJD (What Would Jesus Do) to WDJD... What DID Jesus Do? What did He actually accomplish on behalf of mankind? Let's address a couple of issues and then compare what I view as a fake Jesus to the real One, as in the non-white, Jewish Rabbi of His day.

True context tells me the Jews of times past as well as today don't believe in hell. True context tells me the real Jesus would never use a Latin concocted, pagan word like hell, while teaching and addressing his Jewish brethren. In every instance but one, where the fake Jesus used the word hell, the real Jesus used the word Gehenna. The other word used by Jesus was the Aramaic word for "unseen". Consider reading or rereading my chapter called "Lazarus and the rich man", where the word unseen is found and explained. The Latin Jesus icon was know to use the word hell in the Lazarus story, rather than the word unseen. Will the real Jesus please stand up!

Within the context of how law breakers were punished, it makes complete and practical sense that Jesus would warn people of Gehenna. Why? Because other than trash, the bodies of the criminals who were judged as lawless thieves and murderers-- they were "damned and condemned" by the justice system of their day. Are you getting the strong language and wording that is often used in scripture? Most of the time that's all it is in scripture when reading of judgment--"culturally strong language". One wouldn't know that if all they did was read their Bible through a modern, westernized lens.

Speaking of judgment, it's been declared how Jesus is going to return on His white horse to judge and smite His enemies. Doctrines of men choose to ignore how righteous any judgment from God would be, and that very righteousness is based on love. You can't entirely blame Christendom for being deceived, considering how the "lying pens of the Scribes"(Jer. 8:8) documented God's supposed righteousness that included the slaughter of men, women, and children. Thanks to a few corrupt Scribes, we now have a perverted view of God. This in turn was the foundation for the ancient Latin church to pervert what Christ said and did.

Remember how I earlier and sarcastically said the fake Jesus did not die for the sins of the world, but was going to make the world pay for their own sins through the wrath of God? What did the real Jesus have to say about judgment, as in judging the world? All I'm asking of my reader is to momentarily put aside what your teachers and preachers have told you, and listen to what Jesus is telling you in John 3:17:

"For God did not send his Son to judge the world, but the world might be saved through Him."

What's usually done to verses like this one in John, is a condition of believing in Jesus is attached as a prerequisite for a person not to be judged by Jesus. Which Jesus is it, the one who judges or the One who doesn't? Believe or be judged? That's not what the verse says, nor implies anywhere within the context, but that's how it's presented in church circles. Don't allow them to get away with it. Well... at least not in your own heart and mind.

It's also taught that since the word "might" is used in the above verse--this opens the door for the ignorant to claim that most will still be judged by God, regardless of what Jesus was sent to the world to do. This is another example of "straining a gnat and swallowing a camel" in order to fit a narrative. Let's look into that word "might", shall we? When translating scripture to English, it was common to insert the English word "might" into a passage in order to aid the translation of a different Greek word being used before or after it. In most cases the word for "might" does not appear in the Greek text.

For example, in some translations of Matt. 12:17 the phrase "that it might be fulfilled", would be saying "this was to fulfill" when properly translated. Above, I purposely used the wrong translation of John 3:17 to read, "For God did not send his Son to judge the world, but the world "might" be saved through Him", because that's how some Bibles read. However, the same verse in other translations say, "For God did not send his Son into the world to condemn the world, but to save the world through him." There's nothing conditional or uncertain about it. It's simply a difference in the manner of speaking.

Would you like further proof of how a "manner of speaking" technique is used elsewhere within scripture, when using the word "might"?

- MT 26:56: "But this has all taken place that the writings of the prophets might (WILL) be fulfilled."

- MK 3:6: "Then the Pharisees went out and began to plot with the Herodians how they might (WILL) kill Jesus."

- MK 3:14: "He appointed twelve, designating them apostles that they might (WILL) be with him and that he might (WILL) send them out to preach..."

- JN 9:3: "Neither this man nor his parents sinned," said Jesus, "but this happened so that the work of God MIGHT (WILL) be displayed in his life."

- JN 17:2: "Father, the time has come. Glorify your Son, that your Son may glorify you. For you granted him authority over all people that he MIGHT (WILL) give eternal life (aonian life) to all those you have given him."

- EPH 2:6: "And God raised us up with Christ and seated us with him in the heavenly realms in Christ Jesus, in order that in the coming ages he MIGHT (WILL) show the incomparable riches of his grace, expressed in his kindness to us in Christ Jesus. For it is by grace you have been saved, through faith and this not from yourselves, it is the gift of God – not by works, so that no one can boast."

- 1st JN 3:5: "But you know that he appeared so that he might (WILL) take away our sins. And in him is no sin."

I think I've proven my point in explaining the word "might", so let's continue with the question of which Jesus are we talking about? In John 5:22 we'll see how "The father judges no one but has given all judgment to the Son", but earlier we read how the Son doesn't judge anyone. Even though both verses point out how the Father and Son are in agreement, Christendom chooses to push an agenda of judgment from both. Which Father and Son are real, and which one's are fake? How does believing, confessing, and repenting fit into the judgment scenario? Jesus answered it best in John12:47 by starting out with "If anyone...". Those two very important words include the believer and unbeliever alike.

"If anyone hears my sayings and does not keep them I do not judge him for I did not come to judge the world but to save the world."

Rather than teaching what the real Jesus actually did (WDJD), over hundreds of years the Christian religion has recreated a fake Jesus to better fit the deception, as in to better fit the agenda of their doctrines. Rather than building a doctrine around Jesus, Christendom has built a Jesus to fit their doctrines. This is precisely what Jesus was warning people about in Matthew 24:5:

"For many will come in My name, saying, `I am the Christ,' and will mislead many."

Being a novice historian of ancient history, I love different cultures and languages. Nothing is more ancient than God, so I've researched the differences in how we view God in our modern era as compared to how they did in ancient times. From around the world, dating back to 6000BC, we all have at our disposal clay tablets, scrolls, and the Old Testament being the most recent of the three. I love to know why people believe what they believe--that's why I call myself The Why Guy.

One of my favorite questions I like to ask Christians is what is the source of their information, and why do they believe it's true? Most will claim the source and authority for their beliefs is the Bible, yet very few even know how the Bible came about. One would think if so much of what one believes is based on the Bible, then wouldn't it be prudent to investigate the how, what and why it exists, and most importantly who was involved in its conception? Just by saying "God said..." (fill in the blank) is nothing more than a cop-out! That same Bible instructs those homogeneous group of Christians to "study, and show themselves approved unto God". That's all I'm trying to do when I research culture and language of those stories within its pages.

Isn't that what real context is all about, rather than just reading a verse before or after a particular Bible text? Some will go as far as reading the whole chapter, which is commendable, but it only scratches the surface. I like trying to get into the minds of the people, of how they might have thought back then due to their surroundings. By examining the circumstances and lifestyle of the people of that day of those who were around Jesus, it helps me learn what they thought or perceived of what Jesus said and did at the time--it helps me to know which Jesus I'm reading about. I believe I'm going to make a fair comparison of what Jesus did back then, as compared to what the Christian church is doing today. I'm speaking in general terms when I say church, so your particular church may not fall within the parameters I'm about to lay out.

Everywhere Jesus went, He healed people. This is still going on in some churches, but not as consistently as when the sandal wearing Jesus walked, talked, and sweated with men. I'm a perfect example. I pulverized my left elbow in a hang-gliding accident. There was talk of amputation, but a specialist said he glued and screwed the bone fragments back together the best he could. Three days after surgery, I went to a church service and was completely healed. The X-rays showed no scar on the bone. There's considerably more to this story, but you get the point that Jesus healed back then and He's still doing it in our churches today, but seemingly not very often.

Why don't these kinds of healings happen as often as they did when Jesus was personally doing them? Maybe some are not praying to a loving Father, but instead are praying to a false god who they think heals some while eternally torturing others. I really don't know, but maybe it's some kind of a test of how are we going to treat those who are not healed. Are we going to judge them for not being righteous enough, not believing enough, or for not having enough faith... I've heard all the judgmental puke, because frankly that's what it is--it's puke!

When I read about Jesus turning over tables because of profiteering in His church--His synagogue, it gives me pause. Do you think it's still going on within our church walls of today? You bet it is! I used to be in church leadership so I know exactly what's going on behind the scenes. In defense, I will add that in most cases of what some view as "profiteering"--it's not all malicious, because the concern of expenses is always in the back of the mind of church leaders. However, this isn't what I'm talking about in reference to profiteering.

Gary Amirault, founder of tentmaker.org, has a YouTube video where he did a study on the various Bibles that had hell in them versus the ones that didn't. He obtained the public financial records of the publishers, and he discovered that the Bibles that mentioned hell, sold astronomically more than the ones that didn't. He had statistical proof that fear and hell sells big time! As long as the doctrine of hell is preached, the church is promoting fear, and as long as fear is promoted, churches are financially exploiting that fear. They may think they're doing it for the right reasons, but the bottom line is how many "Benjamins" go in the offering plate. Yes, of course they will say it's all about saving the lost from hell, but without the fear of hell, I often wonder how many people would actually darken their doors.

When the real Jesus challenged church leaders they called Him names, and they eventually crucified Him. In far too many instances, to a degree, the church of today is doing the same thing. Now they will socially crucify you by calling you names like heretic, dissenter, turn coat, deceived, deceiver, and/or rebellious. If you don't leave ashamed or angry on your own, they do their best to kick you out. As far as a Pharisee was concerned, those of us who are nonconforming free thinkers are in good company with the real Jesus,.


In Jesus' day the hungry were fed. In this one area, and on occasion, I believe the real Jesus is standing up. There are a lot of churches that are feeding the hungry, and I give kudos where it's due. Bless you for that, but unfortunately you're few and far in between. The street ministries I've been involved with always seemed to have a hidden, and sometimes personal agenda behind feeding the hungry. Was it done ONLY for the sake of love in order to rid a stranger of their hunger pains? With some who attended church, this was the case, but with many, it was a self-seeking duty to be performed for the sole purpose of obtaining the approval of God. The motive of others was to have an excuse or a platform to warn the street people of hell if they didn't repent and change their ways. Most of these people had to "earn" their meal and/or a warm place to sleep by first listening to some form of the gospel message. More times than not, that message threatened them with hell. Did the real Jesus do that while dividing the five fishes and two loaves?

In His company, the real Jesus welcomed the wealthy, the poor, the prostitute, and tax collector. It didn't matter, they were all welcome. Think about your own particular church, would that be the case? I'm sure the wealthy would be welcome, the poor would be tolerated, the tax collector would probably keep his or her occupation close to the vest, yet what about the prostitute? Let's be honest, I highly doubt a prostitute would be welcome in your church, and guess what? They would instantly know it. Most fellowships I was involved with would unconditionally accept them, and offer a support mechanism if they had a desire to change their occupation.

Song writer Keith Green promoted a street ministry called Agape Force. For a short time, as a teen, I was involved with Agape Force on the streets of East Colfax in Denver, Colorado. Our coffee house was sandwiched in between a nude dancing bar and an X-rated book store, not far from an Air Force Base. I used to go out on the streets at night and talk to prostitutes and drug dealers, so I know what I'm talking about.

I've read stories how Jesus addressed people who were in spiritual bondage, and how He set them free. Yet, in the modern Christian church of today-- as long as a doctrine of hell is preached, people are going to remain in bondage. Anytime a fear based message is used to manipulate and coerce people to believe or act a certain way, is pure, unadulterated BONDAGE! The real Jesus came to show people, including the religious people of his day, how they had God all wrong. At the time, their religious leaders were not sharing the true nature of God with the people of Israel. They had a boat load of rules, regulations, punishments, and laws to put their people in bondage. The Christian church is doing the exact same thing with that insidious doctrine of hell.

Note how the majority of people in Jesus' day slandered God's character by believing scripture of their day that spoke of how He authorized killing people--of how He destroyed groups of people, one after another--wiping out men, women, and children-- including their puppies. I'm telling you folks, God didn't sanction those things. Because of this kind of slander of God's character, there are still people today who refuse to turn to a god like that. As far as I'm concerned, religion and specifically Christianity are to blame for the creation of atheists. The fake Jesus and the god of religion is what people are rejecting.

If only the Christian people would repent of denigrating God--just imagine what impact it would have on the world. The defamation began long before Jesus was born, and it's still being promoted mainly within Christendom and Islam of our day. The real Jesus came to show the opposite of what is being taught--that God is not vengeful, wrathful, and an intolerant judge that Christians claim He is. You don't think so? Say that to the woman caught in adultery, whom everyone but the real Jesus wanted to stone to death.

The real Jesus continued to display a God of love, who is a forgiving Father, yet modern Christian theology depicts a god that should be feared in some fashion, and Jesus (fake) came to save us from that god! Your particular pastor or church leader may or may not say this in so many words, because most of the time, they avoid or dance around the topic, due to fear of offending someone. One cannot be neutral about the hell doctrine--either you're for it or against it! The "damned" hell doctrine does nothing but slander God, excused in big part by how God was falsely portrayed in some of the horrendous stories told in the Old Testament. I hope you're getting how insidious it is how the Christian church continues to promote this crap, and why repentance is in order.

Those who consistently spent their time with the real Jesus were loved, encouraged, and taught, rather than used and exploited. Most of us who have spent a lot of time in church leadership were exploited. Of course we were loved, but it was a conditional love based on one's performance. In my case, it was a 30 year stint of being a praise and worship leader. By the way, there are those who will scoff at the whole thought of praise and worship leaders or praise teams in general.

Those that do scoff are usually in my "no hell" paradigm, and in my defense I would encourage some of you to look for a moment into what might be your self-righteous mirror. Because of the hell doctrine, most of you are anti-church, and I get that, but to be anti praise and worship simply because that was what was done in church is extremely short-sighted on your part. Believe it or not, there were some of us who had a pure heart towards God, and all we wanted was for people to come together in unity. We viewed songs as a literal prayer put to music, resulting in a wonderful communion with God. None of you who are anti-praise and worship are against prayer are you? That's all we wanted to do, so keep that in the back of your judgmental minds--okay?

While using music, I was invited to encourage an intimate communion with God in a variety of churches and denominations such as: Vineyard, Calvary Chapel, Four Square, Southern Baptist, Presbyterian, Catholic, prison Chapels, and even on one occasion, a Mormon Ward. In every case, and on the surface, I experience a form of love from those people. Is appreciation a form of love? No matter what denomination or congregation you're involved with, you will naturally enjoy a quality or quantity of love. However, I guarantee it's not unconditional, not in the way God's love is. The Jesus and/or God you believe in is what's going to determine the kind of love you give or receive.

What gets me, is the same people who believe in hell--some of them actually say that their god has unconditional love for mankind, and yet the vast majority of people, that the aforementioned god loves, are going to end up in hell because they didn't qualify for heaven! It doesn't add up. We are instructed by the real Jesus to love our enemies, yet the fake Jesus is going to return on a white horse to slay his enemies, ushering them to hell. How is that love? Will the real Jesus please stand up!

To help determine who the real Jesus is, and who His real Father is--consider comparing what you know about the journey of man versus God's journey in man.

- When I think of the journey of "religious" man, I think of the warning Jesus gave us of: "For many will come in My name, saying, `I am the Christ,' and will mislead many."

- When I think of the journey of man, I think of the flesh, as in the way man seems to morally degrade without some form of communion with God. But, when I think of God's journey in man, I think of the Spirit, as in His Spirit. The One true Spirit that is able, powerful, and competent to accomplish its goals.

- When I think of the journey of man, I think of a carnal mind, as in man's reasoning and man's thinking about "stuff". Thinking about stuff is something we all do, but when I think of God's journey in man, I consider the mind of Christ.

- Contemplate the mind of Christ when I mention how the journey of religious man requires repentance. To the religious carnal mind and on the surface, repentance sounds reasonable, but God's journey in man operates through His loving kindness that actually causes repentance. (2nd Tim. 2:25)

- The journey of man requires a confession of Jesus as Lord. Again, this requirement sounds reasonable, but with God's journey in man, He first draws man to Christ so man has the ability to confess Jesus as Lord. The first journey is flesh, and the latter one is instigated by God's Spirit. I hope you're catching this.

- In Jn 12:32, the real "Jesus will draw ALL mankind unto Himself", yet the fake Jesus will draw only those that are willing.

- Along these same lines, in Jn 6:44, the real Jesus claims "No one can come to Him UNLESS HE DRAWS THEM.", as in you don't choose Him first. You guessed what's coming next... the fake Jesus wont draw you unless you first choose to be drawn. Ridiculous.

- According to Phil. 2:9: "EVERY tongue will confess Jesus is Lord". This happens AFTER He first draws you of course, but the religious carnal mind will put a condition on "every", even though that would negate the very word "every".

- The journey of man requires an act of your will, thus enabling and giving a legal right for their god to enact his will. However, God's journey in man proclaims "it is God that works in you both to will and to act according to his good purpose." (Phil. 2:13)

- The journey of religious man believes man is saved from sin through their behavior and/or the actions of man. The actions of mankind is defined as: believing, confessing, repenting, baptism, and basic obedience. However, God's journey in man operates through the power of grace alone, and not due to the actions and behavior of man according to 2nd Timothy 1:9: "...who has saved us and called us with a holy calling, not according to our works, but according to His own purpose and grace which was granted us in Christ Jesus from all eternity."

- The journey of man allows only this short lifetime to permit (permit?) God to complete His work in man, but God's journey in man isn't limited to this short lifetime, and He will complete His will in due time according to 1st Tim. 2:6: "Who gave himself a ransom for all, to be testified in due time." Death may stop the god spoken of in Christian theology, but death doesn't stop God in 1st Peter 4:6: "For the gospel has for this purpose been preached even to those who are dead, that though they are judged in the flesh as men, they may live in the spirit according to the will of God."

- The journey of man requires man to heed and obey the words of "a Jesus", and if they don't, they will be severely judged. However, God's journey in man states what the real Jesus had to say about that in John 12:47: "If anyone hears My sayings and does not keep them, I do not judge him; for I did not come to judge the world, but to save the world."
- The journey of man claims their Jesus is going to judge the world, yet God's journey in man through the real Christ is not going to judge the world according to John 3:17: "For God did not send the Son into the world to judge the world, but that the world will be saved through Him." It's further declared in John 5:22 that "the Father judges no one but has given all judgment to the Son."

So let me understand this... God is declaring that neither He nor Christ have come to judge the world, yet Christianity has gone to great lengths and expense to produce movies that claim the opposite! Somebody is lying here! Either God and Christ are lying within scripture, or Christian theology is. You're going to have to choose for yourself. When will Christendom allow the real Jesus to stand up? Christ claimed that He and the Father are one, so when He says He came not to judge the world, but to save the world--how on earth can Christianity take that, twist it, and demand of people to obey, or they will be judged and condemned to hell?

- By ignoring the words of Jesus, the journey of man claims God is going to judge the world, yet I'll share one more time how God's journey in man is not going to judge the world according to John 5:22: "The Father judges no one but has given all judgment to the Son."

- The journey of man requires man to have faith in Christ, and I might add... that's good stuff to have faith in Christ--right? Even so, God's journey in man gives the Faith **OF** Christ as a gift, as the Author and Perfecter of man's faith-- that's who the real Jesus is! It's so nice that no one can boast about their own faith this way.

"Looking unto Jesus the author and perfecter of our faith." (Heb. 12:2)

" Know that a person is not justified by the works of the law, but by the faith of Jesus Christ. So we, too, have put our faith in Christ Jesus that we may be justified by the faith of Christ...". (Gal. 2:16)

One of the two aforementioned faiths requires man to remain faithful to God, and again, that sounds reasonable, especially to the religious carnal mind who wants to take some kind of credit. The key word I used in my statement is "requires", and it becomes problematic when a person strives to fulfill what they deem necessary, and if they're successful, they end up boasting about it. Our faith "in" Christ is supposed to give us confidence in the gift of **HIS** faith and nothing more, otherwise "our faith" is nothing more than a religious rite that accomplishes nothing. On the other hand, the Faith of Christ operating through the journey in man remains faithful when man is faithless as pointed out in 2nd Tim. 2:13: "If we are faithless, He remains faithful, for He cannot deny Himself." "He cannot deny Himself"? Why would Paul use a term like that if it was our faith instead of Christ's?

- The Jesus of Christendom, along with his father, count men's sins against them, for all time, for all eternity in hell. In the mean time, because of what the real Jesus accomplished-- God's journey in man does not count men's sins against them as recorded in 2nd Cor. 5:19: "For God WAS in Christ, reconciling the world

411

to himself, NO LONGER counting people's sins against them. And he gave us this wonderful message of reconciliation."

- The Journey of man demands a person must believe in order for God to have His way in their life.  God's Journey in man says so "what if some don't believe, will this nullify the faithfulness of God?  May it never be.  Let God be found true and let every (journey of) man be found a liar." Ro. 3:3)

The fake Jesus from doctrines of men puts a huge burden and false responsibilities on mankind, just like the Pharisees did to their people.  You know who I mean--the religious clowns, the ones who crucified the real Jesus.  They crucified Christ, but for what reason?  Answer:  For not following their rules, their journey of man.  Doesn't this sound familiar? Christianity has fallen into the same trap as the Pharisees, by requiring hoops to be jumped through to obtain and keep God's favor.  Jesus warned us about this by saying "beware the leaven of the Pharisee."

What journey would you rather have--the journey of religious man or a journey of God in and through you? It's probably obvious by now to my reader that I have left the journey of man. I will also admit that this book is slightly controversial, and that I have barely scratched the surface to understanding God's journey in and through me. I'm "looking through a glass dimly", still wanting, still ignorant, and I have a desire for so much more. I hope you feel the same about yourself as well.

Which Jesus best represents God? Which Father of Jesus claims to love the world, love all mankind by loving "ALL"? Christendom would agree with the assessment of loving God, but will later add a nuance of how God will still love you even though you may be suffering for an eternity in hell. In every scripture I'm about to point out, you as an individual have no part to play in order to be included as the member of the "passive all". Consider rereading chapter five.

This is possibly the umpteenth time I've mentioned faith in this book, but stick with me. If a person claims the Bible is the word of God, that would mean God Himself is stating in Phil. 2:13 that Christ is the Author and the Finisher of your faith. Unfortunately Christianity adds to those words by saying "only if you allow Him to be". Can you hear the arrogance of that statement? Allow Him? Which

Jesus is it that we first must allow Him to be the Author and Finisher of our faith? Also, as the Author--wouldn't that make it His faith, that He gives as a gift, so no one can boast about it being their faith? Will the real Jesus please stand up?

God also claims to be the One "who is at work in you both to will and to act according to His good purposes." Again, Christianity usually responds with "only if we allow God to do it"! Wow, we apparently hold the puppet strings attached to the Creator of the Universe, by perversely presenting this verse, to say how it's the individual's will power that will accomplish what is needed to please God. Which God is telling the truth here, you as a god working in yourself or God the Father of Christ that is the One who is at work in you, both to will and to act according to His good purposes?

Which Jesus was it, who demonstrated by everything He did throughout His life that love keeps no record of wrong? Apparently there's a different Jesus who makes an exception when it comes to hell, which is keeping an eternal record of wrong. Will the real Jesus please stand up?

Which Jesus died for all? (2nd Cor. 5:15) In no uncertain terms Christian theology promotes the notion of how one MUST become a Christian, before one can be included as a member of "the all" that Jesus died for. These same people will also claim that the Bible is inerrant, but they must realize how there must have been a mistranslation of the word "all", because it should have read; "some" instead of "all", according to their teaching. Which Christ is the Bible referring to in 1st Tim. 4:10, Jn 12:47, Jn 4:42, and 1st Jn 4:14 where it's making the case that Jesus is the savior of all? There's that same "passive" all again. But as usual, Christianity puts a condition on these verses by agreeing the verses are true, but only if you become a Christian. When did becoming a Christian become a standard for something being true or not? The word "all" and the word "some" are not interchangeable, they are not one and the same, but they sure are in the minds of Christian people.

Will the real Jesus please stand up who is declaring to all creation that no one can come to Him unless He first draws them. (Jn. 6:44) Apparently a different Jesus is saying how we must first believe, and it's initially up to us! It's first up to us to be willing to believe, confess, and repent. It's amazing how they add these kinds of conditions to scripture, and to this verse specifically, as if it was printed right along with the other words in the passage. I don't think consciously church leaders sit around a table and contemplate how they can add doctrines of men to scriptures, yet boom!... they just stick it right in there. So that's what they're doing, intentional or not.

Also, isn't it a different Jesus that is announcing all will know him, but only if you become a Christian? Call me if you become a Christian. Are not these beliefs the exact opposite of what the real Jesus said? The genuine Jesus says He "will save all and it will be testified in due time" (1st Tim. 2:6). Christianity horribly twists this verse to read all who are willing! The word willing is nowhere in this verse nor in the chapter, but Christian doctrine continues to declare the verse is implying the all means those who are willing, and then they conclude and assert the timing of our salvation is in our control. Again, the opposite of what 1st Timothy is saying.

Which Jesus maintains that it is He who is the atoning sacrifice for your sins?  When I ask the question regarding "your sins", I'm implying "believers", as in those who call themselves Christians.  Christians are in complete agreement with how Christ is the atoning sacrifice for their sins, but the verse doesn't stop there.  It continues to say "but not for ours only, but also for the sins of the whole world." (1st Jn 2:2)  Why do Christians refuse to read, much less understand the second half of this verse?  Weird.  Also note how there are no conditions attached to that verse.

Are you ready for the question always asked up to this point?  "If all are eventually going to be saved, then why should I care if I am now?"  Answer:  It's your "due time" as mentioned in  1st Timothy 2:6, and you just happen to be reaping the benefits now!  You are benefiting now by believing, confessing, and repenting about a salvation that has already been provided long before you were born.

"And He is the atoning sacrifice for our (believers) sins, and not OURS ONLY, but ALSO for the sins of the WHOLE WORLD."  (you still think you're "special" because you're a believer?)

If one's salvation, meaning a vivified life, is by grace alone, not works--a free gift from God, then why do Christians continue to claim that salvation wouldn't happen without the "works" of believing? You don't think believing is a work? I'm glad you've got a handle on it, because I sometimes struggle each and every day. What about repenting, as meaning to change your mind about something? Oh it's work big time! It's hard to change your mind about some things, especially if you don't have a clue what it is you're supposed to change your mind about.

If "to confess" is a prerequisite for grace, then it too is a "work". Look... it all comes down to how Christianity implies that salvation wouldn't happen without the "works" of believing, repenting, and confessing. Once, I finally convinced a Christian that those things are works after all, but the conversation didn't end there--as expected, they used a fall back statement that now makes the bile rise up in my throat. "Yes, salvation is a gift, but it's only a gift if you're willing to receive it!" Where in the hell, that I don't believe in, did they get that notion from, other than the carnal mind? There is absolutely no scripture that hints, implies, or states that!

Was it the real or fake Jesus who encouraged us in scripture to come to Him, because His burden is light , and His yoke is easy?  Christianity invites people to join them to take upon themselves the heavy burden and responsibility for their own salvation--through the power of their own free will.  Choices... so many choices.  Should I trust my ability or what Christ accomplished?  Who should I follow, church teaching or Christ?

Jesus needs your help... at least the fake Jesus does.  Everything I'm about to write in my make-believe want ad below, is based on what I've been taught on and off for 40 years in Christendom.  The beginning of this paragraph is already in the sarcasm mode, so put on your seat belts--there's more to come.

"I can't do it alone!  You can't expect just one man to save the whole world much less reconcile all of creation can you?  Who I AM, my birth, my life, my death, and my resurrection did not accomplish what was needed, so this is where you come in.  To complete what I started, my organization, my church is offering you an opportunity of a lifetime.  Some have reached the top echelon of becoming televangelist, and some have birthed mega churches.  They're making millions of dollars and you can too, if you simply follow my guidelines for success.  To initiate this wonderful journey, come to me as you are. But first, there are baby steps you must take to apply for membership in my organization.

Requirements to qualify for membership in my organization, my church, (but not limited to, nor in any specific order) are as follows:

- Believe in me.
- Confess your sins.
- Repent of your sins.
- Go to church.
- Pay tithe.
- Give up ownership of all you own for my purposes.
- Abide by The Ten Commandments.
- There will be much more to come once you show a maturity for handling responsibility.

This may seem like a lot, but in exchange for your services my father is willing to give you a free gift of Grace!

Grace disclaimer: Grace may or may not be sufficient to give you access to eternal life. Your contributions to grace are necessary to keep from falling from grace. Any other scenario would result in the cheapening of grace. Contributions to grace may include but are not limited to:

- Showing a sincere guilt and shame for the offenses and sins committed.

- You must stop committing those offenses and sins that brought you to the foot of grace in the first place.

Don't pass up this offer.  I'll continue to stand at the door and knock, but only for so long.  This offer is for a limited time only, considering your lifetime is extremely short--some shorter than others.  Act now, or else your only other option will be eternal damnation!

Signed,
The Christian Jesus

Disclaimer:  Even though prepared and written by The Why Guy--all claims of this want ad are not necessarily the views of The Why Guy, his news organization, broadcast network, their affiliates, friends, or family members. (lol)

When my wife read this bogus ad, she sadly pointed out how far too many Christians who might read an ad like this, would see nothing wrong with it.  If this ad has cast a seed of doubt that causes you to go to God about it--then it's a good thing.  Over and over again Jesus would debate with the Pharisees by using their scripture against them.  Throughout this book, that is precisely what I've been doing.  Like Jesus, my purpose is not to be argumentative, but is to make one think.

My next and last chapter will be a mixture of thoughts that simply didn't fit anywhere within the previous 15 chapters.  Enjoy.

# Chapter 16

## Deception & Ending Thoughts

Being deceived does not make someone a bad person, however, the actions someone takes due to that deception can and often will make them a bad person.  Most modern day Christians would think burning someone alive for being called a witch or for demon possession goes way beyond bad, but enters into the realm of evil.  It's been swept under the rug by leaders within Christendom, that at one point in church history, mentally disabled people were publicly burned alive or drowned for demon possession.  My point:  Some will view the pages of this book as Christian bashing.  No, on the contrary, it's deception bashing.  If a Christian chooses to hold onto a deception with all their might, and refuses to investigate the truth, resulting in getting their feelings hurt, that is not my problem.

With those harsh words said, let me reiterate and expound on my sentiment I've written about in previous chapters.  I LOVE THE CHRISTIAN PEOPLE, but I hate the deception they are ignorantly promoting.  Think about this... if I didn't have the kind of love I have, I couldn't care less about the harm they're causing themselves and those around them.  Hate is not the opposite of love--apathy is.

If I were to describe the four cornerstones modern Christianity is built upon, I would say; God, Christ, love, and hell.  I simplistically describe it as: God sent His Son, the Christ, to show us His love by giving us an opportunity to be saved from hell.  When the foundation is flawed, the whole building will be out of alignment and skewed.  Because of one specific erroneous cornerstone of modern Christian theology, dozens upon dozens of doctrines have been established.  Exponentially, deception has been built upon deception for so long, it's now considered truth and orthodoxy.  Hitler said something similar to: Repeat a lie often enough and it becomes truth to the listener.  Jesus said:  "A little leaven leavens the whole loaf."


If Christianity would repent and eliminate just one of the four cornerstones of their belief system, I would have to say about 99% of all deception would be eliminated from the church.  That's how insidious the hell doctrine is.  Consider making your foundation a tripod rather than a square--Father, Son, and love.  Some may be thinking, it is not we who are deceived, it is YOU!  Let's look for a moment how I might be deceived, rather than at my bold indictments referring to the possible millions of people, who over a couple thousand years carefully and meticulously established church dogma.

Since I'm honest and a transparent kind of a guy, I fully understand why people might have the perception that I'm deceived due my claims that I no longer believe in hell. I see where they're coming from, because I used to be right where they're at in their understanding. One of the many problems I see with those who think I'm deceived--is they have never been where I'm at now. It seems kind of one sided, don't ya think? I continually check myself, do you? Every one of us requires a self-examination from time to time, because Jesus warned how believers in Him would lead many astray, and like you, I don't want to be one of those who do that.

It's wise for me to take a real hard look at how I might be deceiving people--for example, in writing this book. I will now openly go over everything I believe and promote, and bear it all in judging myself in the upcoming paragraphs. However, in doing so, I will be using a bit of sarcasm--that's just how I'm wired, so bear with me.

First I'll have to admit that I'm deceiving people by telling them that God loves them and myself more than any of us could possibly understand. I promote that sentiment above all else, so if I am deceiving people by encouraging them to trust God--I'm in big trouble. I also make the assertion, if anything hinders that trust, then they need to examine what it is and why it's hindering. I don't care what you read, or what you think the Bible says, you need to examine why it might be hindering your trust in God. Rather than taking what you read at face value with a limited understanding--wouldn't it be wise to pause for a moment and ask yourself--why is this causing me to question God's love?

I apparently have deceived people by pointing out the finished work of Christ, as in what He did was a work of perfection that doesn't require your participation to finish it. I know I'm going to step on toes with this statement, but His perfected finished accomplishments do not require anyone to believe, confess, or repent to somehow make it better. This is probably where most people think I'm deceived. If I am deceived--due to my deception, if it causes me to give more credit to the competence of God and to the sacrifice of His Son than to the individual--then I choose to remain in deception.

I've deceived people by telling them to judge me! Yes, absolutely judge me if I'm saying anything contrary to what would bring the fruit of the Spirit of God out in you. Usually, those in my camp bring out anger in some--angry that someone has the audacity and gall to come out against their pet doctrines. It doesn't stop there, just try pointing out errors in the Bible, and watch the shit hit the fan. So, ignore me, ignore the facts and some of the opinions I've disclosed. I openly admit how I see through a glass dimly, but most of my opposition refuse to admit that about themselves. It does seem a little silly of me to ask my reader to ignore me considering we're in the last chapter (LOL), but you get the point.

I'm also deceiving people by asking the question of everyone, including myself, why do you believe what you believe? Is it a problem to put seeds of doubt about what you've been taught, and to hold suspect your understanding of scripture? My good friend Joe Lindsey told me that one of the best seeds that God can plant in the heart or a mind of a person is the seed of doubt. When mentioning doubt, I'm not talking about anti-faith. Doubt does not have to be the opposite of believing, but rather an indicator that one might be believing something wrong. I've concluded the seed of doubt is a good thing, because I don't know about you, but the first impulse I have when in doubt, is to go to God. That's not a bad thing, and maybe just maybe you'll get the urge to research some things I've written about in this book.

Yes, I also deceive people by proclaiming that there is no need to fear God. Since God claims He is love, who would it make sense to--to fear love? I deceive people by sharing how words like death or grave have been horribly perverted and mistranslated into a word called hell. If that's deceiving people, then I challenge anyone to prove me wrong by investigating the Hebrew language and culture considering Jesus was a Jew. By doing so, maybe your eyeballs will open wide like mine did when I tried to prove others wrong. That's why I'm where I am today, because I tried proving other people wrong such as: Gary Amirault (tentmaker.org), Rob Bell (Love Wins), Martin Zender (First Idiot In Heaven), and now my new friend Gerry Beauchemin (Hope Beyond Hell). Even though I was already on this track of thinking, I got a bonus by making friends with Julie Ferwerda, author of "Raising Hell". She confirmed everything I had been researching, so at least I didn't have to pooh-pooh her book like I initially did with all the others.

I deceive people by pointing out how there's an inconsistency in language and translations in the Bible, and how those inconsistencies need to be reexamined and researched. That's simply what myself and other's have done in our books and websites. So I wholeheartedly encourage my readers to visit the websites of those I listed above, and if you're questioning the topic of hell, get your hands on Julie's book "Raising Hell", and Gerry's book "Hope Beyond Hell". I have to give a shout out for Gerry's newest book titled: "Hope for All - Ten Reasons God's Love Prevails." Try to read these books with an open mind, and don't let pride become a stumbling block. By reading these books, I was proven wrong, and I'm so glad I was.

I deceive people by exploring how doctrines of men might nullify the accomplishments of Christ. Technically, nothing can invalidate nor neutralize the accomplishments of Christ, but in the minds of men it sure can. Whenever you read the word "nullify" in a scripture, it's in the context of how people think and act towards Christ, rather than the actual achievements of Christ. I find it ironic how Christianity is the largest proponent of nullifying the accomplishments of Christ. How so? By claiming He didn't fulfil God's will and do a completed work, thus requiring mankind to take up the slack! If someone doesn't believe Christ did a completed work, then in their mind they have nullified His completed work-- make sense?

I've deceived people by telling them that they can be confident that He who began a good work in them will complete it unto the glory of God.  Boy am I deceiving people with that one.  I'm deceiving people by telling them that Christ is the Author and the Perfecter of their faith, and they can trust Him with this faith, considering He is going to perfect it! Somehow, I'm deceiving people by openly admitting I see through a glass dimly.  Is it a deception to admit the flaws we all have in humanity, and that we all need each other?  None of us have all the answers to everything, so in admitting that, I'm sorry if that offends you to the point that you feel deceived.

In most cases, the very ones who accuse me of deceiving people are in fact themselves walking in deception.  As long as we all see through a glass dimly or darkly, to one degree or another we are all ignorant.  Ignorant is best defined as a lack of knowledge, so that would mean we are all deceived to one degree or another.  We are all deceived as long as we are only using our brain, our eyes, and our limited understanding when reading scripture.  If you're an American, or you only speak English, then it should be common sense that you would be ripe for deception when reading scripture that originated from a different time, language, and culture.  Far too many have made the huge mistake of trusting translators, from centuries past, over and above trusting in God's character.

If I'm deceiving you by encouraging you to trust God with all of your heart, mind, soul, and strength--if I'm encouraging you to do that, and that's deceiving you, then oh yes, I want to deceive you big time! I know I've mentioned in previous chapters how I now judge things, but it's worth repeating. First, I judge myself. How? By judging everything I believe, and I want to encourage anyone who happens upon this book to judge yourself by the same standard I'm about to explain. More on that standard in a moment. Don't be fearful to judge yourself, because you're just making an assessment, and your evaluation should be based upon a standard.

Usually, when it comes to a standard, the first thing that comes to the religious Christian mind is "The Word of God", i.e. the Bible. To some, that statement carries the stench of pompous arrogance and self-righteousness. The standard I'm referring is so much deeper, yet profoundly simpler than reading a Bible to justify your beliefs. Judging yourself in a way that a child could understand is how I now do so.

So, how do I now judge myself and avoid being deceived? How do I take all that information, most of which was doctrines of men that was pumped into me for 30 to 40 years by Christendom, and not be deceived? How can I help myself not to turn right around and use that information to deceive others?

How do I not do that as most people do--monkey see, monkey do, that's how it works and that's how we're wired. I have finally escaped that cocoon that kept me from getting my head wrapped around some Bible verses. I don't care what you say the Bible says, because that's the problem--it's what you say it says. And frankly, you shouldn't give a rat's rear end what I say either. If I'm willing to dish it out and feed it, then I should be willing to eat it too, and I'm willing--you'll see why.

The reason why is because I'm not afraid, thus I'm not afraid to judge scripture. I'm not afraid to rightly divide the word of truth--from what? From words that are not true! If you're going to just go along with the doctrines of men that says the Bible is inerrant, much less the word of God, ignoring facts and hard evidence to the contrary, then that's your choice. If you're going to completely disregard this book because I happen to write something that opposes what you and I have both been previously taught, then go ahead and keep right on being deceived and promoting deception. But, there's a better way.

There's a way to judge me, and I welcome your judgment, but there is a standard for that judgment. Meaning, there's a right way and a wrong way to judge. Judging something and trusting something are two entirely different things. I expect to be judged, yet I don't expect to be trusted. I don't trust myself fully, and I most certainly don't expect anyone else to. But here's the thing... you shouldn't trust yourself either! I know that sounds kind of weird, doesn't it? Seriously, we cannot trust ourselves, as in we cannot trust our carnal minds. However, we can trust God, but how do we trust Him since most of the time we're using our minds to do so? It's a paradox.

I've discovered the answer is more simple than I expected. The paradox battle of using my mind to trust God, while at the same time not trusting my mind, raged in my head until I finally gave up--I gave in and trusted God alone. The real kind of trust--not the lip service kind. My mind and my ego didn't want to put aside everything I was taught for over 30 years about God. My mind trusted all that stuff, and to give that up was fearful and painful. When I sincerely laid it all down, something "clicked" in my mind. I didn't fully understand at the time, but the "mind of Christ" had been clicked on. Take note: This is not a formula, this is simply how it happened to me.

Now, with the mind of Christ, I can rightly divide my beliefs by using the correct standard for judging. If you've paid attention to previous chapters, this will not be new news. I judge scripture, everything I believe, and everything you say is scriptural, simply by comparing it all to what I now know is God's character. Previously in my religious carnal mind I would say God is love, but now with the mind of

Christ, I KNOW God is love. With the mind of Christ, reading scripture is totally different, as in, everything is read through a lens of who I know God is--love.


As an example of how I judge scripture, let's say I were to read some verses or stories in the Bible that makes me shout: WHAT? I know I'm not the only one, so why do you think that happens? That questioning or feeling of "what" is there for a reason, because our spirit that is actually one with God's Spirit, is giving us a warning. Some stories and verses make us feel terrible, and make us question God's ways. His "way" is always love, because that's His character and that's who He is! Unfortunately, most Christians push that warning aside and operate on blind faith endorsed by doctrines of men, or they simply believe whatever explanation their pastor or priest give.


If I read something in the Bible or elsewhere that doesn't compliment God's character, and bring out His fruit--I view it as words from men, i.e. doctrines of men, and NOT words from God (possibly a horrible mistranslation). In all honesty, most people view the words in the Bible through a lens coated with doctrines of men. However, when I "rightly divide" doctrines of men from words from God, I find TREASURE! It's critical to be honest enough to ask yourself if what you're reading causes you to trust God more, or does it chip away at that trust.

Is my understanding of whatever I'm reading in the Bible or otherwise--does it bring out in me the fruit of the Spirit of God, or fear which is NOT a fruit of The Spirit. You'll be going along, reading something inspirational, giving you hope and peace, but then it's only a matter of time until you'll come across a story or verse that doesn't do that. Something begins to change in you. I guarantee your smile has left your face at that point. JUDGE what is going on--take the time to do it rather than gloss over and ignore it! I'm not implying that a person only reads something that makes them "feel good", but instead, I'm asking you to keep an eye open for those words that slander God's character, causing you to fear Him, and trust Him less.

No matter where words originated, either from the Bible or elsewhere, if "fear" is in the mix, which is usually the case, then it needs to be properly judged by the standard I just pointed out. Fear is the weapon of choice by most deceived Christians. Most of the time when I get accusations thrown at me about deceiving people--do you know what they use every time without fail? FEAR! They threaten me with God's wrath, and then they threaten me with hell. Do you think there's fear behind those threats, trying to get me to be afraid? Sorry folks, it won't work anymore, because the Spirit of God doesn't do that. If fear is involved, it is not of God.

As I've said in previous chapters, but worth repeating again... God's perfect love casts out the kind of fear hell believers promote. In the same Bible verse that clearly says God's perfect love casts out fear--it continues by describing a specific fear, as having a fear of being punished by God. If I'm deceiving people by telling them that they can trust in God's perfect love, then I think I should continue deceiving them--don't you? If anyone is deceiving people, it's those who slander God, and promote how a person should fear God's punishment of hell.

So, if you think that threatening me with hell, which is supposedly a punishment from God, is going to have any effect, you're sorely mistaken. Those kind of threats just go right over my head or right through me, because I have no fear in those regards. Go for it if that makes you happy, because the reason I have no fear of punishment from God is I look forward to punishment from God! WHAT? That should blow a few minds, and pop a few brain cells. Why would I look forward to that? Because God disciplines and punishes those He loves, and I know that any punishment or discipline from God is for my good. I welcome it, because I can trust Him. I know I'm walking in God's perfect love when I can say something like that and mean it!

Honest people will admit they view words in the Bible through a lens coated with doctrines of men. However, when you rightly divide the doctrines of men from the words from God in the Bible, you're going to find treasure like you've never seen before. Verses really do pop out, it's fun, and enjoyable. I used to hate reading the Bible, because it would cause confusion, and confusion is definitely not one of the fruit of the Spirit--thus it's not from God. If this sounds simple, guess what--it is that simple. Simple enough a child could understand it, and it's never proven me wrong. If I'm deceiving you right now with these words, by encouraging you to rightly divide the word of truth from words that are not true, by telling you to look at the fruit of the Spirit of God in your life, and by judging everything through the character of God, which is love--if I'm deceiving you, then by all means I want you to be deceived in this regard!

My two closest friends on this whole planet, other than my wife, my two dogs, my cat, and my backhoe... or would it be my Xbox... anyway, they are Kevin Bogart and Phil Smith. They're my closest buddies. Kevin has had a paradigm shift in his thinking, and he knows there is no hell. Now get this... my buddy Phil definitely believes in the existence of hell. I find this fascinating... I'm as close to my buddy Phil who believes in hell as I am to my buddy Kevin who does not believe in hell. This is called love folks--this is what love is all about. Neither one of my friends think I'm deceiving them, and they have never judged my character, or my worth for any reason. With love, it doesn't matter if I agree with them or not.


Ending Thoughts and Cool Quotes


I'm going to end this chapter with subjects and thoughts that didn't fit anywhere else in this book, along with a few quotes from people who seem to have a wisdom and understanding beyond what I've written. This statement is not my attempt to display a sense of false humility, but it's what I truly believe.

We cannot "save" ourselves for the purpose of, or in order to begin a relationship with God, no matter how much "free will" we apply, and no matter how many good choices we make. By thinking we can--it causes us to focus on ourselves, our abilities, and our strength. These things are good, but they're the wrong mark, meaning the wrong bulls-eye to be aiming for. In this context, the wrong bulls-eye is our free will and choice. By doing so, we are "missing the mark", which is the real definition of sin. Simply put... the doctrine of free will is a sin. Jesus and His accomplishments is the true mark that Christianity is missing, due to the doctrine of free will. One cannot have it both ways by saying Jesus provided salvation, but it takes one's free will to provide salvation. It makes no sense!

Yes, we have been given wills, free or otherwise to choose God's ways or to reject them... but, by choosing wrong, it has no everlasting effect other than robbing one of peace in the here and now. If anything robs a person of peace, it's our damnable free will that has the potential to cause us to fail. In other words, Christians put their trust is their choice rather than ultimately trusting God. So, when it comes to our relationship with God... it is finished! The majority of people, Christian or otherwise, just don't know it yet!

The Good News i.e., The Gospel of Jesus in Luke 4:18:

"THE SPIRIT OF THE LORD IS UPON ME, BECAUSE HE ANOINTED ME TO PREACH THE GOSPEL TO THE POOR. HE HAS SENT ME TO PROCLAIM RELEASE TO THE CAPTIVES, AND RECOVERY OF SIGHT TO THE BLIND, TO SET FREE THOSE WHO ARE OPPRESSED"

How would hell be applicable to this message? In the vein of sarcastic humor, let's see... hmmm?

- First, only the poor will get a chance to accept Jesus as their Lord and savior. ("He anointed Me to preach the gospel to the **poor**") Apparently, everyone else (especially the rich) are automatically destined for hell since any message they receive won't be "anointed".

- Are the people in hell considered "captives" since Christendom claims there is no escape, even though "He has sent Me to proclaim release to the **captives**"?

- Are the people in hell considered spiritually "blind", because Jesus didn't include them in His proclamation to the "recovery of sight to the **blind**"? I think I know what the problem was...

they were not poor enough to have an anointed message preached to them that was capable of opening their eyes.  Now we're getting somewhere.

- Finally... are those in hell "oppressed" (ya think?), even though Jesus said He was sent "to set free those who are **oppressed**"?

- None of this makes sense, even though I wrote it!  Why is that?  Because...

- HELL HAS NOTHING TO DO WITH THE GOSPEL.  It never has and it never will, so why include it?

Christian Irony

According to Christian teaching: Preach Jesus! If you do and your message is rejected, then comes death, and then comes eternal hell.

However, according to Christian teaching:  If you don't preach Jesus, and they never hear, then God will make a way for them because He is just. Otherwise God would be sending people to hell who didn't have a choice.

My answer: Close all church doors, remove all Evangelists from TV and radio. Never mention the name of Jesus ever again, because if you do and someone hears and rejects your message--they'll end up in hell. Christian, if people go to hell it's your fault. KEEP YOUR BIG MOUTHS SHUT!, and God will make a way for them because He is just.

One more bit of Christian Irony...

According to Christian teaching abortions are murder, and if any babies are murdered, not given a chance to accept or reject Christ, and since God is just--they are guaranteed a ticket into heaven. So, wouldn't it be wise to continue all abortions so the baby CAN'T grow up, thus by growing up, doesn't this give them an opportunity to reject Christ and spend an eternity in hell?

Like everyone, I'm still wondering and questioning a lot of things. In other words, I'm on the fence about some things. I've asked people on Social Media for their opinion on: Did Jesus really have to die to accomplish salvation for all? In previous chapters I gave a list of scriptures that have stated that God didn't, nor does He require a sacrifice, yet I was taught that Jesus was a sacrifice for the sins of mankind. However, recently I've discovered there's a huge different between Jesus being sacrificed BECAUSE of the sins of mankind versus Jesus WAS a sacrifice for the sins of mankind. On the surface it seems subtle, so reread it a few times until it sinks in. Below are examples of what others had to say about this, along with some of my favorite off-the-topic quotes.

Jacob M. Wright wrote:

"The cross has nothing to do with the wrath or anger of God. The bloody body of Jesus does not in any way, shape, or form represent God's violence against humanity unleashed onto Jesus. Instead, Jesus is "the fullness of God in bodily form." Therefore the bloody body of Jesus represents the violence of humanity against God. Who was it who scourged, dehumanized, and crucified God? Not God! It was us! We did it! Don't let anyone pull some slight-of-hand theological trickery to spin this into the opposite of what is obvious. The demonic dehumanization of Christ does not represent God's holiness and justice, it represents our wickedness and injustice!

It was the hard-hearted Roman soldiers who tore the flesh off of Christ's back and forced jagged thorns into his skull. It was the deranged minds of barbaric Romans that devised the dehumanizing instrument of the cross to maximize full public humiliation and excruciating torture and pain. Do not associate with God what came from the demonized mind of man.

Again, the cross has nothing to do with the wrath or anger of God against humanity. The cross has everything to do with the unconditional love and forgiveness of God for humanity, the extremity of which is demonstrated in the face of our ultimate enmity and violence against him. For God to submit to be the victim of our demonic wrath and rage, to submit to be the subject of our perverse instruments of torture, to be unanimously condemned and scapegoated by the mob, and to be crucified as subhuman was the extremity of evil through which God revealed the extremity of his love. It was the ultimate way God could reveal his undying love to a race at war with itself, and to reveal the universal reconciling power of forgiveness. It is also how God exposes and overturns our systems of victimization and injustice and brings the world to justice, making peace in all things. Through sheer, pure, unadulterated self-giving love."

Duane Armitage wrote:

"Human beings first and foremost chose to reject God and thus torture God to death. God could have fought back, he chose not to, but rather let human beings see who/what they really were, namely murderers of their own maker. His death effectively exposes (reveals) the true nature of the evil in the world, but also, doubly the absolute love of God."

Raymund Schwager wrote:

"If even the greatest misdeed against his own Son provoked no reaction of revenge, then there is no other thinkable deed which God would not willingly forgive. His goodness and his forgiveness are shown to be unlimited, because they have expressly stepped over the last recognizable limit."

Ray Harthcock Sr had an interesting thought that I consider profound:

"I've wondered this many times. What was God like before He created clay? Are we merely clay with a will, or are we His will competing for top position? Is it the luck of the draw I beat the billions of siblings to land a spot on Earth? Maybe they won and I really lost? I'm asking questions. Maybe I'm here because I don't clearly see. Why do I understand others better than I understand myself? Maybe we should rest our identity solely know His will. I believe God is relationship minded as a heart felt loving God in every unimaginable way. His will is infused is us all. Earthen clay has its own relentless identity. Man will always be seeking his own way and will. I like what Paul says in the book of Philippians: "Let the peace of God transcend your imagination. Be like minded (like Him who created you), and do what is peaceable and good."


Mark Rayner wrote:

"Let me offer a completely different view. (Ref. scripture) The bible is a terrible translation pretty much everywhere. You need to see past things. Let me give you a for example; lets say that a man jumps in front of a shooter trying to shoot me and takes the bullet and dies. It changes my life. Why? Because of the absolute love of that person to go through that. Yes he died instead of me, but that is not the thing that changed me. Yes I could say; "without his blood and sacrifice there could be no salvation of myself" but it was not his blood that changed me. It was the act of love that devastated me and changed me.

So while certain actions took place, those actions are not the point. I could live on and remain a selfish person and say; "what an idiot for taking that bullet". It's only the love that matters. Scripture says it is the goodness of God that brings repentance. The actions are just the means by which the love was displayed, not some magic set of actions that needed to be performed to undo a magic curse. People don't realize the superstition inherent in the idea of actions and words being the source. This is essentially what spells are, actions and words. The point has always been love.

So how does this relate? What was the fall? Man fell out of a love relationship with God and into a relationship with their own knowledge. In that knowledge they now saw God as a source of pain. The image of God was changed for mankind. Jesus went through what he went through to demonstrate the love.

Jesus was very powerful. He could have destroyed every person who opposed him. He could have come down from the cross and wiped out every person who betrayed Him, but He did not. He allowed his own people and religion to hand him over to gentiles to be whipped and scourged and shamed to the worse state, and allowed them to nail him up. All so that he could demonstrate love.... "Forgive them father, they know not what they do".

Then the father raised Him after Jesus took on our sin by saying; "why have you forsaken me" which is what man believed of God.  Then God raised Him to say to us loud and clear, even when you think I have forsaken you, I will raise you.  Jesus says; no matter what you do to me I will forgive you.  What could be worse than killing Gods son?  Can there be a greater crime against God?  Yet... Forgive them father... The father raised him.... Its all love, forgiveness, raised to life in the backdrop of horrible actions. But the actions are not what did the job.  The job was done through the demonstration of love. The greatest crime against God in the history of man was the backdrop for the greatest demonstration of love."


Only an opinion--by The Why Guy:

"I've been wrong on many of occasions and this may be one of those times.  I'm beginning to believe Jesus didn't come to die for the world, but to show the world who the Father is.  As a way of showing who the Father is, Jesus ALLOWED men to murder Him.  Mankind sinned in doing so. (ya think?)  God the Father, forgave the world for doing such a thing.  So yes, technically Jesus did die for the sins of the world, but not in the way Christendom presents it."

Mark Twain said:

"It's easier to fool people than to convince them that they have been fooled."

Unknown author wrote:

"Anyone who believes in hell has had their moral conscience hijacked."

Joe Lindsey wrote:

"The Christians build a safe place to hide from Him while they try to 'serve' Him--this is called religion."

The Why Guy wrote:

"Today's Christianity:  I did it my way, but let's give Jesus the credit anyway.
I'm sure glad God loved the hell out of me"

Frank Clifton wrote:

"Why would a God of love cast us out for being deceived when we started out deceived, and were not condemned by Him?  How much more would He do for us to come out of deception now that we have been awakened to His all forgiving love?

You were in deception and I forgave you.  Now your awake.  I will hold the course and cause the same as I did from the beginning.  My motives have not changed.  I am always the same and I do not waiver from My purpose which isn't for My glory, but for your well being.  So continue on, because I know the beginning from the end and vice-versa."


Mark Twain wrote:

"Man is a religious animal.  He is the only religious animal.  He is the only animal that has the true religion--several of them.  He is the only animal that loves his neighbor as himself and cuts his throat if his theology isn't straight.  He has made a graveyard of the globe in trying his honest best to smooth his brother's path to happiness and heaven."


Ken Nichols wrote:

"Lucifer and satan are transliterated names based on Latin words being turned into names.  But they aren't names.  The people who heard the words at the time they were said would not have thought of them as names.  The "satan" means adversary.  "Lucifer" means morning star, as in the star you can still see in a dawn sky--the brightest star in the sky.

We have taken these words, made them into names, and built elaborate mythologies around them."

My favorite joke that is not so funny:

"Behold, I stand at the door and knock..."

Knock, Knock...

Who's there?

It's me, the Christian Jesus, let me in...

Why?

I have to save you

From what?

From what I'm gonna do to you if you don't let me in!

I hope this book has been an encouragement to you rather than angering you. I have devoted years of research into ancient languages, culture, and history. Due to the Earth suit I reside in, I know this book cannot be error free, but let the result speak for itself. Thank you for reading.

Theme: ALL, EVERY, WORLD

Genesis 12:3 --- ALL peoples on earth will be blessed through Abraham.

Genesis 22:18 --- ALL nations on earth will be blessed through Abraham's offspring.

Psalms 22:27 --- ALL the ends of the earth and ALL the families of the nations will acknowledge God.

Psalms 33:15 – God fashions ALL hearts

Psalms 65:2 – To You (God) ALL flesh shall come

Psalms 86:9 – ALL nations will worship Him

Psalms 145:9-10 --- The Lord has compassion on ALL His creation and ALL He has made will praise Him.

Psalms 145:13 --- The Lord loves ALL His creation.

Psalms 145:14 – He raises ALL WHO FALL (even backsliders?)

Samuel 14:14 – We must ALL die; we are like water spilled on the ground, which cannot be gathered up. But God will NOT take away a life; He will devise plans so as NOT TO KEEP AN OUTCAST BANISHED FOREVER FROM HIS PRESENCE. (do you honestly still believe in eternally being separated from God in hell?)

Isaiah 25:6-8 --- God will prepare a feast for ALL PEOPLE, He will destroy the shroud that enfolds ALL peoples, the sheet that covers up ALL nations. He will eliminate death, wipe away the tears from ALL FACES and remove the disgrace of his people from all the earth.

Isaiah 45:22-23 --- God has sworn an oath that (ALL) every knee will bow before Him and every tongue will swear by Him.

Isaiah 49:6 --- God's salvation will be brought to the ends of the earth.

Jeremiah 31:33-34 --- ALL men will know God, from the greatest to the least.

Matthew 18:13 --- Like the man who owes a hundred sheep and is not willing to lose even one, God is not willing that any one be lost.

Luke 2:10 --- The birth of Jesus is good news for ALL the people. (nowhere in context is this conditional)

Luke 3:6 - ALL flesh shall see God's salvation

Luke 15:4 - If ANY (all) stray He goes after that which is lost until He finds it

John 1:29 --- Jesus is the Lamb of God who takes away the sin of the world. (not conditional)

John 3:35 – The Father has given ALL into His hands (meaning God gave Him ALL things)

John 4:42 – Jesus is Savior of the WORLD

John 5:25 --- Even the dead will hear the sound of Christ and ALL who hear will live.

John 5:28 – ALL in the grave will hear & come forth

John 6:37 --- Everything (ALL) that God has given to Christ will come to him.

John 6:39 – This is the will of the Father Who sent Me, that of ALL He has given Me, I should I SHOULD LOSE NOTHING, but raise them up at the last day.

John 12:32 – Jesus will draw ALL mankind unto Himself

John 12:47 – I do not judge ANYONE who hears my words and does not keep them, for I CAME NOT to judge the world, but to save the WORLD. (Jesus came to save ALL)

John 17:2 – He (Jesus) has authority over ALL flesh to give eternal life. (Jesus gives eternal life to ALL that His Father gave Him)

Acts 3:20 – (Restitution of ALL) And that He may send [to you] the Christ (the Messiah), Who before was designated and appointed for you--even Jesus, Whom heaven must receive [and retain] until the time for the complete (universal) RESTORATION OF ALL that God spoke by the mouth of all His holy prophets for ages past [from the most ancient time in the memory of man].

Romans 3:3-4 --- The unbelief of some will not nullify God's faithfulness.

Romans 5:15 – In Adam ALL condemned, in Christ ALL live

Romans 5:18 – Therefore just as one man's trespass led to condemnation for ALL, so one man's act of righteousness leads to justification and life for ALL

Romans 8:38-39 --- Nothing can separate us from the love of God that is in Christ.

Romans 11:15 – Reconciliation of the WORLD

Romans 11:32  He has shut ALL up in unbelief to show mercy to ALL

1 Corinthians 3:15 – ALL saved, so as by fire

1 Corinthians 15:22 – In Adam ALL die, in Christ ALL live

2 Corinthians 5:15 – Jesus died for ALL

2 Corinthians 5:19 --- Through Christ, God was reconciling the world (ALL) to Himself.

Ephesians 1:10 – ALL come into Him at the fullness of times

Ephesians 1:11 --- God will bring ALL things under heaven and on earth under Christ.

Ephesians 1:22 - Therefore He has put ALL things in subjection to Christ

Ephesians 4:10 --- Christ ascended higher then all the heavens to fill the whole (ALL) universe.

Philippians. 2:9-11 --- Every (ALL) tongue will confess that Jesus is Lord (In 1 Corinthians 12:3, Paul writes that no one can say "Jesus is Lord" except by the Holy Spirit)

Colossians 1:20 – ALL reconciled unto God

1 Timothy 2:4 – God will have ALL to be saved

1 Timothy 2:4 – God desires ALL to come to the knowledge of truth

1 Timothy 2:6 – Salvation of ALL is testified in due time

1 Timothy 4:10 --- God is the Savior of ALL men, especially (not exclusively) those who believe.

Titus 2:11-12 --- God's grace, which brings salvation has appeared to ALL men.

Hebrews 2:9 --- Jesus tasted death for everyone (ALL).

Hebrews 7:25 – Jesus is able to save to the UTTERMOST

Hebrews 8:11 – ALL will know God

II Peter 3:9 - ALL come to repentance

1 John 2:2 – And He is the atoning sacrifice for our (believers) sins, and not OURS ONLY, but ALSO for the sins of the WHOLE WORLD.  (you still think you're "special" because you're a believer?)

1 John 4:14 --- Christ is the Savior of the world (ALL).

Revelation 5:13 --- Every (ALL) creature in heaven, on earth, under the earth, and on the sea will sing praises to him who sits on the throne and to the Lamb (Christ).

Revelation 21:4-5 --- God will dwell with men and he will wipe every (ALL) tear from their eyes, death, mourning, crying, pain and the old order of things will pass and everything will be made new.

# Bibliography

Raising Hell by Julie Ferwerda 2011

Go To Hell by Chuck Crisafulli & Kyra Thompson 2005

Hope Beyond Hell by Gerry Beauchemin 2007 Malista Press

Eternal Security Fact or Fiction by M.J. Roberts 2003 KiwE Publishing

The First Idiot in Heaven by Martin Zender 2012 Starke & Hartmann, Inc

A Dictionary of Early Christian Beliefs by David Bercot  1998 Hendrickson Publishers, Inc.

The Guideposts Parallel Bible 1991 by Zondervan

The New Strong's Exhaustive Concordance of the Bible 1990 by Thomas Nelson Publishers

Christian Authorities - Church Fathers - Bad News About Christianity  badnewsaboutchristianity.com

Douay-Rheims (Roman Catholic) public domain-no copy right

Bishops Bible 1568 public domain-no copy right

Original 1611 King James with Apocrypha public domain-no copy right

"Authorized" King James Version public domain-no copy right

Geneva Bible 1599 public domain-no copy right

New King James Version by Thomas Nelson Publishers

The Voice by Thomas Nelson Publishers (a subsidiary of News Corp)

New Living Translation Copyright 1996, 2004, 2015 by Tyndale House Foundation

American Standard Version (Revision of KJV) by the Lockman Foundation

New American Standard Bible by the Lockman Foundation

Revised Standard Version (Revision of KJV) 1989 by National Council of Churches

New Revised Standard Version 1989 by National Council of Churches

Revised English Bible by the publishing houses of both the universities of Oxford and Cambridge

Amplified by the Lockman Foundation

English Standard Version (ESV) 2001 by Crossway

New International Version Both Zondervan and Thomas Nelson were later acquired by HarperCollins

New English Bible (NET) 2005 Biblical Studies Press, L.L.C

Darby public domain-no copy right

New Century Version by Word Publishing Company

Holman Christian Standard Bible (Southern Baptist) by Holman Bible Publishers

Wesley's New Testament (1755) public domain-no copy right

Scarlett's N.T. (1798) public domain-no copy right

The New Testament in Greek and English (Kneeland, 1823) public domain-no copy right

Young's Literal Translation (1891) public domain-no copy right

Young's Literal Translation (1891) public domain-no copy right

Twentieth Century New Testament (1900) public domain-no copy right

Rotherham's Emphasized Bible (reprinted, 1902) public domain-no copy right

Fenton's Holy Bible in Modern English (1903) public domain-no copy right

Weymouth's New Testament in Modern Speech (1903) public domain-no copy right

The New Testament, James Moffat, (1917) public domain-no copy right

Jewish Publication Society Bible Old Testament (1917) public domain-no copy right

Panin's Numeric English New Testament (1914) public domain-no copy right

The New Testament, Charles B. Williams, 1937 public domain-no copy right

The People's New Covenant (Overbury, 1925) public domain-no copy right

Hanson's New Covenant (1884) public domain-no copy right

Western N.T. (1926) public domain-no copy right

NT of our Lord and Savior Anointed (Tomanek, 1958) public domain-no copy right

Concordant Literal NT (1983) by the Concordant Publishing Concern

The N.T., A Translation (Clementson, 1938) public domain-no copy right

Emphatic Diaglott, Greek/English Interlinear (Wilson, 1942) public domain-no copy right

The New Testament, A New Translation (Greber, 1980)

World English Bible (in progress) by Robinson and Pierpont 1991

Orthodox Jewish Brit Chadasha [NT Only] Afi Intl Publishing

Original Bible Project by Dr. James Tabor, still in translation

Zondervan Parallel N.T. in Greek and English by HarperCollins, a division of News Corp

Holy Bible In Its Original Order, Fred R. Coulter, 2007

Etymological N.T. (An Ultra Literal Translation, 2011, Michael Wine)

Aramaic Peshitta New Testament, 2006, Janet M. Magiera

MirrorWord N.T. (Francois du Toit) still in translation

Victorious Gospel of Jesus Christ, Electronic Ver. (Tentmaker Ministries)

The Source N.T. (Dr. Ann Nyland), 2004, 2007

Jonathan Mitchell N.T. (Jonathan Mitchell) 2009

Tree of Life Version, Baker Bookhouse, 2016

The New Testament (David Bentley Hart) Yale University Press, 2017

The Message Paraphrase (Eugene Peterson, Navpress

Websites:

Greek dictionary  http://www.abarim-publications.com/Interlinear-New-Testament/Romans/Romans-9-parsed.html#.W1S92tVKjb0
Webster's online dictionary
https://hellenisticgreek.com/22.html
http://biblehub.com/lexicon/1_corinthians/15-22.htm
The Emphatic Diaglott
https://www.biblestudytools.com/apocrypha/lxx/
http://www.heraldmag.org/olb/bsl/Library/BIBLES/Diagltt/Diaglott.pdf
https://www.wordhippo.com
https://www.blueletterbible.org/kjv/rom/5/8/t_conc_10
51009
studylight.org
http://concordant.org/version/literal-new-testament-online/

http://www.wrongabouthell.com/

https://zondervanacademic.com/blog/did-jesus-really-descend-into-hell/

http://www.sdmorrison.org/7-theories-of-the-atonement-summarized/

https://www.canva.com/    Free photos for book cover

file:///C:/Users/Admin/Downloads/AncientHell%20(1).htm

http://www.kingdomstudy.com/STFireOfLordGreatorex.html

https://bible-truths.com/

https://www.patheos.com/blogs/formerlyfundie/if-hell-is-real-why-did-god-wait-so-darn-long-to-warn-us-about-it/

http://www.brazenchurch.com/how-hell-invaded-church-doctrine/

11684276R00256

Made in the USA
Monee, IL
14 September 2019